NATHANIEL HAWTHORNE
(From a crayon drawing by Samuel Rowse)

HAWTHORNE
AND HIS CIRCLE

BY

JULIAN HAWTHORNE

ARCHON BOOKS
1968

First published 1903
Reprinted 1968
in an unaltered and unabridged edition

Library of Congress Catalog Card Number: 68-20382
Printed in the United States of America

CONTENTS

INTRODUCTION

Inheritance of friendships — Gracious giants — My own
good fortune—My father the central figure—What did
his gift to me cost him?—A revelation in Colorado—
Privileges make difficulties — Lights and shadows of
memory — An informal narrative — Contrast between
my father's life and mine . . . . Page i

I

Value of dates—My aunt Lizzie's efforts—My father's
decapitation—My mother's strong-box—The spirit of
The Scarlet Letter — The strain of imaginative composition—My grandmother Hawthorne's death—Infantile indifference to calamity—The children's plays and
books — The house on Mall Street — Scarlet fever—
The study on the third floor—The haunted mahogany
writing-desk—The secret drawers—The upright Egyptian—Mr. Pickwick—My father in 1850—The flowered
writing-gown, and the ink butterfly—Driving the quill
pen—The occupants of the second floor—Aunt Louisa
and Aunt Ebe—The dowager Mrs. Hawthorne—I kick
my aunt Lizzie—The kittens and the great mystery—
The greatest book of the age . . . . . Page 1

II

Horatio Bridge's "I-told-you-so"—What a house by the
sea might have done—Unknown Lenox—The restlessness of youth—The Unpardonable Sin and the Death-

iii

CONTENTS

III

IV

CONTENTS

CONTENTS

CONTENTS

CONTENTS

XI

XII

CONTENTS

CONTENTS

XV

XVI

CONTENTS

CONTENTS

XIX

ILLUSTRATIONS

INTRODUCTION

THE best use we can make of good fortune is to share
it with our fellows.   Those to whom good things
come by way of inheritance, however, are often
among the latest to comprehend their own advantage; they suppose it to be the common condition.
And no doubt I had nearly arrived at man's estate
before it occurred to me that the lines of few fishers
of men were cast in places so pleasant as mine.   I
was the son of a man of high desert, who had such
friends as he deserved; and these companions and
admirers of his gave to me in the beginning of my
days a kindly welcome and encouragement generated from their affection and reverence for him.
Without doing a stroke of work for it, I found myself early in the enjoyment of a principality of good
will and fellowship — a species of freemasonry, I
might call it, though the secret was patent enough

—for the rights in which, unaided, I might have contended my lifetime long in vain. Men and women whose names are consecrated apart in the dearest thoughts of thousands were familiars and playmates of my childhood; they supported my youth and bade my manhood godspeed. But to me, for a long while, the favor of these gracious giants of mind and character seemed agreeable indeed, but nothing out of the ordinary; my tacit presumption was that other children as well as I could if they would walk hand in hand with Emerson along the village street, seek in the meadows for arrow-heads with Thoreau, watch Powers thump the brown clay of the "Greek Slave," or listen to the voice of Charlotte Cushman, which could sway assembled thousands, modulate itself to tell stories to the urchin who leaned, rapt, against her knees. Were human felicity so omnipresent as a happy child imagines it, what a world would this be!

In time, my misapprehension was corrected, rather, I think, through the application to it of cold logic than by any rude awakening. I learned of my riches not by losing them—the giants did not withdraw their graciousness — but by comparing the lot of others with my own. And yet, to tell the truth—perhaps I might better leave it untold; only in these chapters, especially, I will not begin with reserves—to say truth, then, my world, during my father's lifetime, and afterwards for I will not say how long, was divided into two natural parts, my father being one of them, and everybody else the other.   Hence I was led to regard the parties of the latter part, rich or poor, giants or pygmies, as being, after all, of much the same stature and value.   The brightness (in the boy's estimation) of the paternal figure rendered distinctions between other brightnesses unimportant.   The upshot was, in short, that I inclined to the opinion that while compassion was unquestionably due to other children for not having a father like mine, yet in other respects my condition was not egregiously superior to theirs.   They might not know the Brownings or the Julia Ward Howes; but then, very likely, the Smiths and the Joneses, whom they did know, were nearly as good.

After fifty years, of course, such prepossessions yield to experience.   My father was the best friend I ever had, and he will always stand in my estimation distinct from all other friends and persons; but I can now recognize that in addition to the immeasurable debt I owe him for being to me what he was in his own person, he bestowed upon me a privilege also immeasurable in the hospitality of these shining ones who were his intimates.   Did the gift cost him nothing?   Nothing, in one sense.   But, again, what does it cost a man to walk upright and cleanly during the years of his pilgrimage: to deal justly with all, and charitably: diligently to cultivate and develop every natural endowment: always to seek truth, tell it, and vindicate it: to discharge to the utmost of his ability every duty that was intrusted to him: to rest content, in the

line of his calling, with no work inferior to his best:
to say no word and do no act which, were they
known, might weaken the struggle against temptation of any fellow-creature? These qualities were
the price at which Hawthorne bought his friends;
and in receiving those friends from him, his children could not but feel that the bequest represented
his unfaltering grasp upon whatever is pure, lofty,
and generous in human life.

Yes, whatever it may cost a man of genius to be
all his life a good man, and to use and develop his
genius to the noblest ends only, that my father's
friends cost him, and in that amount am I his
debtor; and the longer I myself live, and the more
I see of other men, the higher and rarer do I esteem the obligation. Moreover, in speaking of his
friends, I was thinking of those who personally
knew him; but the world is full to-day of friends
of his who never saw him, to whom his name is my
best and surest introduction. Once, only three
years since, in the remote heart of the Colorado
mountains, I chanced to enter the hut of an aged
miner; he sat in a corner of the little family room;
on the wall near his hand was fixed a small book-
shelf, filled with a dozen dog-eared volumes. The
man had for years been paralyzed; he could do little
more than to raise to that book-shelf his trembling
hand, and take from it one or other of the volumes.
When this helpless veteran learned my name, he
uttered a strange cry, and his face worked with
eager emotion; the wife of his broad-shouldered

son brought me to him in his corner; his old eyes glowed as they perused me. I could not gather the meaning of his broken, trembling speech; the young woman interpreted for me. Was I related to the great Hawthorne? "Yes; I am his son." "His son!" Seldom have I met a gaze harder to sustain than that which the paralytic bent upon me. Would I might have worn, for the time being, the countenance of an archangel, so to fill out the lineaments, drawn during so many lonely years by his imagination and his reverence, of his ideal writer! "The son of Hawthorne!" He said no more, save by the strengthless pressure of his hands upon my own; the woman told me how all the books on the little shelf were my father's books, and for fifteen years the old man had read no others. Helpless tears of joy, of gratitude, of wonder ran down the furrows of his cheeks into his white beard. And how could I at whom he so gazed help being moved: on that desolate, unknown mountain - side, far from the world, the name which I had inherited was loved and honored! One does not get one's privileges for nothing. My father gave me power to make my way, and cast sunshine on the path; but he made the path arduous, too!

Be that as it may, I now ask who will to look in my mirror, and see reflected there some of the figures and the scenes that have made my life worth living. As I peer into the dark abysm of things gone by, many places that seemed at first indistinct, grow clearer; but many more must remain impene-

trable.   Upon the whole, however, I am surprised
to find how much is still discernible.   Nearly a
score of years ago I published, in the shape of a
formal biography of Hawthorne and his wife, the
consecutive facts of their lives, and numerous passages from their journals and correspondence.   My
aim is different now; I wish to indite an informal
narrative from my own point of view, as child,
youth, and man.   There will be gaps in it—involuntary ones; and others occasioned by the obligation to retain those pictures only that seem likely
to arouse a catholic interest.   Yet there will be a
certain intimacy in the story; and some matters
which history would omit as trivial will be here
adduced, for the sake of such color and character
as they may contain.   I shall not stalk on stilts,
or mouth phrases, but converse comfortably and
trustfully as between friends.   If a writing of this
kind be not flexible, unpretending, discursive, it has
no right to be at all.   Art is not in question, save
the minor art that lives from line to line.   Gossip
about men, women, and things—it can amount to
little more than that.

In the earlier chapters the *dramatis personæ*
and the incidents must naturally group themselves about the figure of my father; for it was
thus that I saw them.   To his boy he was the
fountain of love, honor, and energy; and to the
boy he seemed the animating or organizing principle of other persons and events.   With his death,
in my eighteenth year, the world appeared disor-

dered for a season; then, gradually, I learned to do my own orientation. I was destined to an experience superficially much more active and varied than his had been; and it was a world superficially very different from his in which I moved and dealt. There must follow a corresponding modification in the character of the narrative; yet that, after all, is superficial, too. For the memory of my father has always been with me, and has doubtless influenced me more than I am myself aware. And certainly but for him this book would never have been attempted.

HAWTHORNE AND HIS CIRCLE

I

Value of dates—My aunt Lizzie's efforts—My father's
decapitation—My mother's strong-box—The spirit of
The Scarlet Letter—The strain of imaginative composition—My grandmother Hawthorne's death—Infantile indifference to calamity—The children's plays and
books—The house on Mall Street—Scarlet fever—
The study on the third floor—The haunted mahogany
writing-desk—The secret drawers—The upright Egyptian—Mr. Pickwick—My father in 1850—The flowered
writing-gown, and the ink butterfly—Driving the quill
pen—The occupants of the second floor—Aunt Louisa
and Aunt Ebe—The dowager Mrs. Hawthorne—I kick
my aunt Lizzie—The kittens and the great mystery—
The greatest book of the age.

My maternal aunt, Miss Elizabeth Palmer Peabody, was a very learned woman, and a great
student of history, and teacher of it; and by the
aid of huge, colored charts, done by my uncle Nat
Peabody and hung on the walls of our sitting-
room, she labored during some years to teach me
all the leading dates of human history—the charts
being designed according to a novel and ingenious
plan to fix those facts in childish memory. But as

a pupil I was always most inapt and grievous, in dates and in matters mathematical especially; so that I gave her inexhaustible patience many a sad hour. To this day I cannot tell in what year was fought the battle of Marathon, or when John signed Magna Charta; though the battle itself, and the scene of the barons with menacing brows gathered about John, stood clearly pictured in my imagination. Dates were arbitrary, and to my memory nothing arbitrary would stick. Nevertheless, when I am myself constructing a narrative, whether it be true or fictitious, I am wedded to dates, and cannot be divorced from them. It must be set down precisely when the events took place, in what years the *dramatis personæ* were born, and how old they were when each juncture of their fortunes came to pass. I can no more dispense with dates than I can talk without consonants; they carry form, order, and credibility. Or they are like the skeleton which gives recognizable shape to men and animals. Nothing mortal can get on without them.

Whether this addiction be in the nature of a reaction from my childish perversity, giving my erudite and beloved aunt Lizzie (as I called her) her revenge so long after our lessons are over; or how else to explain it, I know not; but it leads me to affirm here that the nadir of my father's material fortunes was reached about the year 1849. At that time his age was five-and-forty, and I was three.

MY FATHER'S DECAPITATION

The causes of this financial depression were several. One morning he awoke to find himself deprived, by political chicanery, of the income of a custom-house surveyorship which for some while past had served to support his small family. Now, some men could have gone on writing stories in the intervals between surveying customs, and have thus placed an anchor to windward against the time when the political storm should set in; but Nathaniel Hawthorne was devoid of that useful ability. Nor had he been able to spend less than he earned; so, suddenly, there he was on his beam-ends. Leisure to write, certainly, was now abundant enough; but he never was a rapid composer, and even had he been so, the market for the kind of things he wrote was, in the middle of the past century, in New England, neither large nor eager. The emoluments were meagre to match; twenty dollars for four pages of the *Democratic Review* was about the figure; and to produce a short tale or sketch of that length would take him a month at least. How were a husband and wife and their two children to live for a month on the mere expectation of twenty dollars from the *Democratic Review* — which was, into the bargain, terribly slow pay? Such was the problem which confronted the dark-haired and grave-visaged gentleman as he closed his desk in the Salem custom-house for the last time, and put on his hat to walk home.

Thanks, however, to some divine foresight on my mother's part, aided by a wonderful talent

for practical economy, she had secretly contrived
to save, out of her weekly stipends, small sums
which in the aggregate bulked large enough to
make an important difference in the situation.   So
when her husband disclosed his bad news, she
opened her private drawer and disclosed her bank-
notes, with such a smile in her eyes as I can easily
picture to myself.   Stimulated by the miracle, he
remembered that the inchoate elements of a story,
in which was to figure prominently a letter A, cut
out of red cloth, or embroidered in scarlet thread,
and affixed to a woman's bosom, had been for
months past rumbling round in his mind; now was
the time of times to shape it forth.   Yonder upon
the table by the window stood the old mahogany
writing-desk so long unused; here were his flowered
dressing - gown and slippers down - at - heel.   He
ought to be able to finish the story before the
miraculous savings gave out; and then all he would
have to do would be to write others.   And, after
all, to be rid of the surveyorship was a relief.

But matters were not to be run off quite so
easily as this.   *The Scarlet Letter*, upon coming to
close quarters with it, turned out to be not a story
of such moderate caliber as Hawthorne had hitherto been used to write, but an affair likely to extend
over two or three hundred pages, which, instead of
a month or so, might not be completed in a year;
yet it was too late to substitute something more
manageable for it—in the first place, because nothing
else happened to be at his disposal, and secondly,

4

BIRTHPLACE OF NATHANIEL HAWTHORNE AT SALEM, MASSACHUSETTS

because *The Scarlet Letter* took such intimate hold upon the vitals of his heart and mind that he was by no means able to free himself from it until all had been fulfilled. Only men of creative genius know in what glorious and harrowing thraldom their creations hold them. Having once been fairly begun, *The Scarlet Letter* must inevitably finish itself for good or ill, come what might to the writer of it.

This is a story of people and events, not a study in literary criticism; but the writing of *The Scarlet Letter* was an event of no trifling importance in the story of its author's life. To read the book is an experience which its readers cannot forget; what its writing must have been to a man organized as my father was is hardly to be conveyed in words. Hester, Dimmesdale, and Chillingworth—he must live through each one of them, feel their passion, remorse, hatred, terror, love; and he must enter into the soul of the mysterious nature of Pearl. Such things cannot with impunity be done by any one; the mere physical strain, all conditions being favorable, would be almost past bearing. But my father, though uniformly his bodily health was all his life sound, was never what I would call a robust man; he was exquisitely balanced. At the time he began his book he was jaded from years of office drudgery, and he was in some anxiety as to the issue of his predicament. The house in which he dwelt, small and ill-placed in a narrow side-street, with no possibility of shutting out the noise of traffic and of domestic alarms, could not but make the work tell more heavily upon him. But in addition to this there were fortuitous occasions of emotional stress, all of which I shall not mention; but among them were the distasteful turmoil aroused by his political mishap; and, far more poignant, the critical illness of his mother. Circumstances led to her being housed under his roof; there she lingered long at death's door, and there at last she died. He profoundly loved her; but deep-rooted, too, in both of them was that strange, New England shyness, masking in visible ice the underlying emotion. Not since his boyhood had their mutual affection found free, natural expression; and now, in this final hour, that bondage of habit caused the words of tenderness to stumble on their lips. The awful majesty of approaching death, prompting them to "catch up the whole of love and utter it" ere it be too late, wrought this involuntary self-repression into silent agony.

She died; his own health was shaken to its foundations; his children fell ill, his wife underwent acute suffering; and through all this, and more, *The Scarlet Letter* must be written. No wonder that, when he came to read the story in manuscript to his wife, his voice faltered and broke; and she slipped to her knees and hid her face on her arms in the chair. "I had been suffering," he commentated, long afterwards, "from a great diversity and severity of emotion." Great works of art— things with the veritable spirit of enduring life in

6

them—are destined to be born in sore travail and pain. Those who give them birth yield up their own life to them.

It was at this period—say, about 1850—that my own personal recollections, in a shadowy and incoherent way, begin. The shadows are exclusively of time's making; they were not of the heart. All through the trials of my parents I retained a jocund equanimity (save for some trifling childish ailments) and esteemed this world a friendly and agreeable place. *The Scarlet Letter* dashed my spirits not a whit; I knew not of its existence, by personal evidence, till full a dozen years later; and even the death of my grandmother left me light of heart, for the passing of the spirit from the body can but awaken the transient curiosity of a child of four. For the rest, my physical environment, in itself amusing and interesting enough to me, had its chief importance from the material it afforded on which to construct the imaginary scenes and characters of my play. My sister Una and myself were forever enacting something or somebody not ourselves: childish egoism oddly decking itself in the non-ego. We believed in fairies, in magic, in angels, in transformations; Hans Christian Andersen, Grimm, *The Black Aunt* (oh, delectable, lost volume) were our sober history-books, and *Robinson Crusoe* was our autobiography. But I did occasionally take note of concrete appearances, too; and some of them I remember.

The house—the third which we had inhabited

7

since my father became surveyor—was on Mall Street, and was three stories in height, with a yard behind and at one end; this yard, which was of importance to my sister and myself, had access to the street by a swinging gate. There were three or four trees in it, and space for play. The house was but one room deep, and lying as it did about north and south, the rooms were open to both the morning and the afternoon sunshine. They opened one into the other in a series; and when my father was safe up-stairs in his study, my mother would open all the doors of the suite on the lower floor, and allow the children to career triumphantly to and fro. No noise that we could make ever troubled her nerves, unless it was the noise of conflict; the shriek of joy, however shrill, passed by her harmless; but the lowest mutter of wrath or discontent distressed her; for of such are the mothers of the kingdom of heaven! And so zealous was our regard for her just and gentle law that I really think we gave way as little as most children to the latter.

Of course, whenever the weather permitted, we were out in the yard, or even promenaded for short distances up and down the street. And once—"How are you?" inquired a friend of the family, as he drove by in his wagon. "Oh, we've got the scarlet fever!" we proudly replied, stepping out gallantly along the sidewalk. For we were treated by a homœopathic doctor of the old school, who was a high-dilutionist, and mortal ills could never get a firm grip on us. In winter we rejoiced in the snow; and my father's story of the *Snow Image* got most of its local color from our gambols in this fascinating substance, which he could observe from the window of his study.

The study was on the third floor of the house, secluded from the turmoil of earth, so far as anything could be in a city street. No one was supposed to intrude upon him there; but such suppositions are ineffectual against children. From time to time the adamantine gates fell ajar, and in we slipped. It seemed a heavenly place, tenanted by a being possessed of every attribute that our imaginations could ascribe to an angel. The room and its tenant glimmer before me as I write, luminous with the sunshine of more than fifty years ago. Both were equipped for business rather than for beauty; furniture and garments were simple in those Salem days. A homely old paper covered the walls, a brownish old carpet the floor. There was an old rocking-chair, its black paint much worn and defaced; another chair was drawn up to the table, which stood to the left of the eastern window; and on the table was a mahogany desk, concerning which I must enter into some particulars. It was then, and for years afterwards, an object of my most earnest scrutiny. Such desks are not made nowadays.

When closed, it was an oblong mahogany box, two feet long by half that width, and perhaps nine inches high. It had brass corners, and a brass plate on the top, inscribed with the name, "N. Hawthorne." At one end was a drawer, with a brass handle playing on a hinge and fitting into a groove or socket when down; there was a corresponding handle at the other end, but that was for symmetry only; the one drawer went clear through the desk. I often mused over the ethics of this deception.

Being opened, the desk presented a sloping surface two feet square, covered with black velvet, which had been cut here and there and pasted down again, and was stiffened with many ink-spatterings. This writing surface consisted of two lids, hinged at their junction in the centre; lifting them, you discovered two receptacles to hold writing-paper and other desk furniture. They were of about equal capacity; for although the upper half of the desk was the more capacious, you must not forget that two inches of it, at the bottom, was taken up by the long drawer already mentioned.

But there was, also, a more interesting curtailment of this interior space. Along the very top of the desk, as it lay open, was a narrow channel, perhaps a couple of inches wide and deep, divided into three sections; two square ones, at the opposite ends, held the ink-bottle and the sand-bottle; the long central one was for quill pens. These, in the aggregate, appeared to the superficial eye to account for all that remained of the cubic contents of the structure; but the supreme mystery and charm of the affair was that they did not!

THE SECRET DRAWERS

No; there was an esoteric secret still in reserve; and for years it remained a secret to me. The bottle-sockets and pen-tray did not reach down to the level of the long drawer by nearly an inch. Measurement would prove that; but you would have said that the interval must be solid wood; for nothing but a smooth panel met the eye when you pulled aside the sheets of writing-paper in their receptacle to investigate. But the lesson of this world, and of the desk as a part of it, is that appearances are not to be trusted. The guile of those old desk-makers passes belief.

I will expose it. In the pen-tray lay a sort of brass nail, as long as your little finger, and blunt at the end. Now take the sand-bottle from its hole. In one corner of the bottom thereof you will see a minute aperture, just big enough to admit the seemingly useless brass nail. Stick it in and press hard. With an abrupt noise that makes you jump, if you are four or five years old, that smooth, unsuspected strip of panel starts violently forward (propelled by a released spring) and reveals—what? Nothing less than the fronts of two minute drawers. They fit in underneath the pen-tray, and might remain undiscovered for a hundred years unless you had the superhuman wit to divine the purpose of the brass nail. The drawers contain diamonds, probably, or some closely folded document making you the heir to a vast estate. As a matter of fact, I don't know what they contained; the surprise of the drawers themselves was enough for me. I need not add that I did not guess the riddle myself; but nothing that I can call to mind impressed me more than when, one day, my father solved it for me with his little brass wand. At intervals, afterwards, I was allowed to work the miracle myself, always with the same thrill of mysterious delight. The desk was human to me; it was alive.

There were little square covers for the ink and sand-bottles; and on the under sides of these were painted a pair of faces; very ruddy in the cheeks they were, with staring eyes and smiling mouths; and one of them wore a pair of black side-whiskers. They were done by my father, with oil-colors filched from my mother's paint-box. They seemed to me portraits of the people who lived in the desk; evidently they enjoyed their existence hugely. And when I considered that the desk was also somehow instrumental in the production of stories—such as the *Snow Image*—of a delectable and magical character, the importance to my mind of the whole contrivance may be conceived. When I grew beyond child's estate, I learned that it had also assisted at the composition of *The Scarlet Letter*. If ever there were a haunted writing-desk, this should have been it; but the ghosts have long since carried it away, whither I know not.

On the table were two ornaments; one, the finely moulded figure of an Egyptian in bronze, the wide Egyptian head-dress falling on the shoulders, the arms lying rigidly at the sides, with fists clinched. Generations of handling had made it almost black, but the amiable expression of the little countenance —the figure was about seven inches tall—greatly endeared it to me. Its feet were pressed close together on a small round stand; but one day somebody set it down on a hot stove, where it remained without flinching till the feet were melted off. After some years my mother had an ebony stump affixed to it, preserving the proportions of the figure and setting it once more erect. He was of greater endurance and of finer physical if not of moral development than the Tin Soldier of Hans Christian Andersen. The other ornament, less than half the Egyptian's size, and also made of bronze, was a warrior in mediæval armor, whose head lifted off, showing a sharp-pointed rod the sheath of which was the body. Its use was to pick the wicks of the oil-lamps of that epoch, and its name was Mr. Pickwick. When afterwards I became acquainted with the world's Mr. Pickwick, I supposed his creator had adopted the name from our bronze warrior; but the world's Pickwick was made of stuff more enduring than bronze; he remains, but our little warrior has vanished.

I come now to the human occupant of this chamber of marvels. I see a tall, strong man, whose wide-domed head was covered with wavy black hair, bushing out at the sides. It thinned somewhat over the lofty crown and brow; the forehead was hollowed at the temple and rounded out above, after the Moorish style of architecture. Under heavy, dark eyebrows were eyes deep-set and full of

13

light, marvellous in range of expression, with black eyelashes. All seemed well with me when I met their look. The straight, rather salient nose had a perceptible cleft at the tip, which, I was told, was a sign of good lineage; muddy-mettled rascals lacked it; so that I was much distressed by the smooth, plebeian bluntness, at that time, of my own little snub. The mouth, then unshaded by a mustache, had a slight upward turn at the corners, indicative of vitality and good-humor; the chin rounded out sharply convex from the lip. The round, strong column of the neck well supported the head; my mother compared it with that of the Apollo Belvedere, a bust of which stood in the corner of our sitting-room. The head was deep—a great distance between the base of the ear and the wing of the nostril—and was well filled out behind. Above the blue of the shaven beard the complexion showed clear white and red, announcing a strong heart and good digestion. My father shaved himself daily; I was not permitted to see the operation, but I knew he lathered, and wondered why. He was naturally athletic; broad-shouldered and deep in the chest, lean about the loins, weighing never over one hundred and eighty pounds; his height was five feet ten and three-quarter inches; his legs and feet were slender and graceful, his gait long and springy, and he could stand and leap as high as his shoulder. In the house he wore slippers, which seemed always old and down-at-heel.

In the house, also, he wore a writing-gown, made

for him some years before by my mother; it reached nearly to his heels, and had been a gorgeous affair, though now much defaced. The groundwork was purple, covered all over with conventional palm-leaf in old-gold color; the lining was red. This lining, under the left-hand skirt of the gown, was blackened with ink over a space as large as your hand; for the author was in the habit of wiping his pen thereon; but my mother finally parried this attack by sewing in the centre of the place a penwiper in the shape of a butterfly.

While story-writing, the door of the study was locked against all the world; but after noon he became approachable, except during *The Scarlet Letter* period, when he wrote till evening. He did not mind my seeing him write letters; he would sit with his right shoulder and head inclined towards the desk; the quill squeaked softly over the smooth paper, with frequent quick dips into the ink-bottle; a few words would be written swiftly; then a pause, with suspended pen, while the next sentence was forming in the writer's mind. When he miswrote, instead of crossing out the word, he would smear it out with his finger, and rewrite over the smear; so that his page had a mottled appearance. The writing was accompanied by intermittent nods of the head, as one would say, "*Sic cogito!*" So far as he is concerned, the shadows close in on me here.

But I have said that the house was of three stories, and I have accounted for two of them only. The second was occupied by my grandmother Haw-

thorne and her two daughters, Aunt Louisa and
Aunt Ebe (the latter appellation being an infantile
version of her name invented by my father, who
was her junior, and used by us to distinguish between her and that other Elizabeth who was Aunt
Lizzie Peabody). Of my grandmother Hawthorne
I have no personal recollection at all; she was a
Manning, a beautiful old lady, whom her son resembled. She had been a recluse from society for
forty years; it was held to be good form, in that age
and place, to observe such Hindoo rites after the
death of a husband; hers had died in his thirty-
fourth year in Surinam. But she had also insensibly fallen into the habit of isolating herself in some
degree from her own family; they were all of them
addicted to solitude of the body, though kindly
enough disposed in the abstract. When we went
to live in the Mall Street house, the old lady and
her daughters uprooted themselves from their home
of many years in Herbert Street and dwelt with us;
and that quaint crystallization of their habits was
in a measure broken up. But the dowager Mrs.
Hawthorne, it soon appeared, had come there to
die; she was more than seventy years old. My
aunt Louisa I seem dimly to recall as a tall, fragile,
pale, amiable figure, not very effective. My aunt
Ebe I afterwards came to know well, and shall
defer mention of her. So I was encompassed by
kindly petticoats, and was very happy, but might
have been better for a stout playmate of my own
sex. I had a hobby-horse, which I rode constant-

ly to fairy-land in quest of treasure to bestow upon my friends. I swung with Una on the gate, and looked out upon the wonder of the passing world. The tragedy of my grandmother's death, which, as I have said, interrupted the birth of *The Scarlet Letter*, passed me by unknowing, or rather without leaving a trace upon my memory. On the other hand, I can reconstitute vividly two absurd incidents, destitute of historical value. After my grandmother Hawthorne's death I fell ill; but the night before the disease declared itself, I was standing in a chair at the nursery window, looking out at the street-lamp on the corner, and my aunt Lizzie Peabody, who had just come on from Boston, was standing behind me, lest I should fall off. Now, I was normally the most sweet-tempered little urchin imaginable; yet suddenly, without the faintest warning or provocation, I turned round and dealt my loving aunt a fierce kick in the stomach. It deprived her of breath for a space; but her saintly nature is illustrated by the fact that the very first use she made of her recovered faculties was to gasp out, "Sophie, the child must be ill!" Fortunately for my reputation, the illness was not long in arriving. The other episode must have happened at about the same period, and is likewise concerned with Aunt Lizzie. We had a cat, and the cat had had kittens a day or two before. Aunt Lizzie came into the nursery, where Una and I were building houses of blocks, and sat down in the big easy-chair. The cat was in the room, and she immediately came up to my aunt and began to mew and to pluck at her dress with her claws. Such attentions were rare on pussy's part, and my aunt noticed them with pleasure, and caressed the animal, which still continued to devote its entire attention to her. But there was something odd in the sound of her mewing and in the intent regard of her yellow eyes. "Can anything be the matter with pussy?" speculated my aunt. At that moment my father entered the room, and my aunt rose to greet him. Then the massacre was revealed, for she had been sitting upon the kittens. Their poor mother pounced upon them with a yowl, but it was too late. My dear aunt was rather a heavy woman, and she had been sitting there fifteen minutes. We all stood appalled in the presence of the great mystery.

One day a big man, with a brown beard and shining brown eyes, who bubbled over with enthusiasm and fun, made his appearance and talked volubly about something, and went away again, and my father and mother smiled at each other. *The Scarlet Letter* had been written, and James T. Fields had read it, and declared it the greatest book of the age. So that was the last of Salem.

II

Horatio Bridge's "I-told-you-so"—What a house by the
sea might have done—Unknown Lenox—The restlessness of youth—The Unpardonable Sin and the Deathless Man — The little red house — Materials of culture
—Our best playmates—The mystery of Mrs. Peter's
dough—Our intellectual hen—Fishing for poultry—
Yacht-building—Swimming with one foot on the ground
—Shipwreck—Our playfellow the brook—Tanglewood
—Nuts—Giants and enchanters—Coasting—Wet noses,
dark eyes, ambrosial breath—My first horseback ride—
Herman Melville's stories—Another kind of James—
The thunder-storm—Yearning ladies and melancholy
sinners—Hindlegs—Probable murder—"I abominate
the sight of it!"—The peril of Tanglewood—The truth
of fiction—An eighteen - months' work—We leave five
cats behind.

HORATIO BRIDGE, my father's college friend, was a
purser in the navy and lived in Augusta, Maine,
his official residence being at Portsmouth.   He had
kept in closer touch with the romancer than any of
his other friends had since their graduating days,
and he had been from the first a believer in his coming literary renown.   So, when *The Scarlet Letter*
shone eminent in the firmament of book-land, it
was his triumphant "I-told-you-so" that was
among the earliest to be heard.   And when my

father cast about for a more congenial place than Salem to live in, it was to Bridge that he applied for suggestions. He stipulated that the place should be somewhere along the New England sea-coast.

Had this wish of his been fulfilled it might have made great differences. Hawthorne had always dwelt within sight and sound of the Atlantic, on which his forefathers had sailed so often between the Indies and Salem port, and Atlantic breezes were necessary to his complete well-being. At this juncture physical health had for the first time become an object to him; he was run down by a year of suffering and hard work, and needed nature's kindest offices. A suitable house of his own by the sea-side would probably have brought him up to his best physical condition to begin with, and kept him so; and it would so have endeared itself to him that when, two or three years later, Pierce had offered him a foreign appointment he might have been moved to decline it, and have gone on writing American romances to the end—to the advantage of American letters. Concord had its own attractions; but it never held him as the sea would have done, nor nourished his health, nor stimulated his genius. A house of his own beside the Atlantic might well have added twenty years to his life.

But it was not upon the knees of the gods. Bridge's zealous efforts failed to find a place available, and after an uneasy interval, during which his friend wandered uncomfortably about Boston and the neighborhood (incidentally noting down some side-scenes afterwards to be incorporated in *The Blithedale Romance*), a cottage in the Berkshire Hills was spoken of, and upon examination seemed practicable. Lenox, at that time, was as little known as Mount Desert; it was not until long afterwards that fashion found them out and made them uninhabitable to any but fashionable folks. Moreover, my father had seen something of Lenox a dozen years before.

A dozen years before he was not yet betrothed to Sophia Peabody; he already loved her and she him; but her health seemed an insuperable barrier between them. This and certain other matters were weighing heavily upon his soul, and his future seemed dark and uncertain. He thought of taking a voyage round the world; he thought of getting into politics; he even thought—as young men full of life sometimes will—of death. What he finally did, with native good sense, was to make a two-months' trip in the mountainous region to the westward, to change the scene and his state of mind, and to get what artists call a fresh eye. He chose North Adams as his headquarters, and forayed thence in various directions over a radius of twenty miles. He was then beginning to revolve one of the two great romance themes that preoccupied his whole after-life, neither of which was he destined to write. This was the idea of the Unpardonable Sin; the other was the conception of the Deathless Man. The only essay we have towards the embodiment of the first vision is the short fragment

published in *Mosses from an Old Manse*, called
" Ethan Brand." The other was attempted in various forms, of which *Septimius*, *Dr. Grimshawe's
Secret*, and *The Dolliver Romance*, all posthumously
published, are the most important.

But Stockbridge, Pittsfield, and Lenox had been
included among his haunts during the break-away
above mentioned, and he remembered that the
scenery was beautiful, the situation remote, and
the air noble. Next to the sea it seemed an ideal
place to recuperate and write in. Thither, at all
events, he resolved to go, and early in the summer
of 1850 we arrived at the little red house above the
shores of Stockbridge Bowl, with bag and baggage.
Little though the house was, the bag and baggage
were none too much to find easy accommodation
in it.

A fair-sized city drawing-room of these sumptuous contemporary days could stow away in a corner
the entire structure which then became our habitation, and retain space enough outside it for the
exploitation of social functions. Nevertheless, by
the simple expedient of making the interior divi-
sions small enough, this liliputian edifice managed
to contain eight rooms on its two floors (including
the kitchen). One of the rooms was, in fact, the
entrance-hall; you stepped into it across the threshold of the outer door, and the staircase ascended
from it. It was used as an extension of the drawing-room, which opened out of it. The drawing-
room adjoined the dining-room, with windows fac-

ing the west, with a view of the mountains across
the lake, and the dining-room communicated with
the kitchen. One of the western-looking up-stairs
rooms served as my father's study; my sister Una
had her chamber, I mine (which was employed as
the guest-chamber upon occasion), and our parents
the other. What more could be asked?—for when
Rose was born, her crib stood beside her mother's
bedstead.

When we were not asleep—that is, during twelve
hours out of the twenty-four—Una's existence and
mine were passed mainly in the outer sitting-room
and in the dining-room. There was plenty to entertain us. I had my rocking-horse, which I be-
strode with perfect fearlessness; my porcelain lion,
which still survives unscathed after the cataclysms
of half a century; my toy sloop, made for me by
Uncle Nat; and a jack-knife, all but the edge and
point, which had been removed out of deference to
my youth. Una had a doll, a miniature mahogany
centre-table and bureau, and other things in which
I felt no interest. In common, we possessed the
box of wooden bricks, and the big portfolio containing tracings by my mother, exquisitely done,
of Flaxman's "Outlines of the *Iliad* and *Odyssey*"
and other classic subjects. We knew by heart the
story of all these mythological personages, and
they formed a large part of our life. They also
served the important use of suggesting to my father
his *Wonder-Book* and *Tanglewood Tales* stories, and,
together with the figures of Gothic fairy-lore, they

were the only playmates, with the exception of our father and mother, that we had or desired.

But our father and mother were, of course, the main thing, after all. She was with us all day long; he, from the time he stopped writing, early in the afternoon, till our bed - time. They answered all our questions about things animate and inanimate, physical and metaphysical; and that must have taken time, for our curiosity was magnificent; and "The Old Boy," my father records, "asked me to-day what were sensible questions—I suppose with a view to asking me some." They superintended our projections of creation on the black-board—a great, old-fashioned black-board, the like of which I have not since beheld; they read to us and told us stories. Many of these stories were of incidents of their own child-life; and there was also the narrative of our mother's voyage to Cuba and back, and residence there when she was about eighteen or twenty—a fascinating chronicle. Meal-times were delectable festivals, not only because the bread-and-milk, the boiled rice and tapioca pudding, and eggs and fruit tasted so good, but by reason of the broad outlook out of window over the field, the wood, the lake, and the mountains; supper-time, with the declining sun pouring light into the little room and making the landscape glorious, was especially exhilarating. Ambrosial was the bread baked by Mrs. Peters, the taciturn and serious religious person of color who attended to our cooking; the prize morsels were the ends, golden brown in hue, crunching so crisply between our teeth. I used to wonder how a being with hands so dark as those of Mrs. Peters managed to turn out dough so immaculate. She would plunge them right into the ivory-hued substance, yet it became only whiter than before.

But the life of life was, of course, out-doors. There was a barn containing a hay-mow and a large hen-coop, soon populous with hens and chickens, with an heroic snow-white rooster to keep them in order. Hens are the most audacious and presuming of pets, and they have strong individuality. One of our brood was more intellectual and enterprising than the others; she found a way of getting out of the coop, no matter how tightly it was shut up; and she would jump in our laps as we sat eating a piece of bread in the barn doorway and snatch it away from us; but I think we sometimes sat there with the bread on purpose to have her do it. Once or twice—until I was detected and stopped—I enjoyed the poignant delight of fishing for hens out of the barn loft; my tackle consisted of a bent pin at the end of a string tied to a stick. It was baited with a grain of corn, or a bit of rag would do as well, for hens have no hereditary suspicion of anglers, and are much more readily entrapped than fishes. Pulling them up, squawking and fluttering, was thrilling, but, of course, it was wrong, like other thrilling things, and had to be foregone. A less unregenerate experiment was fastening two grains of corn to the ends of a long bit of thread; two hens would seize each a grain and begin swallowing thread

25

until they interfered with each other, when a dis-gorgement would take place. It was an economical sport—the one bit of thread and the two corn-grains would last all day—and, in view of the joy afforded to the spectators, did not seem too unkind.

My father had mechanical talent, and with an old door-knob and some strips of shingle he would make a figure of a man with a saw; you fixed it to the edge of a table, set the door-knob swinging, and the creature would saw with the most absurd dili-gence. From the same shingle he would construct a pugilist, who, being set up where the wind played upon him, would swing his arms interminably. It was yacht-building, however, that afforded us most entertainment. A shingle was whittled to a point at one end; a stick with a square paper slipped on it was stuck up in the middle, and a rudder made fast to the stern; such a boat would sail boldly out upon the vastness of the lake, till the eye could no longer follow the diminishing white speck. These days beside the lake were full of good things. The water was clear, with a white sand bottom; we were given swimming-lessons in the hot summer weather; having waded in up to our middles, we faced towards the shore, where sat our father with a long fishing-pole, the end of which he kept within our reach, and bade us lean forward on the water and kick up our feet. But, for my part, I kept one foot on the bottom. It was not till years afterwards that I mustered courage to take it off, and that was in a lake three thousand miles from Stockbridge Bowl,

with the towers of the castle of Chillon reflected in
its calm surface.

We also made limited use of a leaky old punt,
which one day capsized and emptied its whole crew
into the water, luckily close to shore. We fished for
gold carp for hours together, and during our two
summers we caught a couple of them; there were
thousands of them swimming about; but a bent pin
with the bait washed off is not a good lure. In winter, the lake had five feet of ice on it, which lasted
far into the spring, and once or twice we got aboard
this great raft and tracked across it, with as much
awe and enthusiasm as ever Kane had felt in his
arctic explorations. In all, we became intimate
friends with the lake idea, new to us then, but never
to grow stale; and our good fortune favored us during after-life with many lovely lakes and ponds, including such gems as Rydal, Walden, and Geneva.

Water, in another enchanting guise, dashed and
gurgled for us in the brook that penetrated like a
happy dream the slumber of the forest that bordered on the lake. The wooded declivity through
which it went was just enough to keep it ever vocal
and animated. Gazing down upon it, it was clear
brown, with glancing gleams of interior green, and
sparkles diamond white; tiny fishes switched themselves against the current with quivering tails; the
shaggy margins were flecked with sunshine, and
beautiful with columbines, violets, arbutus, and
houstonias. Fragments of rock and large pebbles
interrupted its flow and deepened its mellow song;

27

above it brooded the twilight of the tall pines and walnuts, responding to its merriment with solemn murmurings. What playfellow is more inexhaustible than such a brook, so full of life, of motion, of sound and color, of variety and constancy. A child welcomes it as an answer to its own soul, with its mystery and transparency, its bounded lawlessness, its love of earth and its echoes of the sky. In winter our brook had a new charm: it ran beneath a roof of ice, often mounded with snow; its voice sounding cheerful as ever in those inscrutable caverns, as if it discoursed secret wonders of fairy-land, and carried treasures of the elves and gnomes. Zero, with his utmost rigors, could not still its speech for a day or fix his grip upon those elastic limbs. Indeed, the frosty god conspired with it for our delight; building crystal bridges, with tracery of lace delicater than Valenciennes, and spangled stringpieces, and fretted vaultings, whimsical sierras, stalactite and stalagmite. An icicle is one of those careless toys of nature which the decorative art of man imitates in vain. They are among the myriad decorations of children's palaces.

To Tanglewood, as we called it, at all seasons of the year, came Hawthorne and his wife and children. In spring there was the issuing forth of the new life from beneath the winter coverlid; the first discovery of sociable houstonias, and the exquisite tints and fragrance of the mayflower on its dark, bearded stalk. When June became perfect, and afterwards till nuts were ripe, my father loved to lie at full length upon the mossy and leaf-strewn floor, looking up at the green roof, the lofty whispering-gallery of vaulted boughs, with its azure lattices and descending sunlight-shafts; wrapped in imaginings some of which were afterwards to delight the world; but many more of them, no doubt, were fated to join the glorious company of untold tales. Beside him sat our mother, on a throne which we had fashioned for her from the upright stump of a tree; round about them played the little girl and boy. They brought all the treasures which this wonderfully affluent world afforded: flowers in all seasons; strawberries, small but of potent flavor, which the little boy would gather with earnest diligence, and fetch to the persons he loved, mashed into premature jam in his small fist; exciting turtles with variegated carapaces, and heads and feet that went in and out; occasional newts from the plashy places; and in autumn, hatfuls of walnuts. There were chestnuts, too, upon whose prickly hulls the preoccupied children would sometimes inadvertently plump themselves. Our father was a great tree-climber, and he was also fond of playing the rôle of magician. "Hide your eyes!" he would say, and the next moment, from being there beside us on the moss, we would hear his voice descending from the sky, and behold! he swung among the topmost branches, showering down upon us a hail-storm of nuts. There was a big cavern behind the kitchen chimney, which gradually became filled with these harvests, and on winter evenings they were brought forth and cracked with a hammer on the hearth-stone.

The wide field, or croft, which sloped from the house to the wood was thickly grown with mullein-stalks, against which I waged war with an upper section of one of my father's old broken canes, for I took them for giants, and stubborn, evil-minded enchanters. I slew them by scores; but I could make no way against the grasshoppers, which jumped against my bare legs and pricked them. There were wasps, too; one of them stung Una on the lower lip as she was climbing over a rail-fence. Her lip at once assumed a Bourbon contour, and I reached the conclusion, by some tacit syllogism of infancy, that the rail-fence was at least half to blame for the catastrophe, and always carefully avoided it. I likewise avoided the wasps; a certain trick they have of giving a hitch to their after-parts as they walk along always struck me as being obviously diabolical.

When the snows came, two and three feet deep, we got out the family sled from its summer lodging in the barn and went forth, muffled in interminable knit tippets and other woollen armor, to coast down the long slope. Our father sat in front with the reins in his hands and his feet thrust out to steer, and away we went clinging fast behind him. Some-times we swept triumphantly to the bottom; at other times we would collide with some hidden ob-stacle, and describe each a separate trajectory into the snow-banks. We made enormous snow-balls by beginning with a small one and rolling it over and over in the soft snow till it waxed too vast for our strength; two or three of these piled one on another would be sculptured by the author of *The Scarlet Letter* into a snow-man, who would stand stanch for weeks. Snow-storms in Lenox began early and lasted till far into April. The little red house had all it could do, sometimes, to lift its upper windows above them. In the front yard there was a symmetrical balsam fir-tree, tapering like a Chinese pagoda. One winter morning we found upon one of its lower boughs a little brown sparrow·frozen stiff. We put it in a card-board coffin, and dug out a grave for it beneath the fir, with a shingle head-stone. The funeral ceremonies had for the two mourners a solemnity such as is not always felt at such functions in later life.

Of the regular daily routine was the journey to Luther Butler's, quarter of a mile up the road, for milk and butter. I generally accompanied my father, and saw placid Luther's cows, placid as himself, with their broad, wet noses, amiable dark eyes, questionable horns, and ambrosial breath. Mr. Tappan, our landlord, had horses, and once he mounted me on the bare back of one of the largest of these quadrupeds, which, to the stupefaction of everybody, instantly set off at full gallop. Down the road we thundered, the rider, with his legs sticking out at right angles, screaming with joy, for this transcended any rocking-horse experiences. A hundred yards away there was a bend in the road.

Just at that point there was a manure-pile, which had long bided its time. I had hold of a strand of the horse's mane; but when he swerved at the bend I had to let go, and after a short flight in air, the manure-pile received me in its soft embrace. Looking up the road, I saw Mr. Tappan, with dilated eyes and a countenance expressing keen emotion, coming towards me at a wonderful pace, and my father and mother following him at a short distance. I did not myself mind the smell of manure, and the others were glad to put up with it in consideration of my having escaped broken bones.

We did not keep a dog, but Herman Melville, who often came over from Pittsfield, had a large Newfoundland which he sometimes brought with him, and Mr. G. P. R. James, a novelist of the Walter Scott school, had another, and I was permitted to bestride both of them; they were safe enough, but they would turn back their heads and lay their cold noses on my leg; I preferred the now-forbidden horse. But Melville himself made up for everything by the tremendous stories he used to tell about the South Sea Islands and the whale fishery. Normally he was not a man of noticeable appearance; but when the narrative inspiration was on him, he looked like all the things he was describing —savages, sea-captains, the lovely Fayaway in her canoe, or the terrible Moby Dick himself. There was vivid genius in this man, and he was the strangest being that ever came into our circle. Through all his wild and reckless adventures, of which a

HERMAN MELVILLE

small part only got into his fascinating books, he had been unable to rid himself ot a Puritan conscience; he afterwards tried to loosen its grip by studying German metaphysics, but in vain. He was restless and disposed to dark hours, and there is reason to suspect that there was in him a vein of insanity. His later writings were incomprehensible. When we were living in England, he passed through the midst of us on one of his aimless, mysterious journeys round the world; and when I was in New York, in 1884, I met him, looking pale, sombre, nervous, but little touched by age. He died a few years later. He conceived the highest admiration for my father's genius, and a deep affection for him personally; but he told me, during our talk, that he was convinced that there was some secret in my father's life which had never been revealed, and which accounted for the gloomy passages in his books. It was characteristic in him to imagine so; there were many secrets untold in his own career. But there were few honester or more lovable men than Herman Melville.

James (no relation of our distinguished contemporary) was a commonplace, meritorious person, with much blameless and intelligent conversation; but the only thing that recalls him personally to my memory is the fact of his being associated with a furious thunder-storm. My father and I were alone in the house at the time; my mother had gone to West Newton on a three weeks' visit. In the midst of the thunder and lightning, the downpour and the hurricane, the crash of matter and the wreck of worlds, our door burst open, and behold! of all persons in the world to be heralded by such circumstances, G. P. R. James! Not he only, but close upon his heels his entire family, numerous, orthodox, admirable, and infinitely undesirable to two secluded gentlemen without a wife and mother to help them out. But it was a choice between murder and hospitality, and come in they must. Never before or after did our liliputian drawing-room harbor so large an assemblage. They dripped on the carpet, they were conventional and courteous; we made conversation between us; but whenever the thunder rolled, Mrs. James became ghastly pale. Mr. James explained that this was his birthday, and that they were on a pleasure excursion. He conciliated me by anecdotes of a pet magpie or raven who stole spoons. At last, the thunder-storm and the G. P. R. Jameses passed off together.

There were many other visitors, not only old friends, but persons attracted thither out of the void by the fame of the book "along whose burning leaves," as Oliver Wendell Holmes sang of it, "his scarlet web our wild romancer weaves." It was a novel experience for the man who had become accustomed to regarding himself as the obscurest man of letters in America. Lonely, yearning ladies came; enthusiastic young men; melancholy sinners. The little red house was not a literary Mecca only, but a moral one. The dark-browed, kindly smiling author received them all

34

courteously; he was invariably courteous. "I would not have a drunken man politer than I," he once answered me, when I asked him why he had returned the salutation of a toper. What counsel he gave to those who came to him as to a father confessor of course I know not; but later, when I used to sit in his office in the Liverpool consulate, I sometimes heard him speak plain truths to the waifs and strays who drifted in there; and truth more plain, yet bestowed with more humanity and brotherly purpose, I have never heard since. It made them tremble, but it did them good. Such things made him suffer, but he never flinched from the occasion by a hair's-breadth. He must have loved his fellow-creatures.

Somebody gave me a rabbit, which I named Hindlegs. I was deeply interested in him for a while, especially when I learned that he could not drink water; but he lasted only two weeks, and I am under the impression that I killed him. Not that I loved him less; but children are prone to experiment with this singular thing called life when it is in their power. They do not believe that death can be other than a transient phenomenon; the lifeless body may puzzle, but it does not convince them. I was certainly not a cruel urchin, and I can recall none but cordial sentiments towards Hindlegs on my part. I remember no details of the murder, if murder were done; but I do remember feeling no surprise when, one morning, Hindlegs was found dead. After so many years, I will not bring against

the owner of Hindlegs a verdict of positive guilt;
but I suspect him. Hindlegs, at all events, achieved
an immortality which can belong to few of his
brethren; for my father, after pooh-poohing the
imbecile little bundle of fur for a day or two, conceived an involuntary affection for him, and reported his character and habits in his journal in a
manner which is likely to keep his memory alive
long after the hand that (perhaps) slew him is dust.

In default of dogs and Hindlegs, we had abundant cats. My father was always fond of these
mysterious deities of ancient Egypt, and they were
never turned away from our doors; but how so
many of them happened to find us out in this remote region I cannot explain. It seems as if good-
will towards cats spontaneously generated them.
They appeared, one after another, to the number
of five; but when the time came for us to leave the
red house forever, the cats would not and could not
be packed up, and they were left behind. In my
mind's eye I still see them, squatting abreast, sil-
houetted against the sky, on the brow of the hill as
we drove down the road; for they had scampered
after our carry-all when we drove away. Cats
teach Americans what they are slow to learn—the
sanctity and permanence of home.

But Lenox could not be a home for us. It was,
indeed, a paradise for the children; but the children's father was never well there. He had a succession of colds—as those affections are called; it
was ascribed to the variations of temperature dur-

ing the summers; but the temperature would not have troubled him had he not been hard hit before he went to Berkshire. He got out of patience with the climate, and was wont to anathematize it with humorous extravagance, as his way was: "It is horrible. One knows not for ten minutes together whether he is too cool or too warm. I detest it! I hate Berkshire with my whole soul. Here, where I had hoped for perfect health, I have for the first time been made sensible that I cannot with impunity encounter nature in all her moods." It was the summers that disagreed with him. "Upon the whole," he said, "I think that the best time for living in the country is the winter." It was during the winter that he did most of his writing. *The House of the Seven Gables* was written between September of 1850 and January or February of 1851. But composition took more out of him than formerly. He admitted to his sister Louisa that he was "a little worn down with constant work," and added that he could not afford any idle time now, being evidently of the opinion that his popularity would be short-lived, and that it behooved him, therefore, to make the most of it. But "the pen is so constantly in my fingers that I abominate the sight of it!" he exclaimed. This was after he had transgressed his custom of never writing in the hot months. He began in June and finished in forty days the whole volume of *The Wonder-Book*. He also read the tales to his domestic audience as fast as they were written, and benefited, perhaps, by the expert criticism of the small people. Many passages in the intercalated chapters, describing the adventures of Eustace Bright and the Tanglewood children, are based on facts well known to his own two youngsters. And when Eustace tells his hearers that if the dark-haired man dwelling in the cottage yonder were simply to put some sheets of writing-paper in the fire, all of them and Tanglewood itself would turn into cinders and vanish in smoke up the chimney—even the present chronicler saw the point; though, at the same time, he somehow could not help believing in the reality of Primrose, Buttercup, Dandelion, Squash-blossom, and the rest. Thus early did he begin to grasp the philosophy of the truth of fiction.

The House of the Seven Gables and *The Wonder-Book* were a fair eighteen - months' work, and in addition to them Hawthorne had, before leaving Lenox, planned out the story of *The Blithedale Romance;* so that after we got to West Newton—our half-way station on the road to Concord—he was prepared to sit down and write it. Long before we left Concord for England he had published *Tanglewood Tales*, not to mention the biography of Franklin Pierce. Una and her brother knew nothing about the romances; they knew and approved the fairy tales; but their feeling about all their father's writings was, that he was being wasted in his study, when he might be with them, and there could be nothing in any books, whether his own or other authors', that could for a moment bear comparison with his actual companionship. What he set down upon the page was but a less free and rich version of the things that came from his living mouth in our heedless playtimes. "If only papa wouldn't write, how nice it would be!" And, indeed, a book is but a poor substitute for the mind and heart of a man, and it exists only as one of the numberless sorry makeshifts to which time constrains us, while we are waiting for eternity and full communion.

It was a dreary day in the beginning of the second winter that we set out on our eastward journey; but Hawthorne's face was brighter than the weather warranted, for it was turned once more towards the sea. We were destined, ere we turned back, to go much farther towards the rising sun than any of us then suspected. We took with us one who had not been present at our coming—a little auburn-haired baby, born in May. Which are the happiest years of a man's life? Those in which he is too much occupied with present felicity to look either forward or backward — to hope or to remember. There are no such years; but such moments there may be, and perhaps there were as many such moments awaiting Hawthorne as had already passed. His greatest work was done before he left his native land, and within a year or two of his death he wrote to Richard Stoddard: "I have been a happy man, and yet I cannot remember any moment of such happy conspiring circumstances that I would have rung a joy-bell at it."

III

The sky that overhung Hawthorne's departure
from Lenox was gray with impending snow, and
the flakes had begun to fall ere the vehicle in which
his family was ensconced had reached the railway
station in Pittsfield. Travel had few amenities in
those days. The cars were all plain cars, with
nothing to recommend them except that they went
tolerably fast—from twenty to thirty miles an hour.
They were chariots of delight to the children, who
were especially happy in occupying the last car of
the train, from the rear windows of which they
could look down upon the tracks, which seemed to
slide miraculously away from beneath them. The

conductor collected the tickets—a mysterious rite. The gradually whitening landscape fled past, becoming ever more level as we proceeded; by-and-by there was a welcome unpacking of the luncheon-basket, and all the while there were the endless questions to be asked and faithfully answered. It was already dark by the time we were bundled out at the grimy shed which was called the depot, at West Newton, where we were met by the Horace Manns, and somehow the transit to the latter's house, which we were to occupy for the winter, was made. The scene was gloomy and unpleasant; the change from the mountains of the west depressing; and, for my part, I cannot remember anything agreeable in this raw little suburb. American life half a century ago had a great deal of rawness about it, and its external aspect was ugly beyond present belief. We may be a less virtuous nation now than we were then, but we are indescribably more good to look at. And the West Newton of to-day, as compared with that of 1851, will serve for an illustration of this truth.

Horace Mann's house was a small frame dwelling, painted white, with green blinds, and furnished with a furnace stiflingly hot. One of the first things the baby did was to crawl under the sofa in the sitting-room and lay her small fingers against the radiator or register, or whatever it is called, through which the heat came. She withdrew them with a bitter outcry, and on the tip of each was a blister as big as the tip itself. We had no glorious out - door playground in West Newton; it was a matter of back yards and sullen streets. The snow kept piling up, week after week; but there was no opportunity to put it to its proper use of coasting. The only redeeming feature of the physical situation that I recall is the momentous fact of a first pair of red-topped boots. They were very uncomfortable, and always either wet or stiff as iron from over-dryness; but they made their wearer as happy as they have made all other boys since boots began. A boy of six with high boots is bigger than most men.

But if the outward life was on the whole unprepossessing, inward succulence was not lacking. We had the Manns, to begin with, and the first real acquaintance between the two sets of children opened here. Mary Peabody, my mother's elder sister, had married Horace Mann, whose name is honorably identified with the development in this country of common-school education. They had three children, of about our age, all boys. A statue in bronze of Horace Mann stands in front of the State-house in Boston, and the memory of the strenuous reformer well merits the distinction. He took things seriously and rather grimly, and was always emphatically in earnest. He was a friend of George Combe, the phrenologist, after whom his second boy was named; and he was himself so ardent a believer in the new science that when his younger son, Benjamin, was submitted to him for criticism at a very early age he declared, after a strict phrenological examination, that he was not worth bringing up. But children's heads sometimes undergo strange transformations as they grow up, and Benjamin lived to refute abundantly his father's too hasty conclusion in his case. He became eminent as an entomologist; George followed the example of his father on educational lines. Horace, who died comparatively early, was an enthusiastic naturalist, who received the unstinted praise and confidence of the great Agassiz. My uncle Horace, as I remember him, was a very tall man, of somewhat meagre build, a chronic sufferer from headaches and dyspepsia. His hair was sandy, straight, rather long, and very thick; it hung down uncompromisingly round his head. His face was a long square, with a mouth and chin large and immitigably firm. His eyes were reinforced by a glistening pair of gold-bowed spectacles. He always wore a long-skirted black coat. His aspect was a little intimidating to small people; but there were lovely qualities in his nature, his character was touchingly noble and generous, and the world knows the worth of his intellect. He was anxious, exacting, and dogmatic, and was not always able to concede that persons who differed from him in opinion could be morally normal. This was especially noticeable when the topic of abolition happened to come up for discussion; Horace Mann was ready to out-Garrison Garrison; he thought *Uncle Tom's Cabin* a somewhat milk - and - water tract. He was convinced that Tophet was the future home of all slave-holders, and really too good for them, and he practically worshipped the negro. Had he occupied a seat in Congress at that juncture, it is likely that the civil war might have been started a decade sooner than it was. My father and mother were much more moderate in their view of the situation, and my mother used to say that if slavery was really so evil and demoralizing a thing as the abolitionists asserted, it was singular that they should canonize all the subjects of the institution. But, as a rule, all controversy with the indignant zeal of our relative was avoided; in his eyes any approach to a philosophical attitude on the burning question was a crime. Nor were his convictions less pronounced on the subject of total abstinence from liquor and tobacco. Now, my father smoked an occasional cigar, and it once came about that he was led to mention the fact in Horace Mann's hearing. The reformer's bristles were set in a moment. "Do I understand you to say, Mr. Hawthorne, that you actually use tobacco?" "Yes, I smoke a cigar once in a while," replied my father, comfortably. Horace Mann could not keep his seat; he started up and paced the room menacingly. He had a high admiration for my father's genius, and a deep affection for him as a man, and this infidelity to the true faith seemed to him the more appalling. But he would be true to his colors at all costs, and after a few moments he planted himself, tall and tragic, before his interlocutor, and spoke, in a husky voice, to this effect: "Then, Mr. Hawthorne, it is my duty

44

to tell you that I no longer have the same respect for you that I have had." Then he turned and strode from the room, leaving the excommunicated one to his reflections. Faithful are the wounds of a friend, and my father was as much touched as he was amused by this example of my uncle's candor. Of course, there was a great vacuum in the place where my uncle's sense of humor might have been; but there are a time and place for such men as he, and more than once the men without sense of humor have moved the world.

In addition to the Manns, there were visitors—the succession of whom, indeed, was henceforth to continue till the end of my father's earthly pilgrimage. Among the earliest to arrive was Grace Greenwood, wading energetically to our door through the December snow. She was one of the first, if not the first, of the tribe of women correspondents; she had lately returned, I think, from England, and the volume of her letters from that strange country was in everybody's hands. She was then a young woman, large and handsome, with dark hair and complexion, and large, expressive eyes, harmonious, aquiline features, and a picturesque appearance. She wore her hair in abundant curls; she exhaled an atmosphere of romance, of graceful and ardent emotions, and of almost overpowering sentiment. In fact, she had a genuine gift for expression and description, and she made an impression in contemporary letters. We might smile now—and, in truth, we sometimes did then—over some of her pages; but much of her work would still be called good, if resuscitated from the dusty book-shelves of the past. I remember one passage in her *English Letters* which was often quoted in our family circle as a typical illustration of the intensity of the period: "The first tears," wrote Grace, "that I had shed since leaving my dear native land fell fast into the red heart of an English rose!" Nothing could be better than that; but the volume was full of similar felicities. You were swimming in radiant tides of enthusiastic appreciation, quotations from the poets and poetical rhapsodies; incidents of travel, humorous, pathetic, and graphic; swirling eddies of word-painting, of moral and ethical and historical reflection; withal, an immense, amiable, innocent, sprawling temperament. And as was her book, so was Grace herself; indeed, if any one could outdo the book in personal conversation, Grace was that happy individual. What she accomplished when she embarked, full-sailed, upon the topic of *The Scarlet Letter* and *The House of the Seven Gables* may be pictured to themselves by persons endowed with the rudiments of imagination; I must not attempt to adorn this sober page with an attempted reproduction of the scene. Mortal language reeled and cracked under the strain of giving form to her admiration; but it was so honest and well meant that it could not but give pleasure even in the midst of bewilderment. My father bowed his head with a painful smile; but I dare say it did him good when the ordeal was over.

46

At this time the reverberations of the European revolutionary year, 1848, were still breaking upon our shores. President Polk had given mortal offence to Austria by sending over a special commissioner to determine whether the seceding státe of Hungary might be recognized as a belligerent. In 1850 the Austrian representative, Baron Huelsmann, had entered upon a correspondence with our own Daniel Webster. The baron remonstrated, and Daniel mounted upon the national bird and soared in the patriotic empyrean. The eloquence of the Secretary of State perhaps aroused unwarranted expectations in the breasts of the struggling revolutionists, and the Hungarian man of eloquence set out for the United States to take the occasion by the forelock. Not since the visit of Lafayette had any foreigner been received here with such testimonials of public enthusiasm, or listened to by such applausive audiences: certainly none had ever been sent home again with less wool to show for so much cry. In 1851, the name of Kossuth was the most popular in the country, and when it was learned that he had accepted an invitation to speak in our little West Newton, we felt as if we were almost embarked upon a campaign — upon an altruistic campaign of emancipation against the Hapsburg oppressor. The excitement was not confined to persons of mature age and understanding; it raged among the smaller fry, and every boy was a champion of Kossuth. The train conveying the hero from New York to Boston (whence he was to return to West Newton after the reception there) was timed to pass through our midst at three o'clock in the afternoon, and our entire population was at the track-side to see it go by. After one or two false alarms it came in sight round the curve, the smoke-stack of the engine swathed in voluminous folds of Old Glory. The smoke-stacks of those days were not like our scientific present-day ones; they were huge, inverted cones, affording ample surface for decoration. The train did not stop at our station; but Kossuth no doubt looked out of the window as he flew past and bowed his acknowledgments of our cheers. He was to return to us the next day, and, meanwhile, the town-hall, or the church, or whatever building it was that was to be the scene of his West Newton triumph was put in order for his reception. The person who writes these words, whose ears had eagerly devoured the story of the Hungarian revolt, wished to give the august visitor some personal assurance of his distinguished con-sideration, and it was finally agreed by his indul-gent parents that he should print upon a card the legend, "GOD BLESS YOU, KOSSUTH," and be afford-ed an opportunity personally to present it to the guest of the nation. Many cards had been used and cast aside before the scribe, his fingers tremu-lous with emotion, had produced something which the Hungarian might be reasonably expected to find legible. Then, supported by his father and mother, and with his uncles, aunts, and cousins doubtless not far off, he proceeded proudly but falteringly to the scene of the presentation. He dimly recalls a large interior space, profusely decorated with stars and stripes, and also the colors of Hungary. At the head of the room was a great placard with " WELCOME, KOSSUTH " inscribed upon it. There was a great throng and press of men and women, a subdued, omnipresent roar of talk, and a setting of the tide towards the place where the patriot stood to receive our personal greetings. The scribe whom I have mentioned, being as yet brief of stature, was unable to see anything except coat-tails and petticoats, until of a sudden there was a breaking away of these obstacles and he found himself in close proximity to a gentleman of medium height, strongly built, with a mop of dark hair framing a handsome, pale, smiling face, the lower parts of which were concealed by a thick brown beard. It was Kossuth, and there was that in his countenance and expression which satisfied all the dreams of his admirer. He was chatting and shaking hands with the elder persons; and in a minute we were moving on again, and the printed card, for which the whole function had been created, had not been presented. At the last moment, in an agony of apprehension, the boy pulled at his mother's skirt and whispered piteously, "But my card!" She heard and remembered; but need was for haste; we had already passed the vantage-point. She snatched it from the tightly gripping fingers of the bearer, handed it to Kossuth, and at the same moment, with a gesture, directed his attention to her small companion. The Hungarian read the inscription at a glance, looked me in the eyes with a quick smile of comprehension, and, stepping towards me, laid his hand upon my head. It was a great moment for me; but as I went away I suddenly dissolved in tears, whether from the reaction of emotion, or because I had not myself succeeded in delivering my gift, I cannot now determine. But Kossuth thereby became, and for years he continued to be, the most superb figure in my political horizon.

All this while *The Blithedale Romance* was being written. Inasmuch as it was finished on the last day of April, 1852, it could not have occupied the writer more than five months in the composition. Winter was his best time for literary work, and there was winter enough that year in West Newton. In the middle of April came the heaviest snowstorm of the season. Brook Farm (modified in certain respects to suit the conditions) was the scene of the story, and Brook Farm was within a fair walk of West Newton. I visited the place some thirty years later, and found the general topographical features substantially as described in the book. In 1852 it was ten years since Hawthorne had lived there, and though he might have renewed his acquaintance with it while the writing was going on, there is no record of his having done so; and considering the unfavorable weather, and the fact that the imaginative atmosphere which writers seek is enhanced by distance in time, just as the physical effect of a landscape is improved by distance of space, makes it improbable that he availed himself of the opportunity. His note-books contain but few comments upon the routine of life of the community; his letters to his wife (then Sophia Peabody) are somewhat fuller; one can trace several of these passages, artistically metamorphosed, in the romance. The episode of the masquerade picnic is based on fact, and the scene of the recovery of Zenobia's body from the river is a tolerably close reproduction of an event in Concord, in which, several years before, Hawthorne had been an actor. The portrayal in the story of city life from the back windows of the hotel, is derived from notes made just before we went to Lenox; there are the enigmatic drawing-room windows, the kitchen, the stable, the spectral cat, and the emblematic dove; the rain-storm; the glimpse of the woman sewing in one of the windows. There is also a passage containing a sketch of the personage who served as the groundwork for Old Moody. "An elderly ragamuffin, in a dingy and battered hat, an old surtout, and a more than shabby general aspect; a thin face and a red nose, a patch over one eye, and the other half drowned in moisture. He leans in a slightly stooping posture on a stick, forlorn and silent, addressing nobody but fixing his one moist eye on you with a certain intentness. He is a man who has been in decent circumstances at some former period of his life, but, falling into decay, he now haunts about the place, as a ghost haunts the spot where he was murdered. The word ragamuffin," he adds, with characteristic determination to be exact, "does not accurately express the man, because there is a sort of shadow or delusion of respectability about him, and a sobriety, too, and a kind of dignity in his groggy and red-nosed destitution." Out of this subtle correction of his own description arose the conception of making Old Moody the later state of the once wealthy and magnificent Fauntleroy. But one of the most striking and imaginative touches in the passage, likening the old waif to a ghost haunting the spot (Parker's liquor-bar) where he was murdered, is omitted in the book, because, striking though it was, it was a little too strong to be in keeping with the rest of the fictitious portrait. How many writers, having hit upon such a simile, would have had conscience and self-denial enough, not to mention fine enough artistic sense, to delete it!

The craftsman's workmanship may occasionally be traced in this way; but, as a rule, it is difficult to catch a glimpse of him in his creative moments. If he made rough draughts of his stories, he must have destroyed them after the stories themselves were completed; for none such, in the case of his finished products, was left. I have seen the manuscripts of all his tales except *The Scarlet Letter*, which was destroyed by James T. Fields's printers—Fields having at that time no notion of the fame the romance was to achieve, or of the value that would attach to every scrap of Hawthorne's writing. All the extant manuscripts are singularly free from erasures

JAMES T. FIELDS

and interlineations; page after page is clear as a page of print. He would seem to have taught himself so thoroughly how to write that, by the time the series of his longer romances began, he was able to say what he wished to say at a first attempt. He had the habit, undoubtedly, of planning out the work of each day on the day previous, generally while walking in solitude either out-of-doors or, if that were impracticable, up and down the floor of his study. It was this habit which created the pathway along the summit of the ridge of the hill at Wayside, in Concord; it was a deeply trodden path, in the hard, root-inwoven soil, hardly nine inches wide and about two hundred and fifty yards in length. The monotonous movement of walking seemed to put his mind in the receptive state favorable for hearing the voices of imagination. The external faculties were quiescent, the veil of matter was lifted, and he was able to peruse the vision beyond.

But there is an important exception to this rule to be noted in the matter of his fictitious narratives which were posthumously published. These, as I have elsewhere said, are all concerned with a single theme—the never-dying man. There are two complete versions of *Septimius*, of about equal length, and many passages in the two are identical. There is a short sketch on somewhat different lines, called (by the editor) *The Bloody Footstep;* and there is still another, and a much more elaborate attempt to embody the idea in the volume which I have

53

entitled *Doctor Grimshawe's Secret.* All these, in short, are studies of one subject, and they were all unsatisfactory to the author. The true vein of which he had been in search was finally discovered in *The Dolliver Romance*, but the author's death prevented its completion.

In this series of posthumous manuscripts there is a unique opportunity for making a study of the esoteric qualities of my father's style and methods, and on a future occasion I' hope to present the result of my investigations in this direction. There is, furthermore, in connection with them, a mass of material of a yet more interesting and interior character. While writing the *Grimshawe*, he was deeply perplexed by certain details of the plot; the meaning of the Pensioner, and his proper function in the story, was one of these stumbling-blocks. But the prosperity of the tale depended directly upon the solution of this problem. Constantly, therefore, in the midst of the composition, he would break off and enter upon a wrestling-match with the difficulty. These wrestling-matches are of an absorbing significance; they reveal to us the very inmost movements of the author's mind. He tries, and tries again, to get at the idea that continues to elude him; he forms innumerable hypotheses; he sets forth on the widest excursions; he gets out of patience with himself and with his Pensioner, and often damns the latter in good set terms; but he will not give up the struggle; his resolve to conquer is adamantine, and the conflict is always renewed.

And there it all stands in black and white; one of
the most instructive chapters in literary criticism in
the world—the battle of a great writer with himself. The final issue, after all, was hardly decisive,
for although a tolerable *modus vivendi* was reached
and a truce declared, it is evident that Hawthorne
regarded the entire scheme of the story as a mistake, and it is concluded in a perfunctory and indifferent manner.

But it may be doubted whether anything of this
sort ever took place in the making of any of the other
stories. These depend but in a subordinate degree
upon what is called technically plot interest. The
author's method was to take a natural, even a familiar incident, and to transmute it into immortal
gold by simply elucidating its inner spiritual significance. *The Scarlet Letter* is a mere plain story
of love and jealousy; there is no serious attempt to
hide the identity of Roger Chillingworth or the
guilt of the minister. The only surprise in *The
House of the Seven Gables* consists in the revelation
of the fact that Maule reappears after several generations in the person of his modern descendant.
The structure of *The Blithedale Romance* appears
more complicated; but that is mainly because, in a
masterly manner, the author keeps the structural
lines out of sight and concentrates attention upon
the interplay of character. The scaffolding upon
which are hung the splendid draperies of *The Marble Faun* is, again, of the simplest formation, though
the nature of the materials is unfamiliar.

This is a digression; the present volume, as I have already stated, is not designed to include—except incidentally—anything in the way of literary criticism.

Blithedale having been finished and published, the question of where to settle down permanently once more came up for an answer. Of course, our sojourn at Mr. Mann's house had been a temporary expedient only; and for that matter, the Manns, following the example of most Americans before and since, had rented the place merely as a stepping-stone to something else. My father's eyes again turned with longing towards the sea-shore; but the fitting nook for him there still failed to offer itself. People are naturally disposed to return to places in which they have formerly lived, and Concord could not but suggest itself to one who had passed some of the happiest years of his life among its serene pastures and piney forests. This suggestion, moreover, was supplemented by the urgent invitations of his old friends there, and Mr. Emerson, who was a practical man as well as a philosopher, substantiated his arguments by throwing into the scale a concrete dwelling. It was an edifice which not even the most imaginative and optimistic of house-agents would have found it easy to picture as a sumptuous country-seat; it was just four wooden walls and a roof, and they had been standing for a hundred years at least. The occupants of this house had seen the British march past from Boston on the 19th of April, 1775, and a few hours later they had seen them return along the same dusty highway at a greatly accelerated pace and under annoying circumstances. There was a legend that a man had once lived there who had announced that death was not an indispensable detail of life, and that he for his part intended never to die; but after many years he had grown weary of the monotony of his success, or had realized that it would take too long a time to prove himself in the right, and rather than see the thing through he allowed himself to depart. The old structure, in its original state, consisted of a big, brick chimney surrounded by four rooms and an attic, with a kitchen tacked on at the rear. It stood almost flush with the side-path along the highway; behind it rose a steep hill-side to a height of about one hundred feet; in front, on the other side of the road, stretched broad meadows with a brook flowing through the midst of them. Such conditions would not seem altogether to favor a man wedded to seclusion.

But the thing was not at this juncture quite so bad as it had been. Mr. Alcott, whose unselfish devotion to the welfare of the human race made it incumbent upon his friends to supply him with the means of earthly subsistence, had been recently domiciled in the house by Mr. Emerson (how the latter came into possession of it I have forgotten, if ever I knew), and he had at once proceeded to wreak upon it his unique architectural talent. At any rate, either he himself or somebody in his behalf had set up a small gable in the midst of the front, thrown out a double bow-window, and added a room on the west side. This interrupted the deadly, four-square uniformity, and suggested further improvements. Mr. Alcott certainly built the summer-house on the hill-side, and terraced the hill, which was also planted with apple-trees. Another summer-house arose in the meadow opposite, which went with the property, and rustic fences separated the domain from the road. The dwelling was now fully as commodious as the red house at Lenox, though it had no Monument Mountain and Stockbridge Bowl to look out upon.

The estate, comprising, I think, forty-two acres, all told, including upward of twenty acres of second-growth woodland above the hill, perfectly useless except for kindling-wood and for the sea-music which the pine-trees made, was offered to my father at a reasonable enough figure, to be his own and his heirs' forever. He came over and looked at the place, thought "The Wayside" would be a good name for it, and was perhaps helped to decide upon taking it by the felicity of this appellation. It was close upon the highway, undeniably; but then the highway was so little travelled that it might almost as well not have been there. One might, also, plant a high hedge in place of the fence and make shift to hide behind it. One could enlarge the house as need demanded; an affluent vegetable garden could be laid out in the meadow, and fruit and ornamental trees could be added to the slopes of the hill-side. The village was removed to a dis-

THE WAYSIDE
(Showing Nathaniel Hawthorne and his wife)

tance of a trifle over a mile, so that the roar of its traffic would not invade this retreat; and Mr. Emerson sat radiating peace and wisdom between the village and " The Wayside "; while Mr. Alcott shone with ancillary lustre only a stone's - throw away. Thoreau and Ellery Channing were tramping about in the neighborhood, and Judge Hoar and his beautiful sister dispensed sweetness and light in the village itself. Walden Pond, still secluded as when only the Indians had seen the sky and the trees reflected in it, was within a two-mile walk, and the silent Musketaquid stole on its level way beyond the hill on the other side. Surely, a man might travel far and not find a spot better suited for work and meditation and discreet society than Concord was.

But, of course, the necessity of settling down somewhere was a main consideration. Concord was inviting in itself, but it was also recommended by the argument of exclusion; no other place so desirable and at the same time so easy of attainment happened to present itself. It did not lie within sound and sight of the ocean; but that was the worst that could be urged against it. A man must choose, and Concord was, finally, Hawthorne's choice.

At this epoch he had not contemplated, save in day - dreams, the possibility of visiting the Old World. His friend, Franklin Pierce, had just become President-elect, but that fact had not suggested to his mind the change in his own fortunes

59

which it was destined to bring about. He was too modest a critic of his own abilities to think that his work would ever bring him money enough for foreign travel, and, therefore, in accepting Concord as his home, he believed that he was fixing the boundaries of his future earthly experience. It was not his ideal; no imaginative man can ever hope to find that; but as soon as we have called a place our Home, it acquires a charm that has nothing to do with material conditions. The best-known song in American poesy has impressed that truth upon Americans—who are the most homeless people in the world.

IV

A transfigured cattle-pen—Emerson the hub of Concord
—His incorrigible modesty—Grocery-store sages—To
make common men feel more like Emerson than he did
—His personal appearance—His favorite gesture—A
glance like the reveille of a trumpet—The creaking
boots—"The muses are in the woods"—Emerson could
not read Hawthorne—Typical *versus* individual—Benefit from child-prattle—Concord-grape Bull—Sounds
of distant battle—Politics, sociology, and grape-culture—The great white fence—Richard Henry Stoddard
—A country youth of genius—Whipple's Attic salt—
An unwritten romance—The consulship retires literature—Louisa's tragedy—Hard hit—The spiritual sphere
of good men—Nearer than in the world—The return of
the pilgrim.

My father's first look at "The Wayside" had been
while snow was still on the ground, and he had reported to his wife that it resembled a cattle-pen.
But the family advent was effected in June, and although a heavy rain had fallen while the domestic
impedimenta were in transit, wetting the mattresses
and other exposed furniture, yet when the summer
sun came out things began to mend. My mother
and Una came a day ahead of the others, and with
the help of carpenters and upholsterers, and a neighboring Irishman and his wife for cleaning and mov-

ing purposes, they soon got human order into the place of savage chaos. The new carpet was down in the study, the walls had been already papered and the wood-work grained, the pictures were hung in their places, and the books placed on their shelves. By the time the father, the boy, the baby, and the nurse drove up in the hot afternoon a home had been created for their reception.

Mr. Emerson was, and he always remained, the hub round which the wheel of Concord's fortunes slowly and contentedly revolved. He was at this time between forty-five and fifty years old, in the prime of his beneficent powers. He had fulfilled the promise of his unique youth—obeyed the voice at eve, obeyed at prime. The sweet austerity of his nature had been mellowed by human sorrows—the loss of his brothers and of his eldest son; he had the breadth and poise that are given by knowledge of foreign lands, and friendships with the best men in them; he had the unstained and indomitable independence of a man who has always avowed his belief, and never failed to be true to each occasion for truth; he had the tranquillity of faith and insight, and he was alert with that immortal curiosity for noble knowledge the fruit of which enriches his writings. Upon his modestly deprecating brows was already set the wreath of a world-wide fame, and yet every village farmer and store-keeper, and every child, found in his conversation the wisdom and companionship suited to his needs, and was made to feel that his own companionship was a valued gift. Emerson becomes more extraordinary the further we get away from him in years; illustrating the truth which Landor puts into the mouth of Barrow in one of his *Imaginary Conversations*, that "No very great man ever reached the standard of his greatness in the crowd of his contemporaries: this hath always been reserved for the secondary." The wealth contained in his essays has only begun to be put in general circulation, and the harvest of his poetry is still more remote; while the sincere humility of the man himself, who was the best incarnate example of many of his ideals, still puzzles those critics who believe every one must needs be inferior to his professions.

"Though I am fond of writing and of public speaking," said Emerson, "I am a very poor talker, and for the most part prefer silence"; and he went on to compare himself in this respect with Alcott, "the prince of conversers." Alcott was undoubtedly the prince of fluency, and Emerson rarely, in private dialogue, ventured to string together many consecutive sentences; but the things he did say, on small occasion or great, always hit the gold. On being appealed to, or when his turn came, he would hang a moment in the wind, and then pay off before the breeze of thought with an accuracy and force that gave delight with enlightenment. The form was often epigrammatic, but the air with which it was said beautifully disclaimed any epigrammatic consciousness or intention. It was, rather, "I am little qualified to speak adequately, but this, at least, does seem to me to be true." In the end, therefore, as the interlocutor thought it all over, he was perhaps surprised to discover that, little in quantity as Emerson may have said during the talk, he had yet said more than any one else in substance. But it may be admitted that he was even better in listening than in speech; his look, averted but attentive, with a smile which seemed to postpone full development to the moment when his companion should have uttered the expected apple of gold in the picture of silver, was subtly stimulating to the latter's intellect, and prompted him to outdo himself. His questions were often revelations, discovering truth which the other only then perceived, and thus beguiling him into admiration of his own supposed intelligence. In this, as in other things, he acted upon the precept that it is more blessed to give than to receive gratification; he never seemed to need any other happiness than that of imparting it. And so selflessly and insensibly were the riches of his mind and nature communicated to the community that innocent little Concord could not quite help believing that its wealth and renown were somehow a creation of its own. The loafers in Walcott & Holden's grocery store were, in their own estimation, of heroic stature, because of the unegoistic citizen who dwelt over yonder among the pines. Emerson was a great man, no doubt; but then he was no more than their own confessed equal, or inferior!

This will and power to secularize himself is per-

haps Emerson's unique attribute. It is comparatively easy to stand on mountain-tops and to ride
Pegasus; but how many of those competent to such
feats could at the same time sit cheek by jowl with
hucksters and teamsters without a trace of con-
descension, and while rubbing shoulders with the
rabble of the street in town-meeting, speak without arrogance the illuminating and deciding word?
This, at last, is the true democracy that levels up
instead of down. An Emerson who can make common men feel more like Emerson than he himself
did is the kind of man we need to bring America
up to her ideals.

Emerson was ungainly in build, with narrow,
sloping shoulders, large feet and hands, and a projecting carriage of the head, which enhanced the
eagle-like expression of his glance and features.
His head was small; it was covered (in 1852) with
light brown hair, fine and straight; he was clean-
shaven save for a short whisker; the peaked ends
of an uncomfortable collar appeared above the
folds of a high, black silk stock. His long-skirted
black coat was commonly buttoned up; he wore, on
different occasions, a soft felt hat or a high silk one,
the latter, from use, having become in a manner
humanized. On the street he kept his face up as he
walked along, and perceived the approach of an acquaintance afar off, and the wise, slow smile gleamed about his mouth as he drew near. "How do
you do?" was sometimes his greeting; but more
often, "Good-bye!" or "Good-night!"—an original

and more sensible greeting. Though ungainly in formation, he was not ungraceful in bearing and action; there was a fitness and harmony in his manifestations even on the physical plan. On the lecture platform he stood erect and unadorned, his hands hanging folded in front, save when he changed the leaf of his manuscript, or emphasized his words with a gesture: his customary one, simple but effective, was to clinch his right fist, knuckles upward, the arm bent at the elbow, then a downward blow of the forearm, full of power bridled. It was accompanied by such a glance of the eyes as no one ever saw except from Emerson: a glance like the reveille of a trumpet. Yet his eyes were not noticeably large, and their color was greenish-gray; but they were well set and outlined in his head, and, more than is the case with most men, they were the windows of his soul. Wendell Phillips had an eloquent and intrepid eye, but it possessed nothing approaching the eloquence and spiritual influence of Emerson's. In every Lyceum course in Concord, Emerson lectured once or twice, and the hall was always filled. One night he had the misfortune to wear a pair of abominably creaking boots; every slightest change of posture would be followed by an outcry from the sole-leather, and the audience soon became nervously preoccupied in expecting them. The sublimest thoughts were mingled with these base material accompaniments. But there was nothing to be done, unless the lecturer would finish his lecture in his stocking-feet, and we were fain to derive a fortuitous inspiration from observing the unfaltering meekness with which our philosopher accepted the predicament. I have forgotten the subject of the lecture on that occasion, but the voice of the boots will always sound in my memory.

In his own house Emerson shone with essential hospitality, and yet he wonderfully effaced himself; any one but he might hold the centre of the stage. You felt him everywhere, but if you would see him, you must search the wings. He sat in his chair, bending forward, one leg crossed over the other, his elbows often supported on his knee; his legs were rather long and slender, and he had a way, after crossing his leg, of hitching the instep of that foot under the calf of the other leg, so that he seemed braided up. He seldom stood in a room, or paced to and fro, as my father was fond of doing. But the two men were almost equally addicted to outdoor walking, and both preferred to walk alone. Emerson formed the habit of betaking himself to Walden woods, which extended to within a mile or so of his door; thence would he return with an exalted look, saying, "The muses are in the woods to-day"; and no one who has read his *Woodnotes* can doubt that he found them there. Occasionally Channing, Thoreau, or my father would be his companion; Alcott preferred to busy himself about his rustic fences and summer-houses, or to sit the centre of a circle and converse, as he called it; meaning to soliloquize, looking round from face to face with unalterable faith and complacency.

My father read Emerson with enjoyment; though more and more, as he advanced in life, he was disposed to question the expediency of stating truth in a disembodied form; he preferred it incarnate, as it appears in life and in story. But he could not talk to Emerson; his pleasure in his society did not express itself in that form. Emerson, on the other hand, assiduously cultivated my father's company, and, contrary to his general habit, talked to him continuously; but he could not read his romances; he admitted that he had never been able to finish one of them. He loved to observe him; to watch his silence, which was full of a kind of speech which he was able to appreciate; "Hawthorne rides well his horse of the night!" My father was Gothic; Emerson was Roman and Greek. But each was profoundly original and independent. My father was the shyer and more solitary of the two, and yet persons in need of human sympathy were able to reach a more interior region in him than they could in Emerson. For the latter's thought was concerned with types and classes, while the former had the individual touch. He distrusted rules, but had faith in exceptions and idiosyncrasies. Emerson was nobly and magnanimously public; my father, exquisitely and inevitably private; together they met the needs of nearly all that is worthy in human nature.

Emerson rose upon us frequently during our early

struggles with our new abode, like a milder sun; the children of the two families became acquainted, the surviving son, Edward, two years my elder, falling to my share. But Emerson himself also became my companion, with a humanity which to-day fills me with grateful wonder. I remember once being taken by him on a long walk through the sacred pine woods, and on another occasion he laid aside the poem or the essay he was writing to entertain Una in his study, whither she had gone alone and of her own initiative to make him a call! It is easy to compliment a friend upon his children, but how many of us will allow themselves to be caught and utilized by them in this fashion? But Emerson's mind was so catholic, so humble, and so deep that I doubt not he derived benefit even from child-prattle. His wife rivalled him in hospitality, though her frail health disabled her from entering into the physical part of social functions with the same fortitude; in these first months we were invited to a party where we were fellow-guests with all the other children of Concord. There they were, their mothers with them, and everything in sight that a child at a party could require. My new friend Edward mounted me on his pony, and his father was at hand to catch me when I fell off. Such things sound incredible, but they are true. A great man is great at all times, and all over.

Thoreau, Channing, and Alcott were also visible to us at this time, but of none of them do I find any trace in my memory; though I know, as a matter of fact, that Channing and my father once permitted me to accompany them on a walk round the country roads, which inadvertently prolonged itself to ten miles, and I knew what it was to feel foot-weary. But another neighbor of ours, hardly less known to fame, though in a widely different line of usefulness, makes a very distinct picture in my mind; this was Ephraim Wales Bull, the inventor of the Concord grape. He was as eccentric as his name; but he was a genuine and substantive man, and my father took a great liking to him, which was reciprocated. He was short and powerful, with long arms, and a big head covered with bushy hair and a jungle beard, from which looked out a pair of eyes singularly brilliant and penetrating. He had brains to think with, as well as strong and skilful hands to work with; he personally did three-fourths of the labor on his vineyard, and every grape-vine had his separate care. He was married and had three children, amiable but less interesting than himself. He had, also, a tremendous temper, evidenced by his heavy and high-arched eyebrows, and once in a while he let slip upon his helpers in the vineyard this formidable wrath, which could easily be heard in our peaceful precincts, like sounds of distant battle. He often came over and sat with my father in the summer-house on the hill, and there talked about politics, sociology (though under some other name, probably), morals, and human nature, with an occasional lecture on grape-culture. He permitted my sister and me to climb the fence and eat all the grapes we could hold; it seems to me he could hardly have realized our capacity. During our second summer he built a most elaborate fence along the road-front of his estate; it must have been three hundred yards long and it was as high as a man could reach; the palings, instead of being upright, were criss-crossed over one another, leaving small diamond-shaped interstices. The whole was painted brilliant white, to match the liliputian cottage in which the Bull family contrived (I know not how) to ensconce itself. When the fence was built, Mr. Bull would every day come forth and pace slowly up and down the road, contemplating it with the pride of a parent; indeed, it was no puny achievement, and when I revisited Concord, thirty years later, the great white fence was still there, with a few gaps in it, but still effective. But the builder, and the grapes—where were they? Where are Cheops, and the hanging gardens of Babylon?

Among many visitors came Richard Henry Stoddard, already a poet, but anxious to supplement the income from his verses by a regular stipend from the big pocket of Uncle Sam. His first coming was in summer, and he and my father went up on the hill and sat in the summer-house there, looking out upon the wide prospect of green meadows and distant woods, but probably seeing nothing of them, their attention being withdrawn to scenes yet fairer in the land of imagination and memory. Stoddard was then, as always, a handsome man, strong and stanch, black-haired and black-bearded, with strong eyes that could look both fierce and tender. He was masculine, sensitive, frank, and humorous; his chuckle had infinite merriment in it; but, as his mood shifted, there might be tears in his eyes the next moment. He was at that time little more than five-and-twenty years old, and he looked hardly that; he was a New England country youth of genius. Nature had kindled a fire in him which has never gone out. Like my father, he was affiliated with the sea, and had its freshness and daring, though combined with great modesty, and he felt honored by the affection with which he inspired the author of *The Scarlet Letter*. It was not until his second visit, in the winter, that the subject of a custom - house appointment for him came up; for my father, being known as a close friend of the President, whose biography he had written for the campaign, became the object of pilgrimages other than literary ones. He received sound advice, and introductions, which aided him in getting the appointment, and he held it for nearly twenty years— more to the benefit of the custom - house than of poetry, no doubt, though he never let poetry escape him, and he is to-day a mine of knowledge and wisdom on literary subjects. There is an immense human ardor, power, and pathos in Stoddard; better than any other American poet does he realize the conception of his great English brother—the love of love, the hate of hate, the scorn of scorn. The world has proved impotent to corrupt his heroic simplicity; he loved fame much, but truth more.

EDWIN P. WHIPPLE

He is a boy in his heart still, and he has sung songs which touch whatever is sweetest, tenderest, and manliest in the soul of man.

E. P. Whipple, essentially a man of letters, and famous in his day as a critic of literature, appeared often in "The Wayside." His verdict on a book carried weight; it was an era when literary criticism was regarded seriously, and volumes devoted to critical studies had something more than a perfunctory vogue. He had written penetrating and cordial things about my father's books, and foretold the high place which he would ultimately occupy in our Pantheon. He was rich in the kind of Attic salt which was characteristic of Boston in the middle century; the product of an almost excessive culture erected on sound, native brains. He had abounding wit; not only wit of the sort that begets mirth, but that larger and graver wit which Macaulay notices in Bacon's writings—a pure, irradiating, intellectual light. It had often the effect of an actual physical illumination cast upon the topic. He was magnificent as a dinner-table companion. He was rather a short, thick-shouldered man, with a big head on a short neck, a broad, projecting forehead, prominent eyes, defended by shiny spectacles, and bushy whiskers. He is not remembered now, probably because he never produced any organic work commensurate with his huge talent. Analyses of the work of others, however just, useful, and creative, do not endure unless they are associated with writing of the independent sort. Whipple, with all his ability and insight, never entered the imaginative field on his own account, and in the press of wits he falls behind and is forgotten.

My father had come to Concord with the idea of a new romance in his mind; he designed it to be of a character more cheerful than the foregoing ones. It was never written, and but the slightest traces of what it might have been are extant. Herman Melville had spent a day with us at Concord, and he had suggested a story to Hawthorne; but the latter, after turning it over in his mind, came to the conclusion that Melville could treat the subject better than he could; but Melville finally relinquished it also. It seems likely, however, that this projected tale was not the one which Hawthorne had originally been meditating. At all events, it was postponed in favor of a new book of wonder - stories from Greek mythology—the first one having had immediate popularity, and by the time this was finished, the occasion had arrived which led to the writing of Pierce's biography. This, in turn, was followed by the offer by the President to his friend of the Liverpool consulate, then the most lucrative appointment in the gift of the administration; and Hawthorne's acceptance of it caused all literary projects to be indefinitely abandoned.

But even had there been time for the writing of another book, the death of Hawthorne's sister Louisa would doubtless have unfitted him for a while from undertaking it. This was the most painful episode connected with his life; Louisa was a passenger on a Hudson River steamboat which was burned. She was a gentle, rather fragile woman, with a playful humor and a lovable nature; she had not the intellectual force either of her brother or of her sister Elizabeth; but her social inclinations were stronger than theirs. She was a delightful person to have in the house, and her nephew and niece were ardently in love with her. She was on her way to "The Wayside" when the calamity occurred, and we were actually expecting her on the day she perished. Standing on the blazing deck, with the panic and the death-scenes around her, the gentle woman had to make the terrible choice between the river and the fire. She was alone; there was none to advise or help her or be her companion in inevitable death. Her thoughts must have gone to her brother, with his strength and courage, his skill as a swimmer; but he was far away, unconscious of her desperate extremity. She had to choose, and the river was her choice. With that tragic conception of the drowning of Zenobia fresh in his mind, the realization of his sister's fate must have gained additional poignancy in my father's imagination. He was hard hit, and the traces of the blow were manifest on him. After about a month, he made a journey to the Isles of Shoals with Franklin Pierce, and in that breezy outpost of the land he spent some weeks, much to his advantage. This was in the autumn of 1852, and I recall well enough the gap in things which his long absence made for me, and my perfect joy when the whistle of the train at the distant railway station signalled his return. Twenty minutes had to elapse before the railroad carriage could bring him to our door; they were long and they were brief, after the manner of minutes in such circumstances. He came, and there was a moment of indescribable glory while he leaped from the carriage and faced the situation on the doorstep of his home. His countenance was glowing with health and the happiness of home-coming. I thought him, as I always did, the most beautiful of human beings, by which I do not mean beautiful in feature, for of that I was not competent to hold an opinion; but beautiful in the feelings which he aroused in me beholding him. He was beautiful to be with, to hear, touch, and experience. Such is the effect of the spiritual sphere of good men, in whom nature and character are harmonious.

My father got his appointment from Washington in the following March, 1853. His wife had but one solicitude in leaving America; her mother was aged and in delicate health, and their parting might be forever in this world. But a month before the appointment was confirmed, her mother quietly and painlessly died. It was as if she had wished not to be separated from her beloved daughter, and had entered into the spiritual state in the expectation of being nearer to her there than she could be in the world. My mother always affirmed that she was conscious of her mother's presence with her on momentous occasions during the remainder of her own life.

June came; the farewells were said, we were rail-roaded to Boston, embarked on the Cunard steam-ship *Niagara*, Captain Leitch, and steamed out of Boston Harbor on a day of cloudlessness and calm. Incoming vessels, drifting in the smoothness, sa-luted us with their flags, and the idle seamen stared at us, leaning over their bulwarks.   The last of the low headlands grew dim and vanished in the golden haze of the afternoon.   "Go away, tiresome old land!" sang out my sister and myself; but my father, standing beside us, gazing westward with a serious look, bade us be silent.   Two hundred and twenty years had passed since our first ancestor had sought freedom on those disappearing shores, and our father was the first of his descendants to visit the Old Home whence he came.   What was to be the outcome?   But the children only felt that the ocean was pleasant and strange, and they longed to explore it.   The future and the past did not concern them.

V

A paddle-wheel ocean-liner—The hens, the cow, and the carpenter—W. D. Ticknor—Our first Englishman—An aristocratic acrobat—Speech that beggars eulogy—The boots of great travellers—Complimentary cannon—The last infirmity of noble republican minds—The golden promise: the spiritual fulfilment—Fatuous serenity—Past and future—The coquetry of chalk cliffs—Two kinds of imagination — The thirsty island — Gloomy English comforts—Systematic geniality—A standing puzzle — The respirator — Scamps, fools, mendicants, and desperadoes—The wrongs of sailor-men—"Is this myself?"—"Profoundly akin"—Henry Bright—Charm of insular prejudice—No stooping to compromise—The battle against dinner—"I'm glad you liked it!"—An English-, Irish-, and Scotchman—An Englishman owns his country—A contradiction in Englishmen—A hospitable gateway—Years of memorable trifles.

THE steamship *Niagara* was, in 1853, a favorable specimen of nautical architecture; the Cunard Company had then been in existence rather less than a score of years, and had already established its reputation for safety and convenience. But, with the exception of the red smoke-stack with the black ring round the top, there was little similarity between the boat that took us to England and the mammoths that do that service for travellers nowadays. The *Niagara* was about two hundred and fifty feet long, and was propelled by paddle-wheels, upon the summits of whose curving altitudes we were permitted to climb in calm weather. The interior decorations were neat and pretty, but had nothing of the palatial and æsthetic gorgeousness which educates us in these later ages. The company of passengers was so small that a single cow, housed in a pen on deck, sufficed for their needs in the way of milk, and there were still left alive and pecking contentedly about their coop a number of fowls, after we had eaten all we could of their brethren at the ten dinners that were served during the voyage. The crew, from the captain down, were all able seamen, friendly and companionable, and not so numerous but that it was easy to make their individual acquaintance. The most engaging friend of the small people was the carpenter, who had his shop on deck, and from whom I acquired that passion for the profession which every normal boy ought to have, and from the practice of which I derived deep enjoyment and many bloody thumbs and fingers for ten years afterwards.

But we had companionship historically at least more edifying. William D. Ticknor, the senior partner of my father's publishers, was the only figure familiar at the outset. He was one of the most amiable of men, with thick whiskers all round his face and spectacles shining over his kindly eyes; a sturdy, thick - set personage, active in movement and genial in conversation. It was James T. Fields who usually made the trips to England; but on this occasion Fields got no farther than the wharf, where the last object visible was his comely and smiling countenance as he waved his adieux. Conspicuous among the group on the after-deck, as we glided out of the smooth harbor of Boston, was an urbane and dignified gentleman of perhaps sixty years of age, with a clean-shaven mouth and chin, finely mould-ed, and with what Tennyson would call an educated whisker, short and gray, defining the region in front of and below his ears. He spoke deliberately, and in language carefully and yet easily chosen, with intonations singularly distinct and agreeable, giving its full value to every word. This was our first native Englishman; no less a personage than Mr. Crampton, in fact, the British Minister, who was on his way to Halifax. He had fine, calm, quietly ob-servant eyes, which were pleasantly employed in contemplating the beauty of that summer seascape —an opalescent ocean, and islands slumbering in the July haze. Near him stood a light-built, tall, athletic individual, also obviously English, but thirty years younger; full, also, of artistic apprecia-tion; this was Field Talfourd, who was an artist, and many things besides; a man proficient in all forms of culture. His features were high and refined, and, without being handsome, irresistibly attractive. He turned out to be a delightful playmate for the children, and astonished them and the rest of the company by surprising gymnastic feats in the rig-ging. The speech of these two Britishers gave the

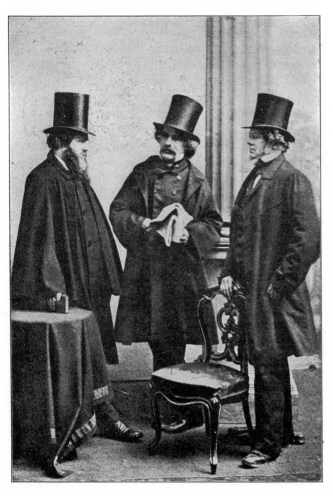

JAMES T. FIELDS, NATHANIEL HAWTHORNE, AND WILLIAM
D. TICKNOR

untravelled American a new appreciation of the beauty and significance of the English language. Not all Englishmen speak good English, but when they do, they beggar eulogy.

George Silsbee was likewise of our party; he was an American of the Brahman type, a child of Cambridge and Boston, a man of means, and an indefatigable traveller. He had the delicate health and physique of the American student of those days, when out-door life and games made no part of our scholastic curricula. He may have been forty years old, slight and frail, with a thin, clean-shaven face and pallid complexion, but full of mind and sensibility. We do not heed travellers now, and I am inclined to think they are less worth heeding than they used to be. It is so easy to see the world in these latter days that few persons see it to any purpose even when they go through the motions of doing so. But to hear George Bradford or Silsbee talk of England, France, and Italy, in the fifties, was a liberal education, and I used sometimes to stare fascinated at the boots of these wayfarers, admiring them for the wondrous places in which they had trodden. Silsbee travelled with his artistic and historic consciousness all on board, and had so much to say that he never was able to say it all.

But to my father himself were accorded the honors of the captain's table, and for him were fired the salutes of cannon which thundered us out of Boston Harbor and into Halifax. These compliments, however, were paid to him not as a man of letters, but

6   81

as a political representative of his country, and, let a man be as renowned as he will on his personal account, he will still find it convenient, in order to secure smooth and agreeable conditions on his way through the world, to supplement that distinction with recommendations from the State Department. Respect for rank is the last infirmity even of noble republican minds, and it oils the wheels of the progress of those who possess it. An American widow of my later acquaintance, a lady of two marriageable daughters and small social pretensions in her own country, toured Europe with success and distinction, getting all the best accommodations and profoundest obeisances by the simple device of placing the word "Lady" before her modest signature in the hotel registers. She was a lady, of course, and had a right so to style herself, and if snobbish persons chose to read into the word more than it literally meant, that was not Mrs. Green's affair.

American commerce still existed in 1853, and the Liverpool consulate was supposed to have more money in it than any other office in the gift of the administration. As a matter of fact, several of my father's predecessors had retired from their tenure of office with something handsome (pecuniarily speaking) to their credit; whether the means by which it had been acquired were as handsome is another question. Be that as it may, Congress, soon after my father's accession, passed a law cutting down the profits about three-fourths, and he was obliged to practise the strictest economy during his residence abroad in order to come home with a few thousand dollars in his pocket. Nevertheless, the dignity, in the official sense, of this consular post was considerable, and it brought him, in combination with his literary fame, a good deal more attention in England than he well knew what to do with. But, in one way or another, he also made friends there who remained to the end among the dearest of his life and more than countervailed all the time and energy wasted on the Philistines.

The Atlantic, all the way across, with the exception of one brief emotional disturbance between lunch and dinner-time, wore a smile of fatuous serenity. The sun shone; the vast pond-surface oilily undulated, or lay in absolute flatness, or at most defiled under our eyes in endless squadrons of low-riding crests. My mother, whose last experience of sea-ways had been the voyage to Cuba, in which the ship was all but lost in a series of hurricanes, was captivated by this soft behavior, and enjoyed the whole of it as much, almost, as her husband, who expanded and drank in delight like a plant in the rain. But, in truth, these must have been blessed hours for them both. Behind them lay nearly eleven years of married life, spent in narrow outward circumstances, lightened only towards the last by the promise of some relaxation from strain, during which they had found their happiness in each other, and in the wise and tender care of their children, and in the converse of chosen friends. They had filled their minds with knowl-

edge concerning the beauties and interests of foreign lands, with but a slender expectation of ever
beholding them with bodily sight, but none the less
well prepared to understand and appreciate them
should the opportunity arrive. And now, suddenly, it had arrived, and they were on the way to the
regions of their dreams, with the prospect of com-
parative affluence added. They had nearly twelve
years of earthly sojourn together before them, the
afternoon sunshine to be clouded a little near the
close by the husband's failing health, but glorified
more and more by mutual love, and enriched with
memories of all that had before been unfulfilled
imaginings. This voyage eastward was the space
of contemplation between the two periods, and the
balm of its tranquillity well symbolized the peace
of soul and mind with which they awaited what
the horizons were to disclose.

The right way to approach England for the first
time is not by the west coast, but by the south,
as Julius Cæsar did, beckoned on by the ghostly,
pallid cliffs that seem to lift themselves like battlements against the invader. It is historically open
to question whether there would have been any
Roman occupation, or any Saxon or Norman one
either, for that matter, but for the coquetry of
those chalk cliffs. An adventurer, sighting the low
and marshy shores of Lancashire, and muddying
his prows in the yellow waters of the Mersey, would
be apt to think that such a land were a good place
to avoid. But the race of adventurers has long

since died out, and their place is occupied by the wide-flying cormorants of commerce, to whom mud flats and rock deserts present elysian beauties, provided only there be profit in them. One kind of imagination has been superseded by another, and both are necessary to the full exploitation of this remarkable globe that we inhabit.

But even the level capes of Lancashire were alluring to eyes that saw England, our venerable mother, loom behind them, with her thousand years' pageantry of warfare and civilization. The egregious little island is a thirsty place; the land drinks rain as assiduously as do its inhabitants beer and other liquors. Heavy mists and clouds enveloped it as we drew near, and ushered us up the Mersey into a brown omnipresence of rain. The broad, clear sunshine of the Atlantic was left behind, and we stood on wet decks and were transported to sloppy wharfs by means of a rain-sodden and abominably smoking little tug-boat—as the way was fifty years ago. Liverpool was a gray-stone labyrinth open to the deluge, and its inhabitants went to and fro with umbrellas over their heads and black respirators over their mouths, looking as if such were their normal plight—as, indeed, it was. Much of this was not needed to quench the enthusiasm of the children. The Waterloo Hotel, to which, by advice of friends, we were driven, seemed by its very name to carry out the idea of saturation, which the activities of nature so insistently conveyed. It was intensely discomfortable, and though the inside of the hotel was well supplied with gloomy English comforts, and the solemn meals were administered with a ceremonious gravity that suggested their being preliminaries to funerals, yet it was hard to be lighthearted. The open-grate coal fires were the most welcome feature of this summer season, and no doubt the wine list offered the best available substitute for sunlight; but we had not been trained to avail ourselves of it. We drank water, which certainly appeared an idle proceeding in such a climate.

In Liverpool, however, or in its suburbs, we were to live for the better part of four years, and we must make the best of it. And there is in English people, when rightly approached, a steady and systematic geniality that not only makes handsome amends for their weather, but also accounts for the otherwise singular fact that the country is inhabited at all. A people with a smaller fund of interior warmth could not have endured it. The French talk about conquering England, but they could not hold it if they did, and it is one of the standing puzzles of history how the Romans, an Italian race, were able to maintain themselves under these skies during four centuries. It may be objected that the present English population is not indigenous to the island; but they are the survival of the fittest and toughest selected from many aspirants. Nor can it be doubted that the British hunger for empire in all parts of the world is due to nothing so much as to their anxiety to have a plausible pretext for living elsewhere than at home.

My father took the rain, as he took everything that could not be helped, philosophically, and it seemed to do him no harm; indeed, his health was uniformly good all through his English residence. It did not suit so well my mother, who was constitutionally delicate in the lungs; she was soon obliged to adopt the English respirator, and finally was driven to take refuge for the greater part of a year in Lisbon and Madeira, returning only a little before the departure of the family for Italy in 1858. But there must have been in him an ancestral power of resistance still effective after more than two centuries of transplantation; he grew ruddy and robust while facing the mist and mirk, and inhaling the smoky moisture that did service for air. Nor was his health impaired by the long hours in the daily consulate—a grimy little room barely five paces from end to end, with its dusty windows so hemmed in by taller buildings that even had there been any sunshine to make the attempt, it could never have succeeded in effecting an entrance through them. Here, from ten in the morning until four in the afternoon, he dealt with all varieties of scamps and mendicants, fools and desperadoes, and all the tribe of piratical cutthroats which in those days constituted a large part of the merchant marine. Calamity, imbecility, and rascality were his constant companions in that dingy little den; and the gloomy and sooty skies without but faintly pictured the moral atmosphere which they exhaled; he entered deeply into all their affairs, projects, and complaints, feeling their troubles, probably, at least as keenly as they did themselves, and yet he came out of it all with clear eyes and a sound digestion. I presume the fact may have been that he unconsciously regarded the whole affair somewhat as we do a drama in a theatre; it works upon our sensibilities, and yet we do not believe that it is real. There was nothing in the experience germane to his proper life; it could not become a part of him, and therefore its posture towards him remained inveterately objective. The only feature of it that quickened a responsive chord in him was the revelation of the intolerable condition of the sailors in many of our ships, and upon these abuses he enlarged in his communications to Washington. Improvements were made in consequence of his remonstrances; but the American merchant service had already begun its downward career, and it is only very lately, owing to causes which are too novel and peculiar to be intelligently discussed as yet, that our flag is once more promising to compete against that of England.

It would be misleading to say, however, that my father was not interested in his consulate work; there was a practical side in him which took hold of the business in man-fashion, and transacted it so efficiently as to leave no room for criticism, and nobody can produce voluntary effects without feeling in himself a reaction from them. He had occasion to look into the privacy of many human hearts, to pity them and advise them, and from such services and insights he no doubt obtained a residue of wisdom which might be applied to his own ulterior uses. These were indirect and incidental issues; but from the consulate *qua* consulate Hawthorne was radically alien, and when he quitted it, he carried away with him no taint or trace of it. As he says in his remarks upon the subject, he soon came to doubt whether it were actually himself who had been the incumbent of the office at all.

But Providence does not deny manna to man in his extremity, and to my father it came in the shape of a few English friends, and in occasional escapes from the office into the outside England where, after the centuries of separation, he found so much with which he could still feel profoundly akin. His most constant friendly visitor was Henry A. Bright, a university man, the son of a wealthy local merchant, who sent ships to Australia, and was related (as most agreeable Englishmen are—though there are shining exceptions) to the aristocratic class. Bright, at this time, could not have been over thirty years of age; he was intensely English, though his slender figure and mental vivacity might make him seem near to the conventional American type. But through him, as through an open window, Hawthorne was enabled to see far into the very heart of England. Bright not merely knew England; he was England, and England at its best, and therefore also at its most insular and prejudiced. It was unspeakably satisfying and agreeable to encounter a man at once so uncompromising and so amiable, so wrong-headed (from the American point of view) and so right-hearted. He was drawn to my father as iron is drawn to the magnet; on every outward point they fought each other like the knight errants of old, while agreeing inwardly, beneath the surface of things, as few friends are able to agree. Each admired the other's onslaughts and his prowess, and, by way of testifying his admiration, strove to excel himself in his counter attacks. The debate was always beginning, and in the nature of things it could never end; the effect of their blows was only to hammer each the other more firmly into his previous convictions. Probably all the things that are English and all the things that are American never before or since received such full and trenchant exposition as was given them by Hawthorne and by Bright. The whole subject of monarchy and aristocracy as against republicanism and democracy was threshed out to the last kernel by champions each of whom was thoroughly qualified to vindicate his cause. Each, constrained by the stress of battle to analyze and expound his beliefs more punctually than ever before, thereby convinced himself while leaving his adversary undaunted; and, of course, both were right. For this world is so constituted that two things incompatible in outward manifestation may in their roots be one and the same, and equally appeal to the suffrages of honest men. England and America are healthy and vigorous in proportion as they differ from each other, and a morbid and vicious tendency in either is noticeable the moment either begins to take a leaf from the other's book. My father and Bright could not have been the life-long friends that they were had either of them yielded his point or stooped to compromise.

Apart from political matters, and such social themes as were nearly allied to them, the two friends had many points of agreement and sympathy. Bright had from the first been an ardent and intelligent admirer of the romancer's writings, and though they might often differ in their estimates of individual works, they were in hearty accord as to the principles which underlie all literature and art. Upon matters relating to society, my father was more apt to accept theories which Bright might propound than to permit of their being illustrated in his own person; he would admit, for example, that a consul ought to mingle socially with the people to whom he was accredited; but when it came to getting him out to dinner, in evening dress and with a speech in prospect, obstacles started up like the armed progeny of the Dragon's Teeth. For, though no one enjoyed real society more than he did, he was ardently averse from conversing as an official with persons between whom and himself as a man there could be little sympathy. Almost as much, too, did he dislike to meet the polite world merely on the basis of the books that he had written, which his entertainers were bound to praise whether or not they had read or comprehended them, and to whose well-meant but inexpert eulogies he must constantly respond with the threadbare and pathetic phrase, "I'm glad you liked it." Bright, of course, insisted that fame and position carried obligations which must be met, and he was constantly laying plots to inveigle or surprise his friend into compliance. He often succeeded, but he failed quite as frequently, so that, as a Mrs. Malaprop might have said, Hawthorne as a social lion was a *rara avis*, from first to last. The foible of artificial, as distinguished from spontaneous, society is that it so seldom achieves simple human relations.

Another chief friend of his was Francis Bennoch. England would never have seemed "our old home" to my father, without the presence and companionship of these two men. Both had literary leanings, both were genial, true, and faithful; but in other respects they were widely dissimilar. Bright was of the pure Saxon type; Bennoch represented Great Britain at large; there were mingled in him English, Irish, and Scotch ancestry. In himself he was a superb specimen of a human being; broad-shouldered, straight, and vigorous, massive but active, with a mellow, joyful voice, an inimitable brogue, sparkling black eyes full of hearty sunshine and kindness, a broad and high forehead over bushy brows, and black, wavy hair. He bubbled over with high spirits, humor, and poetry, being, indeed, a poet in achievement, with a printed and bound volume to show for it—songs, lyrics, and narrative poems, composed in the spirit of Burns and Scott. He was at this time one of the handsomest men in England, with a great heart, warmer than any summer England ever knew, and a soul of ardor and courage, which sent through his face continual flashes of sympathy and fellowship. One naturally thought and spoke of him in superlatives; he was the kindest, jolliest, most hospitable, most generous and chivalrous of men, and his affection and admiration for my father were also of the superlative kind. He had made a fortune in the wool business, and had an office in Wood Street, London; but his affairs permitted him to make frequent excursions to Liverpool, and to act as his American friend's guide and cicerone to many places in England which would otherwise have been unknown to him. My father enjoyed these trips immensely; Bennoch's companionship gave the right keynote and atmosphere to the sights they saw. A real Englishman owns his country, and does the honors of it to a visitor as if it were his private estate. Discussions of politics and of the principles of government never arose between these two, as they did between my father and Bright; for Bennoch, though one of the most loyal and enthusiastic of her Majesty's subjects, and full of traditional respect for the British nobility, was by nature broadly democratic, and met every man as an equal and a brother. One often finds this contradiction in Englishmen; but it is such logically only. A man born to the traditions of monarchy and aristocracy accepts them as the natural background of his ideas, just as the English landscape is the setting of his house and park; he will vindicate them if assailed; but ordinarily they do not consciously affect his mental activities, and he will talk good republicanism without being aware of it. The monarchy is a decoration, a sentiment, a habit; as a matter of fact, England is more democratic in many essentials than we have as yet learned how to be. Bennoch was not a university man, and lacked the historical consciousness that Bright so assiduously cultivated; he lived by feeling and intuition more than by deliberate intellectual judgments. He was emotional; tears would start to his eyes at a touch of pathos or pity, as readily as the laughter of a moment before. So lovable, gallant, honest, boyish a man is seldom born into this modern world—boyish as only the manliest men can be. He died thirty years after the time I write of, the same fresh and ardent character as ever, and loving and serving Hawthorne's children for Hawthorne's sake. I shall have occasion to mention him hereafter; but I have dwelt upon him here, both because he made it forever impossible for any one who knew him well to do other than love the land which could breed such a man, and because, for the American Hawthorne, he was as a hospitable gateway through which the England of his dreams and imaginings was entered upon as a concrete and delightful reality.

With Bright and Bennoch on his right hand and on his left, then, my father began his English experience. The two are frequently mentioned in his English journals, and Bennoch figures as one of the subordinate characters in the posthumous romance called *Doctor Grimshawe's Secret.* It is but a sketch of him, however, and considerably modified from the brilliant and energetic reality. Meanwhile the consul began to accustom himself to the routine of the consulate, and his family, leaving the sombre respectability of the Waterloo Hotel, moved, first, to the hospitable boarding-house of Mrs. Blodgett, and afterwards to a private dwelling in Rock Park, Rock Ferry, on the opposite side of the Mersey, where we were destined to dwell for several years. They were years full of events very trifling in themselves, but so utterly different from everything American as to stamp themselves upon the attention and the memory. It is the trifling things that tell, and give character to nations; extraordinary things may occur anywhere, and possess little national flavor. In another chapter I will attempt some portrayal of this English life of fifty years since.

VI

In a country whose ruling principle is caste, it
might be expected that the line of cleavage between
the upper and the lower grades would be punctually observed. It is assumed that democracy levels and aristocracy distinguishes and separates.
My father was not long in remarking, however, that
there was a freedom of intercourse between the
patrician and the plebeian—between people of all
orders—such as did not exist in America. And the
fact, once perceived, was not difficult of explana-
tion. In a monarchy of a thousand years' standing, every individual knows his place in the social

scale and never thinks of leaving it. He represents a fixed function or element in the general organism, and holds to it as a matter of course, just as, in the human body, the body does not aspire to be the head, nor the liver or heart to take the place of lungs or stomach. The laborer looks back upon an ancestry of laborers; the shopkeeper has been a shopkeeper for unnumbered generations; the artisan on the bench to-day does the same work that his father and grandfathers did before him; the noble inherits his acres as inevitably as the sun rises, and sits in the House of Lords by immemorial usage and privilege. Social position all along the line being thus anchored in the nature of things, as it were, there is no anxiety on any one's part as to maintaining his status. He is secure where he is, and nothing and nobody can change him. There is no individual striving to rise nor fear to fall. Consequently there can and must be entire freedom of mutual conversation; the marquis with a revenue of half a million a year meets as an equal his gardener who gets ten pounds a month, and the tailor in his measuring-room offers a glass of sherry to his noble patron who comes to him for a new coat. Each is at his ease, conscious that he performs a use and fills a place which no one else can fill or perform, and that nothing else matters. The population is a vast mutual-benefit association, without envy on the one side or contempt on the other. And social existence moves as smoothly as a well-oiled and adjusted machine.

This agreeable condition is impossible in a democracy—at all events, in a democracy like ours, which is based upon the assumption that all men are equal. Nevertheless, we are on the right track, and the English are on the wrong one; for the agreeable English system obstructs the insensible infiltration of fresh material into old forms, which is essential to the continued health of the latter; while the democracy, on the other hand, will gradually learn that it is just as honorable and desirable to be a good shoemaker, for example, as a good millionaire; that human life, in short, is a complex of countless different uses, each one of which is as important on its own plane as any of the others. But the intermediate period is undeniably irksome.

So my father noticed, not without a certain satisfaction, that even beggars, in England, are not looked .down upon, and that their rights, such as they are, are recognized. In the steamboat waiting-room at Rock Ferry, and in the boats themselves, he saw tramps and mendicants take the best place at the fire or on the companion-way without rebuke and without consciousness of presumption, and he saw the landlord of a hotel, with a fortune of six hundred thousand pounds, wait at table as deferentially as any footman in his employ. He was struck by the contentment with which, in winter, women went barefoot in the streets, and by the unpretentious composure with which the common herd, on holidays, disported themselves in public, not seeking to disguise their native vulgarity and shabbiness. At the same time, he could not help a misgiving that the portentous inequality between rich and poor must finally breed disaster; the secluded luxury of the rich was too strongly contrasted with the desperate needs of the poor. This contrast was very marked in England fifty years ago, and was comparatively unknown in our own country—though to-day we can hardly lay to our souls the flattering unction of such a difference. The rage for wealth has done for us in a generation what caste did for England in a thousand years.

My father, when opportunity offered, was always finding himself among the poor and their dwellings; he had to be dragged to the rich, though among them, too, he found, when brought in contact with them, many interesting points of dissimilarity from ourselves. His office as consul naturally took him often to the police courts, where magistrates passed upon the squalid cases cited before them, and in the consulate itself he saw specimens enough of human crime and misery. He visited the poor-house and the insane asylum, he was approached by swindlers of all types, and often he went to fairs and other resorts of public out-door amusement and watched the unwashed populace at its play. Beggars followed him on the streets, awaited him in their chosen coigns of vantage on the corners, or haunted him on the ferry-boat that took him each day from his home to his office. Wherever he encountered the forsaken of fortune, he found food for sympathy, and, in spite of assurances that he was only encouraging mendicancy, he often gave them money. It was hard for him to believe that there could be abject poverty where there was work for all, and the appeal of man in want to man in plenty was too strong for him easily to resist it. He liked the very frankness of vulgarity and hopeless destitution of these people, and was appalled by the simplicity with which they accepted things as they were. There was no restlessness, as in America—no protest against fate. It was harrowing enough to see conditions so miserable; it was intolerable to see them acquiesced in by the victims as inevitable. He learned, after a while, to harden himself somewhat against manifest imposition; but the refusal to give cost him quite as much in discomfort as giving did in purse.

The country villages and cottages, however, afforded him compensating pleasure. In the neighborhood of Rock Ferry, on the shore of the Mersey opposite from Liverpool, there were two or three ancient little settlements which he loved to visit. The thatched and whitewashed cottages, with their tiny gardens of hollyhocks and marigolds, seemed like parts of the framework of the land; the passage of centuries only served to weld them more firmly in their places. The villages were massed together, each in a small space, instead of being dispread loosely over a township, as in his native New England, and enduring stone and plaster took the place of timber and shingles. But the churches, small and fabulously ancient, affected him most.

He placed his hand on stones which had been set in place before William the Conqueror landed in England, and this physical survival seemed to bring into his actual presence the long succession of all the intervening ages. These structures, still so solid and serviceable, had witnessed the passing of the entire procession of English history; all the mighty men and events of her career had come and gone while they remained unscathed. Under his feet were the graves of the unknown dead; within the narrow precincts he inhaled that strange, antique odor of mortality that made him feel as if he were breathing the air of long-dead centuries. This apparent evanescence of the spiritual attested by the survival of the material is one of the most singular and impressive of sensations; it takes history out of the realm of the mind, and brings it into sensible manifestation. It is almost as affecting as if the very figures of departed actors of former ages were to reappear and rub shoulders with us of to-day, and cast their shadows in the contemporary sunshine.

On most of these walks in the neighborhood of Rock Ferry I was my father's companion, but, though my legs could march beside his, my mental equipment could not participate in his meditations. He would occasionally make some half-playful, imaginative remark, calculated to help me realize the situation that was so vividly present to himself. His thoughts, however deep, were always ready to break into playfulness outwardly. We often walked through the village of Bebbington, whose church had a high stone steeple, nearly to the summit of which the ancient ivy had clambered. And as it came in view he would always say, in a sort of recitative, perhaps reminiscent of Scott's narrative poems, which he was at that time reading aloud to us, "There is of Bebbington the holy peak!" To which I would as constantly rejoin, "'Of Bebbington the holy *spire*,' father!"—being offended by his use of a word so unmusical as peak. He would only smile and trudge onward. He was somewhat solicitous, I suspect, to check in his son any tendency towards mere poetical sentiment; his own imaginative faculty was rooted in common-sense, and he knew the value of the latter in curbing undue excursions into the fanciful and transcendental.

In Eastham, on the village green, stood an old yew-tree which, six centuries before, had been traditionally called The Old Yew of Eastham, and was probably at least coeval with the village itself, which was one of the oldest in England. It was of enormous girth, and was still in leaf; but nothing but the bark was left of the great trunk; all the wood had decayed away so long ago that the memory of man held no record of it. There was a great conical gap in one side, like an open door, and it was my custom—as it had doubtless been that of innumerable children of ages gone — to enter this door and "play house" in the spacious interior. Meanwhile my father would seat himself on the twisted roots without, and let his thoughts drift back to the time when this huge hulk had first cast a slender shadow over the greensward of primitive, Saxon England. It was a massive tree before the Domesday Book was begun; Chaucer would not be heard of for four hundred years to come; and where was Shakespeare? What was suspected of America? Yet here was this venerable vegetable, still with life enough left in it, perhaps, to see the end of English monarchy. The yew was a fact; but the ghosts were the reality, after all.

These obscure village antiquities, which had no special history attaching to them, were in a way more impressive than the great ruins of England, which had formed the scene and background of famous events. The latter had become conventional sights, which the tourist felt bound to inspect under the voluble and exasperating guidance of a professional showman; and this malice-prepense sort of interest and picturesqueness always tried Hawthorne's patience and sympathy a little. It is the unknown past that is most fascinating, that comes home closest to the heart. The things told of in history books are hackneyed, and they partake of the unreality inherent in the descriptions of the writers. But the unrecorded things are virgin, and enter into our most private sympathies and realization. My father viewed and duly admired the great castles, palaces, and cathedrals of England; but he loved the old villages and their appurtenances, and could dream dreams more moving under the shadow of Eastham Yew than in Westminster Abbey itself.

The historic houses and country-seats which were still inhabited were still more difficult to get in touch with from the historic point of view; the present dazzled the past out of sight. One was told who built this façade, who added that wing, who was imprisoned in yonder tower; where Queen Elizabeth slept, and the foot of what martyr imprinted the Bloody Footstep on the threshold. But you listened to these tales over a cup of tea in the drawing-room, or between the soup and the roast beef at the dinner-table, and they were not convincing. How were these ruddy-cheeked, full-bodied, hospitable personages who sat about you to be held compatible with the romantic periods and characters that they described? The duck and the green pease, the plum-pudding and the port, the white neck-cloths and the bare necks were too immediate and potent. In many cases, too, the denizens of the ancient houses were not lineal descendants of the original founders; they were interlopers, by purchase or otherwise. In themselves they were kind and agreeable, their manners were excellent, they helped one to comprehend the England of the passing moment; but they only clipped the wings of imagination and retrospect. It was only after an interval of some years that Hawthorne was able so far to recover from the effect of their obtrusive existence as to be able to see through them and beyond them to the splendid and gloomy vistas in front of which they were grouped.

Yet England, past and present, rich and poor, real and ideal, did somehow enter into him and become a part of his permanent consciousness, and he liked it better than anything else he had known. Even the social life, though he came to it under some compulsion, rewarded him in the long run. One of the first personal invitations was to the country-seat of the Brights, where he met the family and relatives of his friend Henry Bright. Bright's father was a remarkable figure; he resembled an East-Indian more than an Englishman. He was dark, slender, courteous, and vivid; in long after-years I saw Brahmins like him in India. I would liken him to a rajah, except that rajahs of his age are commonly become gross and heavy from indulgence, whereas he had an almost ascetic aspect. His manners were singularly soft and caressing; he courted his wife, when he returned each day from business, as if they were still in their honeymoon, and his conduct towards all who surrounded him was similarly polished. He did not in the least resemble his Saxon son; and for my part, looking at him from the primitive boy stand-point, I never suspected that he was related to my father's young friend. He had made a fortune in colonial trade, and may possibly have been born in India. At this juncture the dealings of his firm were chiefly with Australia, and the largest merchant steamship then in the world had just been built for them, and Hawthorne was invited to the launching. For a British merchant prince such an occasion could not but be of supreme importance and pride. Mr. Bright's Oriental visage was radiant; his white hair seemed to shine with an added lustre; the reserve of the Englishman was forgotten, and he showed the excitement and emotion that he felt. There was a distinguished company on the great deck to witness his triumph and congratulate him upon it. All went well; at the appointed signal the retaining obstructions were cut away, and the mighty vessel began its descent into the waiting river. A lady of his family smashed a bottle of wine over the graceful bows. For a few moments there was a majestic, sweeping movement downward; then, of a sudden, it was checked. It was as if a great life had been quenched at the instant when its heart first began to throb. A murmur of dismay ran through the assemblage; but it was in the face of Mr. Bright that the full tragedy of the disaster was displayed. Never was seen a swifter change from the highest exultation to the depths of consternation. The color left his cheeks; heavy lines appeared about his handsome mouth; his eyes became fixed, and seemed to sink into his head; his erect figure drooped like that of one who has received a mortal blow. It was only that the ship had stuck in the deep mud of the river bottom; but all ship-owners are super-

stitious, and the old man foreboded the worst.
The ship was floated again some days later; but
the omens were fulfilled; she was lost on her first
voyage. I do not remember seeing Mr. Bright
after this event, but I know he never again was
the same man as before.

Richard Monckton Milnes, who was afterwards
Lord Houghton, was greatly attracted towards my
father, who liked him; but circumstances prevented
their seeing much of each other. Milnes was then
forty-five years old; he was a Cambridge man, and
intimate with Tennyson, Hallam, and other men of
literary mark, and he was himself a minor poet, and
warm in the cause of literature. During his par-
liamentary career, in 1837, he was instrumental in
passing the copyright act. He had travelled in
Greece and Italy in his twenties; was fond of society, and society of him. A more urbane and
attractive English gentleman did not exist; everything that a civilized man could care for was at his
disposal, and he made the most of his opportunities.
His manners were quiet and cordial, with a touch
of romance and poetry mingling with the man-of-
the-world tone in his conversation, and he was quite
an emotional man. I have more than once seen
tears in his eyes and heard a sob in his voice when
matters that touched his heart or imagination were
discussed. There was, indeed, a vein of sadness
and pessimism in Milnes, though only his intimates
were aware of it; it was the pessimism of a man who
has too much leisure for intellectual analysis and

not enough actual work to do to keep him occupied. It lent a fine flavor of irony to some of
his conversation. He was liberal in politics and
liberal in his attitude towards life in general; but
there was not force enough in him, or, at any rate,
not stimulus enough, to lift him to distinction.
Some of his poems, however, betrayed a deep
and radical vein of thought. He was of middle
height, well made, light built, with a large and well-
formed head and wavy, dark hair. His likeness to
Longfellow was marked, though he was hardly so
handsome a man; but the type of head and face
was the same—the forehead and brain well devel-
oped, the lower parts of the countenance small and
refined, though sensuous. His eyes were dark,
brilliant, and expressive. He, like the old poet
Rogers, made a feature of giving breakfasts to
chosen friends, and as he had the whole social
world to choose from, and unfailing good taste, his
breakfasts were well worth attending. They were
real breakfasts—so far as the hour was concerned—
not lunches or early dinners in masquerade; but
wine was served at them, and Milnes was very hospitable and had an Anacreontic or Omar touch in
him. To breakfast with him, therefore, meant—
unless you were singularly abstemious and strong-
minded—to discount the remaining meals of the
day. But the amount of good cheer that an Englishman can carry and seem not obscured by it
surprises an American. A bottle or so of hock of a
morning will make most Americans feel that busi-

RICHARD MONCKTON MILNES

ness, for the rest of that day, is an iridescent dream; but an Englishman does not seem to be burdened by it—at any rate, he did not fifty years ago.

Another hearty companion was Bryan Waller Procter, who, for literary uses, anagrammed his name into Barry Cornwall, and made it famous, fifty years ago, as that of the best song-writer in contemporary England. But he had made a literary reputation before the epoch of his songs; there were four or five dramatic and narrative poems to his credit published during the first quarter of the last century. Procter was, indeed, already a veteran in 1854, having been born in 1787, and bred to the bar, to which he was admitted in 1831. But he spent the active thirty years of his life in the discharge of that function which seems often sought by respectable Englishmen—commissioner of lunacy. He sent my father a small volume containing the Songs, and some fragments; they fully deserved their reputation. The fragments were mostly scraps of dramatic dialogue, of which one at least sticks in my memory:

> " She was a princess; but she fell; and now
> Her shame goes blushing down a line of kings."

As I recollect him, he may have looked like a commissioner of lunacy, but he did not look like a poet; he was rather undersized, with a compact head and a solemn face, and the quietest, most unobtrusive bearing imaginable. He was a well - made little man, and he lived to a great age, dying some time in the seventies, at the age of eighty-seven. He told my father that after leaving Harrow School he was distinguished in athletics, and for a time sparred in public with some professional bruiser. He had been a school-mate of Byron and Sir Robert Peel, and had known Lamb, Kean, and the other lights of that generation. He was a most likeable and remunerative companion. His wife, who survived him (living, I think, to be over ninety), was a woman of intellect and charm, and she retained her attractiveness to the end of her life. There are poets who are consumed early by their own fires, and others who are gently warmed by them beyond the common span of human existence, and Barry Cornwall was one of these, and transmitted his faculty, through sympathetic affection, to his wife.

Of renown not less than the song-writer's was the metaphysical theologian, James Martineau, then in the Liverpool epoch of his career. He was a clean-cut, cold, gentle, dry character, with a somewhat Emersonian cast of countenance, but with the Emersonian humanity and humility left out. Like Emerson, he had ascended a Unitarian pulpit, but, unlike Emerson, he stayed there long after what he was pleased to regard as his convictions had ceased to possess even a Unitarian degree of religious quality. He was always apostolic in his manner, and his utterances were *ex cathedra*, and yet his whole long life was a story of changing views on the subjects he had chosen to be the theme of his career.

A RESPECTABLE FEMALE ATHEIST

He was the great opponent of orthodoxy in his day, yet he led his followers to no goal more explicit than might be surmised from a study of Kant and Hegel. He was, however, sincere in his devotion to the will-o'-the-wisp that he conceived to be the truth, and he was courageous enough to admit that he never satisfied himself. There was chilly and austere attraction about the man; he was so elevated and superior that one could hardly help believing that he must know something of value, and this illusion was the easier because he did know so much in the way of scholarly learning. My father felt respect for his character, but was bored by his metaphysics—a form of intellectual athletics which he had exhausted while still a young man. James's sister Harriet was also of the company. She was so deaf as to be obliged to use an ear-trumpet, and she was as positive in her views (which had become avowedly atheistic) as her brother, and whenever any one began to utter anything with which she disagreed, she silenced him by the simple expedient of dropping the ear-trumpet. In herself, she was an agreeable old lady; but she seldom let her opinions rest long enough for one to get at her on the merely human side, and she cultivated a retired life, partly on account of her deafness, partly because her opinions made society shy of her, and partly because she did not think society worth her time and attention. She was a good woman, with a mind of exceptional caliber, but the world admired more than it desired her.

As a relief from the consideration of these exalted personages, I am disposed to relate a tragic anecdote about our friend Henry Bright. Early in our Rock Ferry residence he came to dine with us—or I rather think it was to supper. At any rate, it was an informal occasion, and the children were admitted to table. My mother had in the cupboard a jar of excellent raspberry jam, and she brought it forth for the delectation of our guest. He partook of it liberally, and said he had never eaten any jam so good; it had a particular tang to it, he declared, which outdid his best recollections of all previous raspberry jam from his boyhood up. While he was in the midst of these rhapsodies, and still consuming their subject with enthusiasm, my mother, who had taken some of the jam on her own plate, suddenly made a ghastly discovery. The jam-pot had been for several days standing in the cupboard with its top off, or ajar, and an innumerable colony of almost microscopic red ants had discovered it, and launched themselves fervently upon it and into it; it had held them fast in its sweet but fatal embrace, and other myriads had followed their fellows into the same delicious and destructive abyss. What the precise color of the ants may have been before they became incorporate with the jam is not known; but as the case was, they could be distinguished from it only by their voluptuous struggles in its controlling stickiness. Only the keenest eye could discern them, and the eyes of Henry Bright were among the most near-sighted in England. Besides, according to his custom, he was talking with the utmost volubility all the time.

What was to be done? My father and mother stealthily exchanged an awful look, and the question was settled. It was too late to recall the ants which our friend had devoured by tens of thousands. It seemed not probable that, were he kept in ignorance of his predicament, they would do him any serious bodily injury; whereas, were he enlightened, imagination might get in her fatal work. Accordingly, a rigorous silence upon the subject was maintained, and the dear innocent actually devoured nearly that whole potful of red ants, accompanying the meal with a continual psalm of praise of their exquisite flavor; and never till the day of his death did he suspect what the secret of that flavor was. I believe the Chinese eat ants and regard them as a luxury. Very likely they are right; but at that period of my boyhood I had not heard of this, and then and often afterwards did I meditate with misgivings upon the predicament of Henry Bright's stomach after his banquet.

VII

THAT life at Rock Park had in it more unadulter-
ated English quality than any other with which we
became conversant while in England. With the
exception of a short sojourn in Leamington, it was
the only experience vouchsafed us of renting a
house. All the rest of the time we lived in lodging
or boarding houses, or in hotels. The boarding-
houses of England are like other boarding-houses;
the hotels, or inns, in the middle of the last century, were for the most part plain and homely com-

pared with what we have latterly been used to; but
the English lodging-house system had peculiarities.
You enjoyed independence, but you paid for it with
inconveniences. The owner of the house furnished
you with nothing except the house, with its dingy
beds, chairs, tables, and carpets. Everything else
necessary to existence you got for yourself. You
made your own contracts with butcher, baker, and
grocer. You did your own firing and lighting.
Your sole conversation with the owner was over
the weekly bill for the rooms. You might cater to
yourself to the tune of the prince or of the pauper,
as your means or your inclination suggested, but
you must do it upon the background of the same
dingy rooms. Dingy or not so dingy, the rooms,
of course, never fitted you; they were a Procrustes
bed, always incompatible, in one way or in another,
with the proportions which nature had bestowed
upon you. You wondered, in your misanthropic
moments, whether there ever was or could be any
one whom English lodgings would exactly fit.
Probably they were designed for the average man,
a person, as we all know, who exists only in the
imagination of statisticians. And if the environment shows the man, one cannot help rejoicing that
there is so little likelihood of one's forming the
average man's acquaintance.

There was nothing peculiar about rented houses
in England beyond the innate peculiarities attaching to them as English. If the house were unfur-
nished, and you had leisure to pick and choose, you

might suit yourself tolerably well, always with the proviso that things English could be suitable to the foreigner. And certainly, in the 1850's, the English commanded living conditions more desirable, on the whole, than Americans did. They understood comfort, as distinct from luxury—a pitch of civilization to which we are even now but just attaining. There was not then, and until the millennium there will probably never be, anything else in the world which so ministered to physical ease and general satisfaction as did the conditions of life among the English upper classes. Kublai Khan, in Xanadu, never devised a pleasure-dome so alluring to mere human nature—especially the English variety of it—as was afforded by an English nobleman's country-seat. Tennyson's Palace of Art is very good in poetry, but in real life the most imaginative and energetic real-estate dealer could not have got so good a price for it as would gladly have been paid for the dwelling of, for example, the Duke of Westminster. "How many gardeners have you got?" asked an American Minister of the duke of the period, after meeting a fresh gardener, during a long afternoon stroll through the grounds, at each new turn of the path. "Oh, I don't know—I fancy about forty," replied the duke, somewhat taken aback by this demand for precise information concerning the facts of his own establishment, which, until that moment, he probably supposed had been attended to by Providence. And really, the machinery of life in such a place is so hidden, it is so nearly automatic, that one might easily believe it to be operated according to some law of nature. The servants are (or were) so well trained, they did their jobs so well, that you were conscious only of their being done; you never saw them a-doing. The thought happened to cross your mind, of a morning, that you would like to take a drive at eleven o'clock; you were not aware that you had mentioned the matter; but at eleven o'clock the carriage was, somehow, at the door. At dinner, the dishes appeared and disappeared, the courses succeeded one another, invisibly, or as if by mere fiat of the will; you must be very wide-awake to catch a footman or butler meddling with the matter. You went up to the bedroom to change your dress; you came down with it changed; but only by an effort could you recall the fact that a viewless but supremely efficient valet had been concerned in the transaction. The coal fire in the grate needed poking; you glanced away for a moment; when you looked at the fire again it had been poked—had, to all appearance, poked itself. And so in all relations; to desire was to get; to picture a condition was to realize it. You were shielded on every side by rose-leaves of culture and refinement; all you had to do was to allow your mind to lapse from one conception to another, and then, lifting your languorous eyelids, behold! there you were — as Mr. James would say.

But I set out to tell not of noblemen's country-seats, but of Rock Park. Rock Park was one of

the typical abodes of the English respectable middle-class, and the English middle-class, respectable,
or not altogether respectable, is the substance of
England. Not until you have felt and smelt and
tasted that do you know what England really is.
Fifty years ago, the people in question were dull,
ignorant, material, selfish, prejudiced, conventional; they were hospitable, on conventional lines;
they were affable and even social, so long as you did
not awaken their prejudices; they were confidential
and communicative, if you conceded at the outset
that England was the best of all countries and the
English the leading nation of the world. They
read a newspaper resembling in every particular
themselves; usually several of them united in a sub-
scription to a single copy, which passed solemnly
from hand to hand. They were slow and method-
ical, never taking short-cuts across lots; but they
were punctual; they knew their own business and
business associates, their circle of relatives, their
dwelling and social place, and *Burke's Peerage;* but
they knew nothing else. In a group of intelligent
persons of this degree, question was raised, once
upon a time, of two English poets; but not one of
the group had heard of either; the poets were Alfred Tennyson and Robert Browning. This may
seem merely absurd· or apocryphal; but consider
the terrible power of concentration which it implies! And consider the effect which the impact
against such a clay wall must make upon a man and
an American like my father!

Well, the very surprise and novelty of the adventure amused and interested him, and even won a good deal upon his sympathies. He loved the solid earth as well as the sky above it, and he was glad of the assurance that this people existed, though he might be devoutly thankful that two hundred years of America had opened so impassable a gulf between him and them. Indeed, the very fact of that impassability may have made his intercourse with them the easier—at any rate, on his side. On their side, they regarded him with a dim but always self-complacent curiosity; had he not been a consul, they would probably not have regarded him at all. Of course they — the Rock Park sort of people—had never read his books; literary cultivation was not to be found in England lower down than the gentleman class. My father, therefore, was never obliged to say, "I'm glad you liked it" to them. And that relief, of itself, must have served as a substantial bond of fellowship.

Rock Park, as I remember it, was a damp, winding, verdurous street, protected at each end by a small granite lodge, and studded throughout its length with stuccoed villas. The villas were mended-on to each other (as one of the children expressed it) two and two; they had front yards filled with ornamental shrubbery, and gardens at the back, an acre or two in extent; they were fenced in with iron pickets, and there were gates to the driveways, on which the children swung. Every normal child supposes that gates are made for no other purpose.

The trees were not large, but there were many of them, and they were thick with leaves. There was a damp, arboreal smell everywhere, mingled with the finer perfume of flowers and of the hawthorns and yellow laburnums. Flowers, especially purple English violets, grew profusely in the gardens, and gooseberry-bushes, bearing immense gooseberries such as our climate does not nourish. There were also armies of garden-snails, handsome gasteropods, which were of great interest to me; for I was entering, at this period, upon a passionate pursuit of natural history. For many years I supposed that the odor of the violets proceeded from snails, and to this day I always associate snails with violets, or *vice versa*. Una, Rose, and I were given each a section of a garden-bed for our own; I cultivated mine so assiduously that it became quite a deep hole; but I do not recall that anything ever grew in it. The soil was a very rich loam, and ceaseless diligence must have been required in me to keep it barren.

Gray skies, frequent showers, a cool or semi-chilly mildness, varied every little while by the intrusion of a yellow fog from Liverpool, over the river—such was the climate of Rock Park. There were occasional passages of sunshine; but never, that I recollect, an entire day of it. The stucco of the villas was streaked with green dampness, and peeling off here and there. I suspect that the fashion of castellated, stuccoed villas may have been set in the eighteenth century by Horace Walpole when he built that marvellous edifice known as Strawberry Hill. I first saw that achieveme1t twenty years after the time of which I now write, and recognized in it, as I thought, the parent of my former Rock Park home and of innumerable of the latter's kindred. Strawberry Hill is sprawling and vast, the progeny are liliputian, but the family likeness is striking. The idea is to build something which shall seem to be all that it is not. The gray-white stucco pretends to be stone, and the lines of the stone courses are carefully painted on the roughened surface; but nobody, since Horace's time, could ever have been deceived by them. The castellated additions and ornamentation are all bogus, of the cheapest and vulgarest sort. It is singular that a people so sincere and solid as the English are supposed to be should adopt this fashion for their dwellings. But then they are used to follow conventions and adopt fashions set them by those whom they esteem to be their betters, without thought, or activity of individual conscience. It is rather matter for wonder, remembering what rascals and humbugs many of their "betters" have been, that middle-class England is not more of a whited sepulchre than it is. I do not mean to cast any reflections upon the admirable and beguiling Horace; but he was a highly civilized person, and had a brother named Robert, and perhaps solid sincerity should not be expected from such a combination.

Our villa, within, was close and comfortable

enough, for its era and degree; but the furniture
was ponderous and ugly to the point of nightmare.
The chairs, tables, and sofas wore the semblance of
solid mahogany, twisted and tortured in a futile
struggle to achieve elegance; the carvings, or
mouldings, were screwed or glued on, and the lines
of structure, intended to charm the eye, accomplished only the discomfort of the body. The
dining-table was like a plateau; the sideboard resembled a cliff-dwelling. The carpets were of the
Brussels ilk: acanthus-leaves and roses and dah-
lias wreathed in inextricable convolutions, glowing
with the brightest and most uncompromising hues.
The lace curtains were imitation lace; the damask
curtains were imitation damask. The bedsteads.
. . . But this is not a History of England. After all,
we were snug and comfortable. On the walls were
portraits of the family whose house this was; by
name, Campbell; the house-painter, or wood-grain-
er, one would suppose, had a leaning towards this
branch of art. I never saw the originals of these
portraits, but, upon the assumption that they had
been faithfully interpreted by the artist, I used to
think, in my childish folly, that the refrain of the
old song, "The Campbells are Coming," was meant
as a phrase or threat to frighten people. Who
would not have run upon such an announcement?

As I have already made one confession in these
pages not reflecting credit upon myself, I may as
well make another now. Just thirty years after
the events I am describing, somebody wrote to me

from Rock Park, stating that the local inhabitants were desirous of putting up on the house which Hawthorne had occupied there a marble or bronze slab, recording the fact for the benefit of pilgrims. The committee, however, did not know which of three or four houses was the right one, and the writer enclosed photographs of them all, and requested me to put a cross over our former habitation. Now, all the houses in Rock Park had been turned out of the same mould, and I knew no more than my interrogator which was which. But I reflected that the committee had been put to trouble and expense for photographs, postage-stamps, and what not, and that all that was really wanted was something to be sentimental over. So, rather than disappoint them, I resorted to a kind of *sortes Virgilianæ;* I shut my eyes, turned round thrice, and made a mark at hazard on the line of photographs. The chances against my having hit it right were only four to one; the committee were satisfied, the pilgrims have been made happy, and it is difficult to see where harm has been done. Nevertheless, the matter has weighed somewhat on my conscience ever since, and I am glad to have thus lightened myself of it. What would one better do in such circumstances? Is history written in this way?

The custom of our family in America had been to take all our meals together; but in England the elders take lunch at noon, tea at four or five, and dinner at seven or eight, while the children dine at noon and sup at six. This arrangement was adopted in

Rock Park. My father used to leave home for the consulate at nine, and return—unless kept away by an official or social engagement—at five or six. There was appointed for us children a nurse or governess, to oversee and administer our supplies; our father and mother dining, with such guests as might happen to be present, late in the evening. We were sometimes allowed to come in at dessert, to eat a few nuts and raisins and exhibit our infantile good manners. This domestic separation was a matter of much speculation and curiosity to our immature minds; we used to haunt the hall through which the servants carried the dishes, smoking and fragrant, from the kitchen to the dining-room, and once in a while the too-indulgent creatures would allow us to steal something. How ravishingly delicious things thus acquired taste! And we, fancying, of course, that they must be not less delicious for the folks at table, used to marvel how they could ever bear to leave off eating. The dinners were certainly rather elaborate compared with the archaic repasts of Salem or of Concord; but they were as far inferior in grandeur and interminableness to the astonishing banquets at which, in some great houses, our father and mother were present. Consider, for example, this dinner, in no way remarkable among such functions, at the Hollands's, about this time. There were twelve persons at table. The service was of solid silver; two enormous covers were on the table before the soup was served; being removed, they revealed turbot and fried fish. Then followed boiled turkey and roast goose, and between them innumerable smaller dishes, including chicken-pies, ragouts, cutlets, fricasées, tongue, and ham, all being placed in their silver receptacles on the table; on the sideboard was a vast round of boiled beef, as a precaution against famine. With the sweets were served grouse and pheasants; there were five kinds of wine, not including the champagne, which was consumed as a collateral all the way along. The pudding which followed these trifles was an heroic compound, which Gargantua might have flinched from; then came the nuts and raisins, then the coffee, then the whiskey and brandy. There were people in England, half a century ago, who ate this sort of dinners six or seven times a week, and thought nothing of it. They actually ate and drank them—did not merely glance at them and shake their heads. The ancient Scandinavians, Gauls, Saxons, and Normans, of whom they were descendants, could not have done more. One cannot help respecting such prodigious trencher-men and women, or wonder that the poverty-stricken class were ill-fed. Dinner in England had become a very different thing when I lived there twenty years later, and though port and Madeira were generally on the table, the only man whom I saw habitually drink them was Robert Browning! Possibly this is the reason the British got such a thrashing in South Africa the other day.

After dinner at Rock Park—or, if it were to be a late affair, before—we would have family prayers,

in which the servants joined. This was in deference to English custom; not that we were irreligious,
but we had not before been accustomed to express
our religious feelings in just that manner. All being grouped in a semicircle, my father would open
the Bible and read a chapter; then he would take a
prayer-book containing thirty or forty well-con-
sidered addresses to the Almighty, and everybody
would kneel down and cover their eyes with their
hands. The "Amen" having been reached, and
echoed by every one, all would rise to their former
positions, and the servants would file out of the
room. It must have been somewhat of an effort
for my father to go through this ceremony; but I
think he did it, not only for the reason above mentioned, but also because he thought it right that
his children should have the opportunity of gain-
ing whatever religious sentiment such proceedings
might inculcate. But I do not think that he had
much faith in the practice as an English institution.
Indeed, he has somewhere written that the English
"bring themselves no nearer to God when they
pray than when they play cards."

I understood long afterwards, as I did not at the
time, how closely my father and mother studied in
all things the welfare and cultivation of their children. They were not formal or oppressive about
it; all went pleasantly and with seeming spontane-
ity, as if in accordance with our own desire; but we
were wisely and heedfully guided. We were never
sent to school during our seven years in Europe;

ROBERT BROWNING

but either we were taught our lessons by our parents at home or by governesses. In addition to the constant walks which I took with my father, he encouraged me to join a cricket club in the Park, and sent me to Huguenin's gymnasium in Liverpool, to the Cornwallis swimming-baths, and to a dancing-academy kept by a highly ornamental Frenchman, and he bought me an enormous steel hoop, and set me racing after it at headlong speed. Nor did he neglect to stimulate us in the imaginative and æsthetic side. From the date of our settlement in England to the end of his life, he read aloud to us in the evenings many of the classics of literature. Spenser's *The Faerie Queene*, the *Don Quixote* of Cervantes, the poems and novels of Scott, Grimm's and Andersen's *Fairy Tales*, much of Defoe and Swift, Goldsmith's *Vicar of Wakefield*, Coleridge's *Ancient Mariner* (he himself was very fond of that poem), and many other things, and I cannot overestimate the good they did me. His talks to me during our walks gave me, under the guise of pleasantry, not so much specific information concerning things (though that was not wanting), but —character; that is, the questions he put to me, the remarks and comments he made, the stories he told, were all calculated to give me a high idea of human duties and aspirations; to encourage generosity, charity, courage, patriotism, and independence. From the reading of *The Faerie Queene* and of *Don Quixote* I conceived a vehement infatuation for mediæval chivalry and knight-errantry; I adopted the motto of the order, "Be faithful, brave, and true in deed and word"; and I indulged in waking dreams of heroic adventures in quest of fair renown, and to succor the oppressed. All this he encouraged and abetted, though always, too, with a sort of twinkle of the eye, lest I should take myself too seriously and wax priggish. He permitted me to have a breastplate and a helmet with a golden dragon crest (made by our nurse out of pasteboard covered with tinsel-paper), and he bought me a real steel sword with a brass hilt wrought in open-work; I used to spend hours polishing it, and picturing to myself the giants and ogres I would slay with it. Finally—with that humorous arching of the eyebrow of his—he bade me kneel down, and with my sword smote me on the shoulder, and dubbed me knight, saying, "Rise up, Sir Julian!" It was worth many set moral homilies to me. He knew the advantage of leading a boy to regard the practice of boyish and manly virtues not as a burden but as a privilege and boon, and of making the boy's own conscience his judge. His handling of the matter was, of course, modified so as to reach the inner springs of my particular nature and temperament, which he thoroughly understood. Withal, he never failed to hold up to ridicule anything showing a tendency to the sentimental; he would test me on this point in various ways, and always betrayed pleasure when he found me quick to detect the sentimental or mawkish taint in literature or life. I breathed a manly, robust, and bracing

128

atmosphere in his company, and when I reflect upon what were my proclivities to folly during this impressionable period, I thank my stars for such a father.

There was abundant quiet and seclusion in Rock Park, and had my father been able to do any writing, he could hardly have found a retreat more suitable. The tradesmen called early at the houses in the Park, their wagon‑wheels making no sound upon the unpaved street, and the two policemen, who lived in the stone lodges, kept the place free from beggars and peddlers. These policemen, pacing slowly along in their uniforms, rigid and dignified, had quite an imposing aspect, and it was some time before we children discovered that they were only men, after all. Each had a wife and children, who filled to overflowing the tiny habitations; when their blue coats and steel-framed hats were off, they were quite humble persons; one of them eked out his official salary by mending shoes. After following with awe the progress along the sidewalk of the officer of public order, stalking with solemn and measured gait, and touching his hat, with a hand encased in a snow-white cotton glove, to such of the denizens of the Park as he might encounter, it was quite like a fairy-tale transformation to see him squatting in soiled shirt-sleeves on his cobbler's bench, drawing waxed thread through holes in a boot-sole. I once saw one of them, of a Sunday afternoon, standing at ease in the doorway of his lodge, clad in an old sack-coat which I recognized as having been my father's. I am constitutionally reverent of law and order; but the revelation of the domestic lives of these policemen gave me an insight, which I have never since lost, into the profound truth that the man and the officer are twain.

There were perhaps twenty families living in the Park, of whom we became acquainted with two only; the people who lived next door to us (whose name I have forgotten), and Mr. and Mrs. Squarey, who dwelt higher up the street. The people next door had two boys of about my own age, with whom I played cricket, and it was from the back windows of their house that I saw for the first time an exhibition of fireworks in their garden; I remember that when, just before the show began, they put out the lamp in the room, I asked to have it relighted, in order that I might see the as yet unexperienced wonder. There are folks who go hunting for the sun with a lantern.

Mr. Squarey was tall and stiff of figure, with a singularly square countenance, with a short whisker on each side of it; but spiritually he was most affable and obliging; so was his wife; but as she was short and globular, my father was wont to refer to her, in the privacy of domestic intercourse, as Mrs. Roundey. They were profuse in invitations to go with us to places—to Chester, to the Welsh show-places, and so forth; and although I think my father and mother would rather have gone alone, they felt constrained to accept these suggestions. It was in their company, at all events, that I first saw Chester

"Rows"; and also, from some coign of vantage on those delightful old walls, an English horse-race, with jockeys in silk caps and jackets tinted like the rainbow. Mr. Squarey's demeanor towards my sisters and myself was like that of the benevolent tutor in *Sandford and Merton*, with which excellent work we were very conversant at that time; as, likewise, with Edgeworth's *Parents' Assistant*, and with still another engaging volume called, I think, the Budget of something; at any rate, it had two or three little boys and girls in it, who were anxious to acquire useful and curious information on many subjects, which was afforded them in generous measure by their highly cultivated elders. Such flower-garlanded instruction was the best specifically juvenile literature which those primitive ages afforded. "Pray, mamma, why does the sun rise in the east instead of in the west?" "Pray, papa, why was King Alfred called 'The Good'?" Mrs. Markham's *History of England* was constructed upon the same artless principle. What a distance we have travelled since then!

But it was a good and happy life in Rock Park, and I think our father and mother enjoyed it almost as much as we children did. They were meeting people many of whom were delightful—I shall try to paint the portraits of some of them in the next chapter—and they were seeing towns and castles and places of historic and picturesque interest; and my father was earning more money than ever before, though less than a quarter as much as he would have earned had not Congress, soon after his accession to office, cut down the emoluments. This was England; the Old Home, and the Old World, for the understanding of which they had prepared themselves all their lives previous. My father once said, "If England were all the world, it would still have been worth while for the Creator to have made it." The children were radiantly content with their lot; and it is on record that the little boy once remarked, "I don't remember when I came down from heaven; but I'm glad I happened to tumble into so good a family." The same individual, rolling on the floor in excess of mirth over some childish comicality, panted out, "Oh, mamma, my ball of jolly is so big I can't breathe!" The ball of jolly became a household word for years thereafter. It was well nourished in those days.

VIII

Cataclysmic adventures—On the trail of dazzling fortunes
—"Lovely, but reprehensible Madham"—The throne
saves the artist—English robin redbreast—A sad and
weary old man—"Most indelicate woman I've ever
known"—Perfectly chaste—Something human stirred
dimly—"She loves me; she loves me!"—The Prince of
Wales and half-a-crown—Portentous and thundering
title—Honest English simplicity—"The spirit lacking"
—Abelard, Isaac Newton, and Ruskin—A famous and
charming woman of genius—Deep and wide well of
human sympathy—The whooping-cough.

In the spring of 1854 we were visited by John O'Sullivan, his wife and mother, and a young relative of
theirs, Miss Ella Rogers. O'Sullivan had been appointed Minister to the Court of Portugal, and was
on his way thither. He was a Democrat of old
standing; had edited the *Democratic Review* in 1837,
and had made my father's acquaintance at that
time through soliciting contributions from him;
later they became close friends, and when my sister
Una was born, he sent her a silver cup, and was ever
after called "Uncle John" in the family, and, also,
occasionally, "the Count"—a title which, I believe,
had some warrant in his ancestry. For, although
an American, Uncle John was born at sea off the

coast of Spain, of an Irish father and a mother of aristocratic connections or extraction (I am a little uncertain, I find, on this point); I think her parents were Italian. Uncle John had all the charming qualities of the nations mentioned, and none of their objectionable ones; though this is not to say that he was devoid of tender faults, which were, if anything, more lovable than his virtues. Beneath a tranquil, comely, and gentle exterior burned all the fire and romance of the Celt; his faith and enthusiasm in "projects" knew no bounds; he might be deceived and bankrupted a hundred times, and would toe the mark the next time with undiminished confidence. He was continually, and in the quietest way, having the most astonishing and cataclysmic adventures; he would be blown up, as it were, by a dynamite explosion, and presently would return from the sky undisturbed, with only a slight additional sparkle in his soft eyes, and with the lock of hair that fell gracefully over his forehead only a trifle disordered. The most courteous and affectionate of men, with the most yielding and self-effacing manners, he had the spirit of a paladin, and was afraid of nothing. He would empty his pockets—or if, as too often happened, they were already empty, he would pledge his credit to help a friend out of a hole; and, on the other hand, he was always hot upon the trail of a dazzling fortune, which, like Emerson's *Forerunners*, never was overtaken. It would not long have availed him, had it been otherwise, for never was there a Monte Cristo who lavished wealth as O'Sullivan habitually did in anticipation, and would undoubtedly have done in fact had the opportunity been afforded him. He was gifted with a low, melodious, exquisitely modulated voice, and a most engaging and winning manner, and when he set out to picture the simple and easy methods whereby he proposed to make millions, it was next to impossible to resist him. He was like a beautiful, innocent, brilliant child, grown up, endowed with an enchanter's wand, which was forever promising all the kingdoms of the earth to him, but never (as our modern phrase is) delivered the goods. He regarded my father as a king of men, and he had, times without number, been on the very edge of making him, as well as himself, a multifold millionaire. However, President Pierce did what he could for him by giving him the Portuguese mission (after first offering it to my father), and O'Sullivan did excellent work there. But he became interested—abstractly—in some copper-mines in Spain, which, as he clearly demonstrated, could be bought for a song, and would pay a thousand per cent. from the start. Partly to gratify him, and partly with the hope of at least getting his money back, my father finally, in 1858 or 1859, advanced him ten thousand dollars to finance the scheme. I saw the dear old gentleman, a generation later, in New York; he had the same clear, untroubled, tranquil face as of old; his hair, though gray, was as thick and graceful as ever; his manner was as sweet and attractive;

135

but though, in addition to his other accomplishments, he had become an advanced spiritualist, he
had not yet coined into bullion his golden imagination. He had forgotten the Spanish copper-mines,
and I took care not to remind him of them. Peace
to his generous, ardent, and loving soul!

Uncle John's wife was a good mate for him, in
her own way as brilliant and fascinating as he and
with an unalterable belief in her husband's destiny.
She was a tall, slender woman, with kindling eyes, a
lovely smile, and a wonderful richness and vivacity
of conversation; nor have I ever since known so
truly witty a woman. But she lacked the delightful mellowness and tenderness for which Uncle John
was so remarkable. The mother, Madame O'Sullivan, as she was called, was a type of the fine-
grained, gently bred aristocrat, every outline soft-
ened and made gracious by the long lapse of years
through which she had lived. She sat like a picture of reverend but still animated age, with white,
delicate lace about her pale cheeks and dark, kindly,
weary eyes, and making a frost-work over her silvery hair. As for Miss Ella Rogers, it is with some
embarrassment that I refer to her; inasmuch as I
fell violently in love with her at first sight, and I
have reason to think that she never fully appreciated or adequately responded to my passion,
though, at the time, I was nearly one-third of her
age—she being five-and-twenty. She was a dark
and lively beauty, thoroughly self-possessed, and
versed in social accomplishments, and gifted with

dramatic talent. She afterwards made a great impression in the court of the Portuguese monarch, and more than once the King himself chose her as his partner in the ball. Reports of these gayeties came to my ears; and I found the other day part of a letter which I addressed to her, remonstrating against these royal flirtations. It is written in pencil, upon the blue office-paper of the consulate, and I can recall distinctly the small, indignant boy and knight-errant, sitting at the desk opposite his hugely diverted father, and beginning his epistle thus: "Lovely, but reprehensible Madham!" I suspect that I consulted my father as to the spelling of the second adjective, for it shows signs of having been overhauled; but after that my feelings became too strong for me, and the remainder of the letter is orthographically so eccentric that it was probably cast aside and a copy made of it. But the rough draught, by some inconceivable chance, was kept, and turns up now, after half a century, with a strange thread of pathos woven by time into the texture of its absurdity. Poor, little, lovely reprehensible Madham! Her after-career was not a happy one.

These agreeable persons filled our stuccoed villa full, and gave poignant addition to the quiet, gray beauty of that English spring. A year or so later, when my mother's health compelled her to escape to a warmer climate from fog-ridden Liverpool, she went with my sisters to Lisbon, where the O'Sullivans were by that time established, and spent several months with them, and saw all the splendors of the naïve but brilliant little court of Dom Pedro V. She brought home a portfolio of etchings presented to her, and done by his youthful Majesty; which indicate that his throne, little as he cared for it, preserved him from the mortification of failing as an artist.

Early in the winter of the following year (1855), Mr. James Buchanan, appointed Minister to the Court of St. James, found his way to my father's retreat in Rock Park. The English winter was a mild affair compared with our recent experiences of the arctic snows of Lenox; there was no coasting, and not much snow-balling; but we had the pleasure of making friends with the English robin-redbreast, a most lovable little creature, who, every morning, hopped confidingly on our window-sill and took bread-crumbs almost from our hands. The old American diplomatist and President that was to be (though he vehemently disclaimed any such possibility) distracted our attention from robin for a day or two. He had the aspect, perhaps cultivated for political and democratic purposes, of a Pennsylvania farmer; he was, I believe, born on a farm in Franklin County, in that State, at the beginning of the last decade of the eighteenth century. He was tall and ungainly in figure, though he bore himself with a certain security and dignity; his head was high and thinly covered with gray hair; he carried it oddly, a little on one side; it was said at the time that this was due to his having

once attempted suicide by cutting his throat.   His
visage—heavy, long, and noticeable—had the typical traits of the American politician of that epoch;
his eyes were small, shrewd, and twinkling; there
was a sort of professional candor in his bearing,
but he looked like a sad and weary old man.   He
talked somewhat volubly to my father, who kept
him going by a question now and then, as his way
generally was with visitors.   There was a flavor of
rusticity in his speech; he was not a man of culture
or polish, though unquestionably of great experience of the world.   He was dressed in a wide-skirt-
ed coat of black broadcloth, and wore a white
choker put on a little askew.   The English, who
were prone to be critical of our representatives,
made a good deal of fun of Mr. Buchanan, and told
anecdotes about him which were probably exagger-
ated or apocryphal.   It was alleged, for example,
that, speaking of the indisposition of a female relative of his, he had observed that it was due to the
severity of the English climate.   "She never enjoyed
delicate health at home," he had declared; "in fact,
she was always one of the most indelicate women
I've ever known."   And it was asserted that he had
been admonished by the Lord High Chamberlain,
or by the Gold Stick-in-Waiting, for expectorating
upon the floor of her Majesty's palace at a levee.
Such ribaldries used to be popular in English mouths
concerning American visitors before the war; they
were all of similar tenor.   Mrs. Abbott Lawrence
was described as having bought a handsome shawl

at a shop on Lord Street, in Liverpool, and to have walked down that populous thoroughfare with her new purchase on her shoulders, ignorant that it bore the legend, inscribed on a white card, which the salesman had neglected to remove, "Perfectly chaste." The same lady was reported as saying, in asking an invitation to a ball on behalf of Mrs. Augustus Peabody, of Boston, "I assure you, on our side of the water, Mrs. Peabody is much more accustomed to grant favors than to ask them." Such anecdotes seem to bear upon them the stamp of the British manufacturer. There would not seem to be much harm in them, yet it is such things that sometimes interfere most acutely with the *entente cordiale* between nations. We had another glimpse of Mr. Buchanan, in London, about a year later, and he then remarked to my mother, indirectly referring to such reports, that the Queen had treated him very kindly. For the present, he faded from the Rock Park horizon, and we returned to the robin; nor have I been able to understand how it happened that he made so distinct an impression upon my memory. But a child's memory is unaccountable, both in what it loses and in what it retains.

One Sunday forenoon, when it was not too cold for the young folks to be swinging on that gate which has been mentioned, and the elders were in-doors, enjoying the holiday in their own way, we descried an old gentleman approaching up the winding street. As he drew nearer he presented rather a shabby, or, at least, rusty appearance. His felt hat was not so black as it had been; his coat was creased and soiled; his boots needed a blacking. He swung a cane as he stumped along, and there was a sort of faded smartness in his bearing and a knowingness in his grim old visage, indicating some incongruous familiarity with the manners of the great world. He came to a halt in front of the house, and, after quizzing it for a moment, went up the steps and beat a fashionable tattoo with the knocker.

Summoned in-doors soon afterwards, we found this questionable personage sitting in the drawing-room. His voice was husky, but modulated to the inflections of polite breeding; he used a good many small gestures, and grinned often, revealing the yellow remains of his ancient teeth, he laughed, too, with a hoarse sound in his throat. There was about him an air of determined cheerfulness and affability, though between the efforts the light died down in his wrinkled old eyes and the lines of his face sagged and deepened. He offered to kiss my sisters, but they drew back; he took my hand in his own large, dry one with its ragged nails and swollen joints. At length he inveigled my younger sister to his knee, where she sat gazing unflinchingly and solemnly into him with that persistence which characterizes little girls of four or five who are not quite sure of their ground. Her smooth, pink-and-white cheeks and unwinking eyes contrasted vividly with his seamed yellowness and blinking grin; for a long time he coquetted at her, and played peep-bo, without disturbing her gravity, making humorous side comments to the on-lookers meanwhile. There was a ragged and disorderly mop of gray hair on his head, which showed very dingy beside the clear auburn of the child's. One felt a repulsion from him, and yet, as he chatted and smirked and acted, there was a sort of fascination in him, too. Some original force and fire of nature still glowed and flickered in his old carcass; something human stirred dimly under the crust of self-consciousness and artificiality. Rose's adamantine seriousness finally relaxed in a faint smile, upon which he threw up his hands, emitted a hoarse cackle of triumph, and exclaimed, "There—there it is! I knew I'd get it; she loves me—she loves me!" He then permitted her to slip down from his knee and withdraw to her mother, and resumed the talk which our entrance had interrupted. It was chiefly about people of whom we youngsters knew nothing—though our ignorance only argued ourselves unknown, for he named persons all famous in their day. He had seen George IV., Napoleon, Talleyrand, Wellington; he had been intimate with Coleridge, De Quincey, Wordsworth, Lamb, Monk Lewis; he was a sort of elder brother or deputy uncle to Tennyson, Browning, Dickens; he had quaffed mountain-dew with Walter Scott and had tramped the moors shoulder to shoulder with Kit North; the courts of Europe were his familiar stamping-grounds; he had the nobility and gentry at his finger-ends; he was privileged, petted, and sought after everywhere; if there were any august door we wished to enter, any high-placed personage we desired to approach, any difficult service we wanted rendered, he was the man to help us to our object. Who, then, was he?

He has long been utterly forgotten; but he was well known, or notorious, during the first half of the last century; he was such a character as could flourish only in England. His name was William Jerdan; he was born in 1785, and was now, therefore, about seventy years old. He had started in life poor, with no family distinction, but with some more or less useful connections either on the father's or the mother's side. He had somehow got an English education, and he had pursued his career on the basis of his native wits, his indomitable effrontery and persistence, his faculty of familiarity, his indifference to rebuffs, his lack of shame, conscience, and morality. How he found the means to live nobody could tell, but he uniformly lived well and had enjoyed the good things of the world. After maintaining his ground during the first twenty or thirty years, it had probably been easier for him to forge along afterwards, for he could impose upon the new generation with his stories of success in the former one. Uncouth and ugly though he was by nature, the external polish and trick of good form which he had acquired, and, no doubt, some inner force of social genius in him, had influenced men to tolerate and often to likè him, and had given him extraordinary good-fortune with women. He had

143

not only been twice married, and had many children born in wedlock, but his intrigues and liaisons had been innumerable, and they had by no means been confined to the lower ranks of society. That he was a practised liar there can be no doubt, but he had the long memory which the proverb recommends to liars, and he was so circumspect that few of his claims and pretensions lacked solid basis enough to make them pass current in a hurrying and heedless world. Now, however, in his age, he was wellnigh at the end of his tether; what we should call his "pull" was losing its efficiency; he was lapsing to the condition where he would offer to introduce a man to the Prince of Wales or to Baron Rothschild, and then ask him for the loan of five pounds—or half a crown, as the case might be. He was a character for Thackeray. He haunted my father for a year or two more, and then vanished I know not where.

Poor, dingy old Jerdan purported to be himself a literary man, though the only thing of his that I ever heard of was a work in four pretentious volumes of "wretched twaddle"—as my father called them—which he published under the title of *My Autobiography*. It contained a long array of renowned names, with passages appended of perfectly empty and conventional comment.

But other men crossed our path who had much sounder claims to renown in literature; among them Samuel Warren, author of half a dozen books, two of which are still sometimes heard of—*The Diary of a Late Physician* and *Ten Thousand a Year*. He lived upon the reputation which these brought him, though they were published, the first as long ago as 1830 and the other only ten years later. Like many other authors, he fancied himself capable of things far better than belonged to his true *métier;* and among the books in my father's library is one called *The Moral and Intellectual Development of the Present Age*— a thin volume, despite its portentous and thundering title—it carries the gloss, in Warren's handwriting, " the fruit of many a long year's reflection." So does every light comedian imagine that he can play Hamlet. Of Warren himself I barely recall a slight, light figure with a sharp nose and a manner lacking in repose; indeed, he was very much like a light comedian in light comedy, eager to hold the centre of the stage, full of small movements and remarks, and—which more interested us children— with a gift for turning himself into other people by slight contortions of countenance and alterations of voice. The histrionic abilities of Dickens probably affected the social antics of many writers at this epoch. Warren also told stories in a vivacious and engaging manner, though, as they were about things and people out of the sphere of his younger auditors, I remember only the way of the telling, not what was told. I recalled, later, his anecdotes of Kit North, who was a friend of his, on account of the contrast between the stalwart proportions of that old worthy and the diminutive physique of the novelist; they must have looked, together, like a bear and a monkey. Warren was born in Wales, though whether of Welsh ancestry I know not. When we saw him he was only a trifle over five-and-forty years of age, so his famous books must have been written when he was hardly more than a boy.

As for Layard, eminent in his time for his work in Nineveh and Babylon, and afterwards as a states-man, he did not, I think, come to Rock Park, nor am I sure that I ever saw him. And yet it seems to me that I have the picture in my mind of a vigor-ous, frank, agreeable personage who was he; not a large man, still less a handsome one, but full of life, manliness, and honest English simplicity. He was at this time, like so many of his countrymen, very anxious concerning the Crimean War, then in its first stages, and vehemently opposed to the policy which had brought it about, for, up to that time, England and Russia had been on friendly terms, and Layard could see no promising or useful future for the Turk. My father shared his views, and he wrote the following passage in commenting upon the general European situation of that day and the prospects for England. It has never been printed, because it stood only for the sentiment of the moment, but may be opportunely quoted now that the aspect of European politics shows symptoms of soon undergoing vital changes. "The truth is," wrote my father, "there is a spirit lacking in England which we in America do not lack; and for the want of it she will have to resign a foremost position among the nations, even if there were not enough other circumstances to compel her to do so. Her good qualities are getting out of date; at all events, there should be something added to them in the present stage of the world." England has a good deal changed since those words were written, and the changes have probably been mainly for the better, though all the important ones have caused our old mother discomfort and embarrassment. The medicine of a new age, the subtle infiltration of anti-insular ideas, the slow emergence of the democracy have given her many qualms, but they are wholesome ones. Her best and most cultivated minds are now on the side of progress, instead of holding by the past, and, should the pinch come, these may avail to save her better than martinet generals or unwieldy fleets. The "spirit lacking" in her in 1855 may, perhaps, be found in them. Whether the spirit in question be as conspicuous with us as it used to be is another matter.

Henry Bright was still our most frequent visitor, and he brought us the news and gossip of the world. It was in 1855 that Millais married the lady who had been Mrs. Ruskin. English society was much fluttered by this event, and many of Ruskin's friends cut him for a time in consequence of it. Ruskin was a man of a rare type, not readily understood in England, where a man is expected, in the fundamental qualities of his nature at least, to be like everybody else. There are two noted characters in history with whom, in some respects, he might be compared, Isaac Newton being one and Abelard the other. All three were men in whom, owing to causes either natural or accidental, the intellect was able to absorb all the energies of the nature. The intellect thus acquired extraordinary power and brilliance, and appropriated to itself, in a sort of image, as it were, the qualities which no longer possessed manifestation on the material plane. Nothing out of the way would, therefore, be noticed, unless or until some combination of circumstances should bring the exceptional condition into every-day light. This happened with Ruskin, and he was, of course, unable to regard the matter in the same light as his critics did. He viewed his wife's disinclination towards him by the light of mere cold logic; and the reason his friends were alienated from him was, not that her grounds of objection to him were justifiable, but that Ruskin (according to the common report of the time, as quoted by Mr. Bright) did not see why he and she and Millais should discontinue their life in common as before. Neither Millais nor Mrs. Ruskin would, of course, accede to this proposition, and the divorce was accordingly obtained. Ruskin intended simply to show magnanimity, and in the course of years this was recognized and he was forgiven, just as we forgive a person for being color-blind. In our present stage of civilization we must, in certain matters, follow strict convention on peril of ostracism, and nothing is less readily condoned in a man's conduct than any suspicion of complaisance. I did not see either Ruskin or Millais until 1879 or 1880, of which beholding I will speak when the time comes.

But we had with us for a short time a famous and charming woman of genius, who made me for a season forget my infatuation for the beautiful Ella Rogers. This was Charlotte Cushman. The acquaintance then begun was renewed in Italy, and maintained till the end of her life. Such is the power of the spiritual in nature and character to dominate and even render invisible the physical, that I was astonished, in after years, to hear Charlotte referred to as a woman of plain or unattractive features. To me, won from the first by the expression, the voice, the sphere, the warmth, strength, and nobility of her presence, she had always seemed one of the handsomest as well as most delightful of women. She was in her fortieth year, but she had already announced her purpose of retiring from the stage. Some of her best work was done in the following twenty years. Critics might call her face plain, or ugly, if they chose, but there was no doubt that its range of expression was vast and poignant, that it could reflect with immense energy the thoughts of the mind, and could radiate the very soul of tragedy. Her figure was tall and superb and her carriage stately without any stiffness, and appalling though she was as Lady Macbeth or Meg Merrilies, in our little drawing-room she was only simple, sincere, gentle, and winning. Born actress though she was, her horizon was by no means restricted to things histrionic; she talked well on many subjects, and was at no loss for means to entertain even so small and inexperienced a person as myself. I had never seen a theatre, and did not know what an actress was, but I loved her, and she was good to me. It was not the interest of the stories she told me, so much as the personal influence that went with them, that entranced me. I was sensible of her kindness, and of the hearty good-will with which she bent her great and gracious self to the task of making me happy. That wonderful array of tiny charms on her watch - chain was beautiful and absorbing, owing less to anything intrinsic in themselves than to some sparkling and lovable communication from their wearer. If a woman be only large enough and vigorous enough to begin with, the stage seems to develop her as nothing else could—to bring out the best in her. It was perhaps the deep and wide well of human sympathy in Charlotte Cushman that was at the bottom of her success in her profession, though, of course, she was greatly aided by her mental and physical gifts. I suppose there may be women now capable of being actresses as great as she was, but the audience to call forth their latent powers and ambition seems, just at present, to be lacking.

Our social diversions at Rock Park were interrupted, at about this period, by the whooping-cough, which seized upon all of us together, and I well remember my father almost climbing up the wall of the room in some of his paroxysms; but he treated it all as a joke, and was always ready to laugh as soon as he got through coughing. It left no ill effects except upon my mother, who had bronchial trouble which, as I have intimated, finally led to the breaking-up of our household. She was not made for England.

IX

Two New England consciences—Inexhaustible faith and energy—Deep and abiding love of England—"How the Water Comes Down at Lodore "—" He took an' he let go " —Naked mountains—The unsentimental little quadruped—The human element in things sticks—The coasts of England—A string of sleepy donkeys—Unutterable boy-thoughts—Grins and chuckles like an ogress—Hideous maternal parody—The adorable inverted bell-glass — Strange things happen in the world — An ominous clouding of the water—Something the world has never known—Overweening security—An admonition not to climb too high—How vice may become virtue by repetition—Corporal Blair's chest—Black-Bottle Cardigan—Called to Lisbon.

EMERSON, as a matter of principle, was rather averse from travel, though he made the trip to England twice; but he fortified his theory by his practice of searching out great men rather than historic or picturesque places. Ruskin's *Modern Painters* had not been written when Emerson first left home, and I doubt if he read it at any time. He found his mountain scenery in Carlyle and his lakes and vales elsewhere among agreeable people. My father's conscience worked in a different way; he thought himself under obligations to see whatever in the way of towns, ruins, cathedrals, and scenery was accounted worthy a foreigner's attention; but I think he would have enjoyed seeing them much more had that feeling of obligation not been imposed upon him. Set sights, as he often remarked, wearied him, just because they were set; things that he happened upon unpremeditatedly, especially if they were not described in guide-books, pleased him more and tired him less. It can hardly be affirmed, however, that he would have missed the set sights if he could have done so, and no doubt he was glad, after the job was done, that he had done it. And he was greatly helped along by the inexhaustible faith and energy in such matters of his wife; she shrank from no enterprise, and seemed always in precisely the right mood to appreciate whatever she beheld. She could go day after day to a picture-gallery, and stay all day long; she would make herself as familiar with churches, castles, and cathedrals as she was with her own house; she would wander interminably and delightedly about old towns and cities, or gaze with never-waning joy upon lakes and mountains, and my father, accompanying her, was, in a measure, recuperated and strengthened by her enthusiasm. In the end, as is evidenced by *Our Old Home* and *The Marble Faun*, he got a good deal out of Europe. On the other hand, he seemed to think himself justified in avoiding persons as much as he decently might, even the most distinguished; and if he had not been a consul, and a writer of books that had been read, I doubt if he would have formed any acquaintances during his foreign residence, and he would thereby have missed one of the greatest and most enduring pleasures of memory that he took back with him. For no one cared more for a friend, or was more stimulated and emancipated by one, than he. It may have been that he had passed the age of youthful buoyancy, of appetite for novelties; that he had begun to lack initiative. "I have seen many specimens of mankind," he wrote down, in a mood of depression, in one of his note-books, "but come to the conclusion that there is little variety among them all." That was scarcely a full thought, and he would never have let it pass in one of his considered books. He made and published many other remarks on similar subjects of quite an opposite tenor, and these more truly represented his true feeling. But he did flag a little, once in a while, and the deep and abiding love of England which was his final sentiment had somewhat the appearance of having been forced upon him against his inclination. We may surmise that he feared disappointment more than he craved gratification.

From Liverpool we explored the strangeness of the land in all directions. Bennoch or Bright sometimes took off my father alone; sometimes my father and mother would go with me, leaving my sisters at home with the governess. Once in a while we all went together, as, for example, to the Isle of Man or to Rhyl. So far as practicable, we children were made acquainted with the literature of places we were to visit before going there. Thus, before jour-

FRANCIS BANNOCH

neying to the Lakes and Scotland, I had by heart a good deal of Wordsworth, Southey, Burns, and Walter Scott, and was able, standing amid the lovely uproar of Lodore, to shout out the story of how the water comes down there; and, again, on the shores of Loch Katrine, at sunset, after spending a long hour on the little white beach opposite Ellen's Isle, I ran along the road in advance of my parents, and, climbing a cliff, saw the breadth of the lake below me, golden under the sunset clouds, and very aptly recited, as they came up, Sir Walter's descriptive verse:

> " One burnished sheet of living gold,
>   Loch Katrine lay, beneath him rolled!"

But I was not always so well attuned to the environment. I had got hold of a hook and line at some hotel on the Lakes, and the old passion for fishing, which had remained latent since Lenox days for lack of opportunity, returned upon me with great virulence. So, one day, when we had set out in a row-boat to visit Rob Roy's cave, I requested, on arriving there, to be permitted to stay in the boat, moored at the foot of the cliff, while the others climbed up into the cave, and, as soon as they had disappeared, I pulled out my line, with a dried-up worm on the hook, and cast it over the side. I wanted to see the cave, but I wanted to catch a fish more. Up to that time, I think, I had caught nothing in all our pilgrimages. If ever Providence is going to give me success (I said to myself, devoutly), let it be now! Accordingly, just before the others came back, I felt a strong pull on my line and hauled in amain. In a moment the fish, which may have been nine inches long, but which seemed to me leviathan himself, broke the surface, wriggling this way and that vigorously; but that was the extent to which my prayer was granted, for, in the words of a rustic fisherman who related his own experience to me long afterwards, "Just as I was a-goin' to land 'im, sir, he took an' he let go!" My fish not only took and let go, but he carried off the hook with him.

I remember wandering with my father through a grassy old church-yard in search of Wordsworth's grave, which we found at last, looking quite as simple as his own most severely unadorned pastoral; but I had not attained as yet to the region of sentiment which makes such things impressive. The bare mountains, the blue lakes, and the gray ruins filled me with riotous intoxication. The North of England and Scotch mountains were much more effective in their nakedness than the wooded hills I had seen in Berkshire of Massachusetts, and their contours were more sharply modelled and various. They were just large enough to make their ascent seem easy until you undertook it, then those seemingly moderate slopes lengthened out unaccountably. The day we reached the hotel at the base of Helvellyn, I started, nothing doubting, to climb to its summit before supper; the weather was clear, the top looked close at hand, and I felt great surprise that the young gentleman mentioned in Scott's poem ("I climbed the dark brow of the mighty Helvellyn," etc.) should have allowed himself to be lost. But after a breathless struggle of fifteen or twenty minutes, finding myself apparently no nearer my goal than at first, I thought differently. Mr. Bright told my father, by-the-way, that the legend of the fidelity of the dead adventurer's little dog, "who scared the hill-fox and the raven away," was far from being in accordance with the prosaic facts. This unsentimental little quadruped had, in truth, eaten up a large part of her master by the time his remains were discovered, and had, furthermore, brought into the world a litter of pups. Well, nothing can deprive us of the poem; but it is wholesome to face realities once in a while.

Unless one have a vein of Ruskin in him, one does not recollect scenery, however enchanting, with the same particularity as persons. It is the human element in things that sticks to us. Scenes are more punctually recalled in proportion as they are steeped in historic or personal interest. The thatched cottages of Burns and of Shakespeare stand clear in my memory; I recall our ramble over the battlements of Carlisle, where imprisoned Queen Mary had walked three centuries before; I remember the dark stain on the floor of the dark room in which one of her lovers was slain; I can see the gray towers of Warwick rising above the green trees and reflected in the still water; and, entering the keep

157

of the castle, I behold myself again trying on the ponderous helmet of the gigantic Guy, and climbing into his monstrous porridge-pot. But vain would be the attempt to marshal before my mind's eye the glorious pageantry of the Trosachs, though, at the time of its actual revelation, it certainly seemed to make a far more vivid impression. The delight and exhilaration which such magnificence inspired are easily summoned back, but not the incarnate features of them. Wild nature takes us out of ourselves and refreshes us; but she does not reveal her secret to us, or ally herself with anything in us less deep than the abstract soul—which also is beyond our reach.

I am not sure that my father did not like the seaside sojourns as well as anything else, apart from the historical connections; for the spirits of many seafaring forefathers murmured in his heart. But he did not so much care for the soft, yielding, brown sands on which the sea-waves broke. The coasts to which he had been used in his youth were either rocky or firm as a macadamized road. Nor was he beguiled into forgetting the tedium of walking over them, as his companion was, by the fascination of the shells and sea curiosities to be picked up on them. Many a mile have I trotted along beside him or behind him, gathering these treasures, while he strode forward, abstracted, with his gaze fixed towards the long ridge of the horizon. The sands at Rhyl, near which Milton's friend was said to have been lost, were like a rolling prairie; at low tide the white fringe of the surf could scarcely be descried at their outermost verge, yet within a few hours it would come tumbling back, flowing in between the higher levels, flooding and brimming and overcoming, till it broke at our feet once more. Behind us rose the tumultuous curves and peaks of the Welsh hills; before us, but invisible across the Irish Channel, the black coast of rainy Ireland. One night, during a gale, a ship came ashore, so far out that it still seemed, in the morning, to be at sea, except for its motionlessness, and the drenched and draggled crew came straggling in—or some of them. At Southport the beach was narrower and the little sea-side settlement larger and livelier; a string of sleepy donkeys always waited there, with the rout of ragged and naughty little boys with sticks to thrash them into a perfunctory and reluctant gallop for their riders. There was always one boy, larger and also naughtier than the rest, who thrashed the thrashers and took their pennies away from them. The prevailing occupation of the children at these places, as on all civilized shores, apparently, was the building of sand-mountains and the digging of pits with their little wooden spades. One day an elderly gentleman, with a square, ruddy face, edged with gray whiskers, who had stood observing my labors in this kind for a long time, stepped up to me as I paused, and said, with a sort of amused seriousness, " You'll do something when you grow up, my little lad; your hill is bigger than any of the others'." He nodded kindly to me and walked off, and I sat down beside my mountain and watched the tide come up and level it, thinking unutterable boy-thoughts.

The only approach to sea-side cliffs that we saw was at Whitby, on the Yorkshire coast, where the abbey of St. Hilda stood, after whom the American maiden in *The Marble Faun* was named. But the German Ocean was bleak and cold, and my experiences in it were even more harrowing than elsewhere; I can imagine nothing more dispiriting to a small boy than to be dragged down over a harsh beach in an old-fashioned British bathing-machine, its damp floor covered with gritty sand, with a tiny window too high up for him to look out of; undressing in the cold draughtiness and trying to hang up his clothes on pegs too high for him to reach; being tossed from side to side, and forward and backward, meanwhile, by the irregular jerking and swaying of the dismal contrivance, drawn by the amphibious horses of the region; until at last he hears the waves begin to dash against it, and it comes to a pause in a depth which he feels must be fathomless. Then comes a thumping at the door, and he knows that the bathing-woman is hungrily awaiting his issuing forth. Nothing else is so terrible in the world— nothing even in *Alice in Wonderland*—to a small, naked, shivering boy as the British bathing-woman. There she stands, waist-deep in the swelling brine; she grins and chuckles like an ogress; her red, grasping hands stretch forth like the tentacles of an octopus; she seizes her victim in an irresistible embrace, and with horrid glee plunges him head-under the advancing wave. Ere he can fetch his breath to scream, down again he goes, and yet again. The frigid, heavy water stings his cowering body; he has swallowed quarts of it; his foot has come in contact with a crab or a starfish; before him rolls the tumultuous expanse of desolation, surging forward to take his life; behind him are the rickety steps of the bathing-machine, which, but now a chamber of torture, has become his sole haven of refuge. Buffeted by the billows, he makes shift at last frantically to clamber back into it; he snatches the small, damp towels, and attempts to dry his shivering limbs; his clothes have fallen on the wet floor; he cannot force his blue toes into his oozy socks. At the moment he is attempting to wriggle himself into his trousers the horse is hitched-to again, and the jerky and jolty journey back up the beach begins. If the hair of a boy of ten could turn white in a single morning, there would be many a hoary-headed youngster in British watering-places. John Leech, in *Punch*, used to make pictures of the experiences I have outlined, and I studied them with deep attention and sympathy. The artist, too, must have suffered from the sea-ogresses in his youth, else he could not have portrayed the outrage so vividly. The mock-cheerfulness and hideous maternal parody of their "Come, my little man!" has no parallel in life or fiction. Nevertheless, such is the fortunate recuperative faculty of boyhood that day after day I would forget the horrors of that hour, and be happy in climbing over the decayed chalk acclivities of Whitby, picking up the fossil shells that nestle there. Yonder on my table, as I write, lies a coiled ammonite found there; it had been there ten thousand years or ages before I detached it from its bed, and, for aught I know, my remotest posterity may use it, as I have done, for a paper-weight. Thanks to eternal justice, the bathing-machines and the bathing-women will have gone to their place long ere then!

My father had given me a book called *The Aquarium*, written by Philip Henry Gosse (father of the present poet, essayist, and critic), illustrated with pictures of sea-anemones and other marine creatures done from his own drawings in color, and so well done that nothing which has been done since in the way of color-reproductions surpasses them. It was delightfully written, and I absorbed it into my very soul, and my dreams by night and longings by day were for an aquarium of my own. At last—I think this was at Southport—a glass jar was given me; it was an inverted bell-glass, mounted on a wooden stand, and it cost ten shillings. I wonder if men often love their wives or children with the adoring tenderness that I lavished upon that bell-glass and its contents! I got sand and covered the bottom; I found two jagged stones and leaned them against each other on the sand; I gathered fronds of *ulva latissima;* I persuaded a boatman to bring me a bucket of salt-water from beyond the line of breakers, and I poured it carefully into the jar.

During the next twenty-four hours I waited impatiently for the water to settle and clear; then I began to introduce the living inmates. I collected prawns and crabs and sea-snails, and a tiny sole or two, a couple of inches long, and by good chance I found a small sepiola, or cuttle-fish, as big as a beetle, which burrowed in the sand and changed color magically from dark brown to faintest buff. I also had a pair of soldier-crabs, which fought each other continually. When the sunlight fell on my aquarium, I saw the silver bubbles of oxygen form on the green fronds of the sea-weed; the little snails crawled along the sides of the glass, sweeping out their tiny, scythelike tongues at every step; the prawns hovered in the shade of the stones or darted back and forward light as thoughts; the soles scuffled over the surface of the sand or hid themselves in it from the stalking, felonious crabs. But I had no sea-anemones; they are not found on sandy coasts, and without sea-anemones my felicity could not be complete.

But strange things happen in this world occasionally, good as well as bad. There came up a heavy storm, and the next morning, walking with my father on the beach, strewn with deep-sea flotsam and jetsam, we came upon the mast of a ship, water-logged till it had the weight of iron; it might have been, as my father remarked, a relic of the Spanish Armada. And it was covered from end to end with the rarest and most beautiful species of sea-anemones!

This was fairy-land come true. I chipped off a handkerchiefful of the best specimens, wishing I could take them all, and carried them to my aquarium. I deposited them, each in a coign of vantage, and in the course of an hour or two they had swelled out their tinted bodies and expanded their lovely tentacles, and the cup of my joy was full. This prosperity continued for near a week, during which I remained with my nose against the glass, as the street boys of Liverpool held theirs against the windows of pastry-cooks' shops. At length I noticed an ominous clouding of the water, which, as Mr. Gosse had forewarned me, signified disaster of some sort, and, searching for the cause, I finally discovered the body of the little sepiola, which had died without being missed, and was contaminating with his decay the purity of the aquarium. The water must be changed at once. I sent out the servant for a fresh bucketful from the sea, while I poured the polluted liquid from the jar.

Presently the bucket of water was brought in. It was unusually clear. I filled the jar with it, and then, as bedtime was near, I left the aquarium to settle down to business again. The next morning I hastened to it in my night-gown, and was confronted by a ghastly spectacle. The crabs lay dead on the bottom, stomachs upward; the prawns hung lifeless and white from the rocks; the soldier-crabs were motionless, half out of their shells; the sea-anemones had contracted themselves into buttons, and most of them had dropped from their perches.

Death had been rampant during the night; but what could be the cause?

A sudden suspicion caused me to put a finger in the water and apply it to my tongue. It was not salt-water at all, but had been taken fresh from the cistern. That traitress servant-girl, to save her indolence a few steps, had destroyed my aquarium! I was too heart-broken to think of killing her; but she had killed something in me which does not readily grow again. My trust in my fellow-creatures was as shrunken and inanimate as the sea-anemones. We left Southport soon after, and that was my last aquarium.

Let us turn to lighter matters. I accompanied my father and mother on that pilgrimage to Old Boston which is described in *Our Old Home*. The world does not know that it is to my presence on the little steamer on the trip down the level river, through the Lincolnshire fens, with nothing but the three-hundred-foot tower of St. Botolph's Church, in the extreme distance, to relieve the tedium of a twenty-four-mile journey made at the rate of never more than six miles per hour—it is not known, I say, that to that circumstance is due my father's description of the only incident which enlivened the way—the tragedy, namely, of the duck family. For it was that tragedy which stood out clearest in my memory, and when I learned, in Concord, that my father was preparing his paper about Old Boston for the *Atlantic Monthly*, I besought him to insert an account of the episode. The duck and her five ducklings had probably seen the steamer many times before, and had acquired a contempt for its rate of progression, imagining that it would always be easy to escape from it. But, somehow, in their overweening security, they lingered on this occasion a little too long, and we succeeded in running them down. Even then, as my father notes, it was only one of them that was carried under; but the shock to the nerves of the other youngsters must have stunted their growth, and the old bird cannot but have suffered tortures from anxiety and remorse.

The sadness caused by this event, added to the chilliness of the sea-wind which blew against us all the way down the river, rendered my first impressions of the ancient town, which had given its name to the one I was born in, somewhat gloomy. But the next morning it brightened up, and our own spirits were correspondingly improved; insomuch that I struck my head a violent blow against the stone roof of the topmost pinnacle of St. Botolph's tower, such was the zeal of my ascent into it. All this happened two years after the aquarium, in 1857, when I was older and wiser, but had not yet outgrown the ambition to climb to the top of all high places; this bump may have been an admonition not to climb too high. We went down and strayed into Mr. Porter's little book-shop, and he transformed himself into a new and more genial proprietor of a virtuoso's collection, and showed us treasures, some of which his predecessor in *Mosses from an Old Manse* might not have despised. I

have never since then heard of his portrait in crayon
of the youthful Sterne; it would be worth a good
deal to any latter-day publisher of his works in a
de luxe edition. As for the green tassel from the
bed of Queen Mary, in Holyrood House, there is a
passage in my father's description of it in his journal which, out of regard, doubtless, for the feelings
of Mr. Porter, he forbore to quote in his published
article; but as the good old gentleman (unless he
has lived to be more than one hundred and twenty
years old) must have gone to the place where treasures are indestructible, I will reproduce it now.
"This tassel," says my father, "Mr. Porter told us
(with a quiet chuckle and humorous self-gratula-
tion), he had personally stolen, and really, for my
part, though I hope I would not have done it myself,
I thought it no sin in him—such valuables being
attracted by a natural magnetism towards such a
man. He obeys, in stealing them, a higher law
than he breaks. I should like to know precisely
what portion of his rich and rare collection he has
obtained in a similar manner. But far be it from
me to speak unkindly or sneeringly of the good
man; for he showed us great kindness, and obliged
us so much the more by being greatly and evidently
pleased with the trouble that he took on our behalf." It may be added that each new stealing
enhances the value of all the previous ones, and
therefore creates an obligation to steal yet more.
Thus does an act which would, standing by itself, be
criminal, become a virtue if often enough repeated.

I am not arranging this narrative in chronological sequence; but I think it was in this year that we went to Manchester to see the exposition. The town itself was unlovely; but, as we had Italy in prospect, it was deemed expedient to accustom ourselves in some measure to the companionship of works of art, and the exhibition professed to contain an exceptionally fine and catholic collection of them. My father made a thorough study of them, going to learn and not to judge, and he learned much, though not quite to believe in Turner or to like the old masters. For my own part, when not taken on these expeditions, I busied myself with the building of a kite six feet high, of engineer's cambric, with a face painted on it, and used to go out and fly it on a vacant lot in the rear of our lodgings, accompanied by a large portion of the unoccupied population of Manchester. The kite broke its string one day, and I saw it descend over the roofs of a remote slum region towards the south, and I never recaptured it. But my chief energies were devoted to acquiring the art of fencing with the small-sword from one Corporal Blair, of the Fourth Dragoon Guards—a regiment which had distinguished itself in the Crimean War. The corporal was a magnificent-looking creature, and he was as admirable inwardly as outwardly — the model of an English non-commissioned officer. He used to come to our lodgings in his short scarlet jacket and black trousers, and my father once asked him, remarking the extraordinary prominence of his chest, what kind of padding was used to produce so impressive a contour. "There's nothing here but my linen, sir," answered the corporal, modestly, and blushing a good deal; a fact which I, having often taken my lessons at the barracks, in the private quarters of the corporal, where he permitted himself to appear in his shirt-sleeves, already knew. My experience of the British army not being so large as that of some other persons, I am unable to say whether there were many other soldiers in it fit to be compared with Blair; but my acquaintance with mankind in general would lead me to infer that there could not have been then, and that there are still less of such to-day. An army of six-footers like him, with his intelligence, instincts of discipline, capacity and expertness, physical strength and activity, and personal courage, would easily account for more than all of England's warlike renown and success; the puzzle is, how to account for anything but disaster without them—though, to be sure, other armies might be equally lacking in Blairs. He was well educated, modest, and moral; he was a married man, with a wife who was the model of a soldier's consort, and two or three little sons, all of them experts with the foils and the broadsword. It was against the regulations of the service for privates or non-commissioned officers to have families, and, when Blair's connubial condition became known to the authorities, he was degraded in rank from sergeant to corporal, though he wore the Balaklava medal; for he had taken part in that immortal charge, and I only wish I could recall the story of it as he told it to me. His regiment had been under the command of Lord Cardigan— "Black-Bottle Cardigan," as he was nicknamed in the army, on account of the well-known (real or apocryphal) incident. It was my good-fortune, by-the-way, once to see this eminent captain. I was taking my lesson at the barracks, when Blair told me that his lordship was expected to visit them that afternoon. The hour appointed was three o'clock. Punctually at three o'clock a carriage drove rapidly through the gates of the barracks, and the guard turned out on the run and lined up to salute the noble occupant. But, much to their disgust, the occupant turned out to be some one else, not meriting a salute. The men returned to the guard-room feeling as men do when they have been betrayed into exertion and enthusiasm for nothing. However, in about ten minutes more, another carriage drove up, and out came the guard again and ranged themselves smartly, to please the eye of their martinet commander, when lo! they had again been deceived. Again they retired with dark looks, not being at all in a mood to recognize the humor of the situation. This same thing actually occurred twice more, by which time it was near four o'clock, and the men were wellnigh mutinous, and it became evident that, for some reason, Cardigan had been prevented from coming. Such being the case, the approach of still another carriage attracted no attention whatever, until it came to a half-pause, and I saw, thrust out of the window, a stern, dark, warlike, soldierly face, full of surprise and indignation—and this was Cardigan himself. The unhappy guard tumbled over themselves in vain efforts to get into form; it was too late, and the haughty and hot-tempered commander drove on without his salute. Blair, not being on guard duty, had no part in this catastrophe, but I well remember his unaffected sorrow over it. He was a grave man, though of an equable and cheerful temper, and he felt his comrades' misfortune as his own. But I never heard that any casualties occurred in consequence of the mishap.

I have left two years of our English sojourn unaccounted for. In the summer of 1855, my father nearly made up his mind to resign his consulship (since it had become hardly worth keeping from the money point of view), and, after making a visit to Italy, going back to Concord. This plan seemed the more advisable, because my mother's lungs could not endure the English climate. But while he was weighing the matter, John O'Sullivan wrote from Lisbon, urgently inviting my mother and sisters to come out and spend a few months with him and his family there. The Lisbon climate was a specific for bronchial disease; my father could complete his term, and we could go to Italy the following year. There was only one objection to this—it involved the parting of my father from my mother, a thing which had never before happened. But it did not take him long to decide that it would be a good thing for her, and, therefore, in the long run, for him. Each loved the other unselfishly, and had the courage of such love. Liverpool without my mother would be a dismal trial for him to face; Lisbon without my father would be tenfold an exile for her. But they made up their minds, each for the other's sake, to undergo the separation, and accordingly, in the autumn of the year, she and my sisters sailed from Southampton, and my father and I went back to Liverpool. How we fared there shall be told in the next chapter.

X

If there were boarding-houses in paradise—Blodgett, the
delight of mankind—Solomon foresaw her—A withering retort—A modest, puny poise about her—Hidden
thoughts derived from Mother Eve and Grecian Helen—
The feminine council that ruled the Yankee captains—
Bonds of fraternity, double-riveted and copper-fastened—Through the looking-glass—Men only of the
manliest sort—The lady-paramount—Hands which were
true works of art — Retained his dignity without putting it on—Sighed heavily over my efforts—Unctuous
M. Huguenin—"From dawn to eve I fell"—The *multum-in-parvo* machine — "Beauty and the Beast"—
Frank Channing—"Blood—and water!"—A lapful of
Irish stew.

IT was observed a little way back that English
boarding-houses were much like other boarding-
houses in the civilized world. The rule is proved
by the exception of Mrs. Blodgett's establishment.
There never was such another; there never will be;
it was unique. It has vanished from earth long
since; but if there were boarding-houses in paradise,
I should certainly expect it to be found again there.

Who was Mrs. Blodgett? Save that she was a
widow of the British middle class, I doubt if any
one of her boarders knew. She had once been rich,
and had lived at Gibraltar. I have often meditated

with fruitless longing about what manner of man Mr. Blodgett could have been. He must have been, like the Emperor Titus, the delight of mankind in his day. He was a man, we must surmise, whose charms and virtues were such that his wife, having felt the bliss and privilege of knowing and living with him, registered a vow over his bier that she would devote her future career to the attempt to make others as happy as he had made her; that she would serve others as faithfully and generously as she had served him. It was a lofty and beautiful conception, for she must have perceived that only in that way could she keep his blessed spirit near her; that the little heaven she would make in Duke Street, Liverpool, would attract him from the kindred heaven above; that he would choose to hover, invisible, above her plenteous table, inhaling the grateful aromas that arose from it as from a savory sacrifice, basking in the smiles and sympathizing in the satisfaction of the fortunate guests, triumphing in their recognition of his beloved consort as a queen among women. One might almost fancy that the steam arising from the portly soup-tureen assumed as it arose something suggesting a human form; that from its airy and fragrant mistiness a shadowy countenance beamed down upon the good lady in black, with the white cap, who ladled out the delicious compound to her waiting devotees. The murmur of the tea-urn would seem to fashion itself into airy accents, syllabling, "Mary, thy Blodgett is here!" His genial spirit would preside over her

labors in the kitchen, suggesting ever more delight-
some dishes and delicate desserts.   He would warn
her against undesirable inmates and intractable
servants, and would inspire her tradesmen to serve
her with the choicest comestibles and to temper
their bills to the unprotected widow.   At night he
would bless her lonely pillow with peace, and would
gently rouse her in the morning to a new day of
beneficences.

Mrs. Blodgett was about five feet four inches
high, and may have weighed twelve stone; into
such limits were her virtues packed.   She was perhaps in the neighborhood of her fiftieth year; her
dark hair was threaded with honorable gray.   Her
countenance was rotund and ruddy; it was the
flower of kindness and hospitality in full bloom;
but there was also power in the thick eyebrows and
in the massy substance of the chin—of the chins,
indeed, for here, as in other gifts, nature had been
generous with her.   There was shrewdness and
discernment in the good-nature of her eyes; she
knew human nature, although no one judged it
with more charity than she.   Her old men were her
brothers, her young men were her sons, all children
were her children.   Solomon foresaw her in the
most engaging of his Proverbs.   Her maid-servants
arose at six in the morning and called her blessed,
for though her rule was strict it was just and loving.   She was at once the mistress and the friend
of her household; no Yankee captain so audacious
that he ventured to oppose her law; no cynic so

cold as not to be melted by her tenderness. She
was clad always in black, with a white cap and rib-
bons, always spotless amid the grime of Liverpool;
in her more active moments—though she was always active—she added a white apron to her attire.
She was ever anywhere where she was needed; she
was never anywhere where she could be dispensed
with. Wherever she went she brought comfort and
a cheerful but not restless animation. Her boarders were busy men, but it was always with an effort
that they wrenched themselves from her breakfast-
table, and they sat down to dinner as one man.
She made them happy, but she would not spoil
them. "You're a pretty young man!" she said,
severely, to complacent Mr. Crane, when, one morning, he came late to breakfast. "I always knew
that," returned he, reaching self-satisfiedly for the
toast-rack. "Well, I'm sure your glass never told
you so!" was the withering retort. Mr. Crane did
not lift his neck so high after that. The grin that
went round the table was too crushingly unani-
mous.

Mrs. Blodgett was helped in her duties by her
niece, Miss Maria, and by her sister, Miss Williams.
Miss Maria was a little wisp of a woman; I do not
know her age then, but I think, were she alive to-
day, she would confess to about eighty-three. She
wore ringlets, after the fashion of the early nine-
teenth-century books of beauty. Her face was
thin and narrow, and ordinarily pale; but when
Miss Maria had been a little while in conversation

with one or more of the gallant Yankee captains
you might see in the upper corner of each cheek a
slight touch of red. For though I would not call
the little lady coquettish—that is too coarse and
obvious a word—yet there was in her that inalien-
able consciousness of maidenhood, that sentiment,
at once of attraction and of recoil, towards creatures of the opposite sex, that gentle hope of pleasing man, that secret emotion of being pleased by
him, that tremor at the idea of being desired, and
that flush at the thought of being desirable, which,
I suppose, may animate the mystic sensibilities of
spinsterhood. She was anything but aggressive
and confident, yet there was a modest, puny poise
about her; she was like a plant that has always
lived in a narrow, city flower-pot, at a window too
seldom visited by the sun, which has never known
the freedom of the rain, but has been skimpingly
watered out of a toy watering-pot; which has never
so much as conceived of the daring and voluptuous
charms of its remote sisters of the forest and garden, but has cherished its rudimentary perfume and
its incipient tints in a light reflected from brick
walls and in the thin, stale atmosphere of rear
sitting-rooms. Yet it knows that it is a flower, and
that it might, somehow, fulfil its destiny and be
beautiful. So Miss Maria had, no doubt, hidden
thoughts remotely derived from Mother Eve and
from Grecian Helen; she was aware of the potentiality in herself of all virgin privileges and powers,
and assumed thereupon her own little dignity. Nev-

er but once did I see a masculine arm round Miss Maria's trig, stiff little waist, and that was at Christmas-time, when there were sprigs of mistletoe over every doorway; but, mistletoe or not, the owner of that arm, if he did succeed in ravishing a kiss, got his ears smartly boxed the next moment. I don't know precisely what was Miss Maria's function in the economy of the household; I can fancy her setting the table, and adding touches of neatness and prettiness; dusting the ornaments and fine china on the shelves of the whatnot; straightening the frames of the pictures on the walls; and, in her less romantic moments, hemming towels or sheets, or putting up preserved fruits. I know she was always amiable and obliging and that everybody loved her.

Miss Williams was a good deal the elder of her sister, and was of a clear white pallor and an aged delicacy and shyness that were very captivating. She had judgment and a clear, dispassionate brain, and I presume she acted the part in the little firm of a sort of court of appeals and final adviser and referee. She talked little and had little to do with outward affairs, but she sat observant and penetrating and formed conclusions in her mind. There had been no brother of The Blodgett to induce her to change her maidenly state, but I think there must have been a quiet, touching romance somewhere hidden in the shadows of the previous forty or fifty years. She admired and delighted in her energetic, practical sister as much as the latter adored her for her serenity and wisdom. There was between them an intimacy, confidence, and mutual understanding that were charming to behold. When the blessed Blodgett had died, one can imagine the vital support and consolation which Miss Williams had been able to afford to her afflicted sister. Each of them seemed, in some way, to explain and enlarge one's conception of the other. Widely different as they appeared outwardly, there was a true sisterly likeness deep down in them. Such was the feminine council that ruled the destinies of the Yankee captains and of their consul.

These captains and this consul formed nine-tenths of the population of the house, and such other denizens as it had were at least Americans. I never learned the cause of this predilection for representatives of the great republic and for the seafaring variety of them in particular. Be that as it might (and it is an interesting inquiry in itself), it can be readily understood that it worked out well as a business idea. There were no quarrels or heart-burnings among the jolly occupants of Mrs. Blodgett's table; first, because they were all Americans in the country of their hereditary enemies, and, secondly, because they were all men of the same calling, and that calling the sea. The bonds of fraternity between them were double-riveted and copper-fastened. Thus all who had experienced the Blodgett régime proclaimed its excellence far and wide, and the number of applicants always exceeded the accommodations; in fact, during this year 1855–56, our hostess was compelled to buy the house adjoining her own, and I had the rare delight of watching every stroke of work done by the carpenters and bricklayers who had the job of cutting a doorway through the wall from the old house to the new one. There was something magical and adventurous in stepping through that opening for the first time—crossing a boundary which had maintained itself so long. Probably the sensation resembled that which Alice afterwards experienced when she stepped through the looking-glass into the room on the other side. The additional accommodations were speedily filled; but after the first fascination had worn off nobody regarded the new house as comparable with the old one, and the people who roomed in it were looked down upon by their associates of the original dwelling. They were, I believe, as much alike as two houses could be, and that is saying much in this age, but the feeling was different, and the feeling is everything if you have a soul.

If the Blodgett house, or houses, were unique, so were the Yankee boarders. The race of our merchant-marine captains disappeared with their ships, and they will return no more. The loss is irretrievable, for in many respects they held the ideal of patriotic and energetic Americanism higher than it is likely to go again. When at sea, in command of and responsible for their ships and cargoes, they were, no doubt, upon occasion, despots and slave-drivers; but their crews were often recruited from among the dregs of men of all nations, who would

interpret kindness as timidity and take an ell
where you gave them an inch. No doubt, too,
there were incarnate devils among these captains—
actual monomaniacs of cruelty and viciousness—
though none of these were known at Mrs. Blodgett's. Round her board sat men only of the manliest sort. They had the handiness and versatility
of the sailor, wide and various knowledge of all
quarters of the globe and of types of mankind,
though, to be sure, their investigations did not proceed far beyond their ports, and you were sometimes more astonished at what they did not know
than at what they did. They had the self-poise
and self-confidence of men who day by day and
month by month hold their lives in their hands,
and are practised in finding a way out of danger and
difficulty. They had a code of good manners and
polite behavior which was not highly refined, but
contained the sound, essential elements of courtesy;
not expressed in fancy, but honest and solid. They
had great shrewdness, and were capable of really
fine diplomacy, for the school they attended demanded such proficiency. They had a dry, chuck-
ling humor; a homely philosophy, often mingled
with the queerest superstitions; a racy wit, smack-
ing somewhat, of course, of the quarter-deck, or
even of the forecastle; a seemingly incongruous sensibility, so that tears easily sprang to their eyes if
the right chord of pathos were touched; a disposition to wear a high-colored necktie and a broad,
gold watch-chain, and to observe a certain smart-

ness in their boots and their general shore rigging; a good appetite for good food, and not a little discernment of what was good; a great and boylike enjoyment of primitive pleasures; a love of practical jokes and a hearty roar of laughter for hearty fun; a self - respecting naturalness, which made them gentlemen in substance if not in all technical details; a pungent contempt for humbug and artifice, though they might not mind a good, swaggering lie upon occasion; a robust sense of honor in all matters which were trusted to their honorable feeling; and, to make an end of this long catalogue, a practical command of language regarded as a means of expressing and communicating the essential core of thoughts, though the words might not always be. discoverable in Johnson's dictionary or the grammatical constructions such as would be warranted by Lindley Murray. They were, upon the average, good-looking, active, able men, and most of them were on the sunny side of forty. They were ready to converse on any subject, but if left to themselves they would choose topics proper to their calling—ships and shipwrecks, maritime usages of various countries, of laws of insurance, of sea-rights, of feats of seamanship, of luck and ill luck, and here and there a little politics of the old-fashioned, elementary sort. They boasted themselves and their country not a little, and criticised everybody else, and John Bull especially, very severely often, but almost always very acutely, too. They would play euchre and smoke cigars from nine o'clock till eleven, and would then go to bed and sleep till the breakfast-bell. Altogether, they were fine company, and they did me much good. Such were the captains of our merchant marine about the middle of the last century.

Some of them would bring their wives with them for the voyage; uniformly rather pretty women, a trifle dressy, somewhat fragile in appearance, but really sound enough; naïve, simple, good souls, loving their husbands and magnifying them, and taking a vicarious pride in their ships and sea-craft. The lady-paramount of these, in my estimation, was the wife of old Captain Howes, the inventor of Howes' patent rig, which he was at that time perfecting. He would sometimes invite me up to his room to see the exquisitely finished model which he had made with his own hands. He was the commodore of the captains, the oldest, wisest, and most impressive of them; a handsome, massive, Jovelike old gentleman, with the gentlest and most indulgent manners, and a straightforward, simple mariner withal. He had ceased to make voyages, and was settled, for the time being, in Liverpool. Mrs. Howes seemed, to my boyish apprehension, to be a sort of princess of exquisite and gracious refinement; I could imagine nothing in feminine shape more delicate, of more languid grace, of finer patrician elegance. She was certainly immensely good-natured and indulgent towards me, and, in the absence of my mother, tried to teach me to be less of an Orson; she had hands which were true works of art, flexible, fine-grained, taper-fingered, and lily-white; these she used very effectively, and would fain have induced me to attempt the regeneration of my own dirty and ragged little fists. She would beseech me, also, to part my hair straight, to forbear to soil my jacket, and even to get my shoes blacked. I was thankful for these attentions, though I was unable to profit by them. Sometimes, at table, I would glance up to find her eyes dwelling with mild reproach upon me; doubtless, I was continually perpetrating terrible enormities. Had she herself been less perfect and immaculate, I might have felt more hopes of my own amendment; but I felt that I was not in her class at all, and I gave up at the start. She was a wonderful human ornament, the despair, I thought, of all pursuit, not to mention rivalry. Beside the heroic figure of her captain, she looked like a lily mated with an oak; but they were as happy a pair, and as well mated, as one could hope to see.

I was, perhaps, more in my proper element among the captains down in the smoking-room, which was at the back of the house, at the end of the hallway, on the left. My father sat there foot to foot with them, played euchre with them, listened to their yarns, laughed at their jokes, and felt, probably, the spirit of his own old sea-captain ancestors stirring within him. Some of them were a little shy of his official position at first, and indeed he was occasionally constrained to adopt towards one or another of them, in the consulate, a bearing very different from the easy comradeship of the Blodgett evenings; but in process of time they came to understand him, and accepted him, on the human basis, as a friend and brother. My father had the rare faculty of retaining his dignity without putting it on. No one ever took liberties with him, and he took none with anybody; yet there was no trace in his intercourse of stiffness or pose; there did not need to be, since there was behind his eye that potentiality of self-protection which renders superfluous all outward demonstration of personal sanctity. On the other hand, he obviously elevated the tone of our little society; the stout captains, who feared nothing else, feared their worser selves in his presence. None of them knew or cared a straw for his literary genius and its productions; but they were aware of something in him which they respected as well as liked, and there was no member of the company who was more popular or influential.

Without letting me feel that I was the object of special solicitude or watchfulness, my father knew all that I did, and saw to it that my time was decently occupied. In addition to the dancing-lessons already mentioned (in which I became brilliantly proficient, and achieved such feats in the way of polkas, mazurkas, hornpipes, and Scotch reels as filled my instructor and myself with pride)— in addition to this, I was closeted twice a week with a very serious and earnest drawing-master, who taught me with infinite conscientiousness, and sighed heavily over the efforts which I submitted to him. The captains, who were my champions and abettors in all things, might take in their large hands a drawing of mine and the copy by the master which had been my model, and say, one to the other, "Well, now, I couldn't tell which was which —could you?" But the master could tell, and the certainty of it steeped his soul in constant gloom. I doubt if he recovered from the pangs I gave him. The fact was, I thought an hour of dancing with lovely Mary Warren was worth all the art in the world. Another instructor to whom I brought honor was thick-shouldered, portly, unctuous M. Huguenin, a Swiss, proprietor of the once-famous gymnasium which bore his name. He so anointed me with praise that I waxed indiscreet, and one day, as I was swinging on the rings, and he was pointing out to some prospective patrons my extraordinary merits, my grasp relaxed at the wrong moment and I came sailing earthward from on high. It seemed to me that, like Milton's Lucifer, "from dawn to eve I fell," M. Huguenin sprinting to intercept my fall; but I landed on a mat and was little the worse for it. I fear the prospective patrons were not persuaded, by my performance, of the expediency of gymnastic training. On the other hand, M. Huguenin managed to dispose to my father of one of his *multum-in-parvo* exercising-machines, on the understanding that it was to be taken back at half-price on the expiration of our stay in Liverpool; but, when that time came, M. Huguenin failed to

remember having been a party to any such understanding; so the big framework was boxed up, and
finally was resurrected in Concord, where I labored
with it for seven or eight years more during my
home-comings from Harvard.

In the intervals of my other pursuits, I was, at
this period, sent into society. The society at Mrs.
Blodgett's was, indeed, all that I desired; but it
was doubtless perceived that it was not all that my
polite development required; my Orsonism was too
much indulged. I was sent alone to Sandheys, the
Brights' and Heywoods' place, where I was mod-
erately ill at ease; and also to the house of a lady in
town, who received a good deal of company, and
there I was, at first, acutely miserable. The for-
malities of the drawing-room and the elegant conversation overwhelmed me with the kind of torture
which Swedenborg ascribes to those spirits of the
lower orders who are admitted temporarily into the
upper heavens. Unlike these unfortunates, however, I presently got acclimated; other boys of my
age appeared, and numbers of little girls (Mary
Warren among them), and now society occupied all
my thoughts. The lady of the house got up private theatricals—" Beauty and the Beast " was the
play. I was cast for the parts of the Second Sister
and of the Beast; Mary Warren was the Beauty. I
got by heart not only my own lines, but those of
all the other performers and the stage directions.
The play was received with applause, and after it
was done the actors were fêted; my father was not

present, but he appeared greatly diverted by my account of the proceedings. He was probably testing me in various ways to see what I was made of, and whether anything could be made of me. He encouraged my predilection for natural history by getting me books on conchology and taking me to museums to study the specimens and make pencil drawings of them. In these avocations I was also companioned by Frank Channing, whose specialty was ornithology, and who was making a series of colored portraits of the birds in the museum, very cleverly done.

Frank was the son of the Rev. William Henry Channing, who was pastor of a Unitarian church in Liverpool; he had brought his family to England at about the same time that we came. He was a nephew, I believe, of the William Ellery Channing who was one of the founders of American Unitarianism, and the brother, therefore, of the Ellery Channing of Concord. Frank inherited much of the talent of his family. He was afterwards sent to Oxford, where he took the highest honors. All intellectual operations came easy to him. He also showed a strong proclivity to art, and he was wonderfully clever in all kinds of fine handwork. He was at this time a tall and very handsome boy, about two years my senior. He was, like myself, fanatically patriotic, an American of Americans, and this brought us together in a foreign land; but, aside from that, I have seldom met a more fascinating companion. I followed him about with joy and

WILLIAM HENRY CHANNING, 1855

admiration. He used to make for me tiny little three-masted ships, about six inches long, with all the rigging complete; they were named after the famous American clippers of the day, and he painted microscopic American flags to hoist over the taffrail. He tried to teach me how to paint in watercolors, but I responded better to his eloquence regarding the future of our country. He proved to me by a mathematical demonstration, which I accepted without in the least understanding it, that in fifty years New York would be larger and more populous than London at the end of the same period. This brilliant boy seemed fitted for the highest career in his native country; his father did not contemplate a permanent stay in England, and in after years I used to look for his name in our Senate, or among the occupants of the Supreme Bench. But, as it turned out, he never revisited America, except for short periods. His father was induced to remain abroad by the success of his preaching, and Frank, after his career at Oxford, was overpowered by the subtle attractions of English culture, and could not separate himself from the old country. I saw him once while I was at Harvard. He was an Englishman in all outward respects, and seemed to be so inwardly likewise. The other day I heard of a Frank Channing in Parliament; probably the same man. But either the effect upon him of his voluntary expatriation—his failure to obey at eve the voice obeyed at prime—or some other cause, has prevented him from ever doing anything to attract attention, or to appear commensurate with his radiant promise. Henry James is the only American I know who has not suffered from adopting England; and even he might have risen higher than he has done had he overcome his distaste to the external discomforts of the democracy and cast in his lot with ours.

Frank's father was a tall, intellectual, slender Yankee, endowed with splendid natural gifts, which he had improved by assiduous cultivation. In the pulpit he rose to an almost divine eloquence and passion, and a light would shine over his face as if reflected from the Holy Spirit itself. My father took a pew in his church, and sent me to sit in it every Sunday; he never went himself. He was resolved, I suppose, if there was any religion in me, to afford it an opportunity to come out. Now, I had a religious reverence for divine things, but no understanding whatever of dogma of any sort. I never learned to repeat a creed, far less to comprehend its significance. I was moved and charmed by Mr. Channing's discourses, but I did not like to sit in the pew; I did not like "church." I remember nothing of the purport of any of those sermons; but, oddly enough, I do recall one preached by a gentleman who united the profession of preacher with that of medicine; he occupied Channing's pulpit on a certain occasion, and preached on the text in John xix., 34: "But one of the soldiers with a spear pierced his side, and forthwith came thereout blood and water." The good doctor, drawing on his physiological erudition, demonstrated at great length how it was possible that blood should be mingled with the water, and showed at what precise point in Christ's body the spear must have entered. I seem to hear again his mellifluous voice, repeating at the close of each passage of his argument, "And forthwith came thereout blood—AND WATER!" I did not approve of this sermon; I was not carried to heaven in the spirit by it, as by Channing's; but somehow it has stuck in my memory all these forty-eight years.

Often I stayed for a few days at a time at Channing's house; his wife was a handsome, delicate, very nervous woman; his daughter Fanny was a beauty, and became still more beautiful in after years; she was married, when past her first youth, to Edwin Arnold, author of "The Light of Asia," and of many rhetorical leading articles in the London *Telegraph*. She died a few years ago. They were, all of them, kind to me. I did the best I could to be a good little boy there; but I recollect Mrs. Channing's face of sorrow and distress when, one day at dinner, I upset into my lap my plate, which she had just filled with Irish stew—one of my best-loved dishes. "Frank never does that," she murmured, as she wiped me up; "never—never!" Nobody looked cheerful, and I never got over that mortification.

XI

Bennoch and Bright like young housekeepers—"What did you marry that woman for?"—"Mrs. Caudle's Curtain Lectures"—"The worst book anybody ever wrote"—"Most magnificent eye I ever saw"—A great deal of the feminine in Reade—Fire, pathos, fun, and dramatic animation—A philosophical library in itself—Amusing appanage of his own book—Oily and voluble sanctimoniousness—Self - worship of the *os - rotundus* sort—Inflamed rather than abated by years—"Every word of it true; but—"—Better, or happier, because we had lived — Appropriated somebody else's adventure —Filtering remarks through the mind of a third person —A delightful Irishman—Unparalleled audacity—An unregenerate opinion—The whole line of Guelphs in it— "Oh, that somebody would invent a new sin!"—"The Angel in the House"—Very well dressed—Indomitable figure, aggressively American—Too much of the elixir of life—A little strangeness between us—Sunshine will always rest on it.

THE central event of 1856 was the return from Lisbon and Madeira of my mother and sisters. Measuring time, as boys do (very sensibly), not by the regulated pace of minutes, but by the vast spaces covered by desire, it appeared to me, for some decades, that they had been absent in those regions for years—two years at least; and I was astonished and almost incredulous when dates seemed to prove

that the interval had been six or eight months only.
It was long enough.

In the course of the previous spring my father
made two or three little excursions of a few days or
a week or so in various directions, commonly con-
voyed by Bright or Bennoch, who were most enterprising on his behalf, feeling much the same sort
of ambition to show him all possible of England and
leading English folk that a young housekeeper feels
to show her visiting school-friend her connubial
dwelling and its arrangements, and to take her up
in the nursery and exhibit the children. Had my
father improved all his opportunities he would have
seen a great deal, but the consulate would have
been administered by the clerks. He took trips
through Scotland and the north of England, and
south to London and the environs; dined at the
Milton Club and elsewhere, visited the Houses of
Parliament, spent a day with Martin Farquhar
Tupper, author of *Proverbial Philosophy*, and still
was not remarkably absent from the dingy little office down by the docks, or from the euchre games
in Mrs. Blodgett's smoking-room. For the most
part, I did not accompany him on these excursions,
being occupied in Liverpool with my pursuit of universal culture; yet not so much occupied as to prevent me from feeling insolvent while he was away,
and rich as Aladdin when he got back. For his
part, he struggled with low spirits caused by anxiety
lest the next mail from Portugal should bring ill
news of the beloved invalid there (instead of the

cheerful news which always did come); his real life was suspended until she should return. Partings between persons who love each other seem to be absolute loss of being; but that being revives, with a new spiritual strength, when all partings are over.

Of the people whom he met on these sallies, I saw some, either then or later: Disraeli, Douglas Jerrold, Charles Reade, Tom Taylor, Bailey, the author of that once-famous philosophic poem, "Festus"; Samuel Carter Hall, and a few more. Disraeli, in 1856, had already been chancellor of the exchequer and leader of the house, and was to hold the same offices again two years later. He had written all but two of his novels, and had married the excellent but not outwardly attractive lady who did so much to sustain him in his career. At a dinner of persons eminent in political life, about this juncture, Mr. and Mrs. Disraeli were present, and also Bernal Osborne, a personage more remarkable for cleverness and aggressiveness, in the things of statesmanship, than for political loyalty or for a sense of his obligations to his associates. This gentleman had drunk a good deal of wine at dinner, and had sat next to Mrs. Disraeli; when the ladies had left the table he burst out, with that British brutality which often passes for wit, " I say, Disraeli, what on earth did you marry that woman for?" All talk was hushed by this astounding query, and everybody looked at the sallow and grim figure to whom it was addressed.

Disraeli for some moments played with his wine-glass, apparently unmoved; then he slowly lifted his extraordinary black, glittering eyes to those of his questioner. "Partly for a reason," he said, measuring his words in the silence, "which you will never be capable of understanding — gratitude!" The answer meant much for both of them; it was never forgotten, and it extinguished the clever and aggressive personage. It was ill crossing swords with Disraeli.

Douglas Jerrold was at the height of his fame and success in this year; he died, I think, the year following, at the age of fifty-four. He was very popular during his later lifetime, but he seems to have just missed those qualities of the humorist which insure immortality; he is little more than a name to this generation. He was the son of an actor, and had himself been on the stage; indeed, he had tried several things, including a short service as midshipman in his Majesty's navy. He wrote some two-score plays, and was a contributor to *Punch* from its outset; there are several books to his credit; and he edited *Lloyd's Weekly Newspaper*, which was first called by his own name. But people who have read or heard of nothing else of his, have heard of or read "Mrs. Caudle's Curtain Lectures." Douglas Jerrold, however, is by no means fully pictured by anything which he wrote; his charm and qualities came out in personal intercourse. Nor does the mere quotation of his brightnesses do him justice; you had to hear and see him say them in order to understand them or him. He was rather a short man, with a short neck and thick shoulders, much bent, and thick, black hair, turning gray. His features were striking and pleasing; he had large, clear, prominent, expressive black eyes, and in these eyes, and in his whimsical, sensitive mouth, he lived and uttered himself. They took all the bitterness and sting out of whatever he might say. When he was about to launch one of his witticisms, he fixed his eyes intently on his interlocutor, as if to call his attention to the good thing coming, and to ask his enjoyment of it, quite apart from such application to himself as it might have. It was impossible to meet this look and to resent whatever might go with it. Thus a friend of his, who wished to write telling books but could not quite do it, came to him in haste one day and exclaimed, aggrievedly, " Look here, Douglas, is this true that was told me— that you said my last book was the worst I'd ever written?" Douglas gazed earnestly into the flushed and troubled face, and said, in his softest tones, " Oh no, my dear fellow, that isn't what I said at all; what I did say was that it was the worst book anybody ever wrote." Such a retort, so delivered, could not but placate even an outraged author.

Of Charles Reade my father saw little, and was not impressed by what he saw; but Reade, writing of him to my sister Una, five-and-twenty years after, said, " Your father had the most magnificent eye that I ever saw in a human head." Reade was just past forty at the time he met my father, and had just published *It Is Never Too Late to Mend*—the first of his great series of reform novels. *Christie Johnstone* and *Peg Woffington* were very clever, and written with immense vigor and keenness, but did not give the measure of the man. I doubt if my father had as yet read any of them; but later he was very fond of Reade's writings. Certainly he could not but have been moved by *The Cloister and the Hearth*, the greatest and most beautiful of all historical novels. He saw in him only a tall, athletic, light-haired man with blue eyes. I was more fortunate. I not only came to know Reade in 1879, but also knew several persons who knew him intimately and loved and admired him prodigiously; they were all in one story about him. He was then still tall and athletic, but his wavy hair and beard were gray; his face was one of the most sensitive men's faces I ever saw, and his forehead was straight and fine, full of observation and humor; his eyes were by turns tender and sparkling. There was a great deal of the feminine in Reade, together with his robust and aggressive masculinity. The fault of his head was its lack of depth; there was not much distance from the ear to the nostril, and the backhead was deficient. It was high above. There was a discord or incongruity in his nature, which made his life not what could be called a happy one. He had the impulses of the radical and reformer, but not the iron or the impassivity which would have enabled him to endure unmoved the attacks of conservatism and ignorance. He kicked against the pricks and suffered for it. He was passionate, impatient, and extreme; but what a lovely, irresistible genius! He was never a society figure, and withdrew more and more from personal contact with people; but he kept up to the last the ardor of his attack upon the abuses of civilization—or what he deemed to be such. He fell into some errors, but they were as nothing to the good he effected even in external conditions; and the happiness and benefit he brought to tens of thousands of readers by the fire, pathos, fun, sweetness, and dramatic animation of his stories, and by the nobility and lovableness of many of the characters drawn in them, are immeasurable, and will touch us and abide with us again when the welter of the present transition state has passed. His devotion to the drama injured his style as a novelist, and also led him to adopt a sort of staccato manner of construction and statement which sometimes makes us smile. But upon the ground proper to his genius Reade had no rival. A true and full biography of him, by a man bold enough and broad enough to write it, would be a stirring book.

Bailey, the amiable mystical poet, whom my father mildly liked, was another man my glimpses of whom came at a date much later than this. He was a small, placid, gently beaming little philosopher, with a large beard and an oval brow, and though he wrote several things besides "Festus," they never detached themselves in the public mind from the general theme of that production. Bailey

himself seemed finally to have recognized this, and
he spent his later years (he lived to a great age) in
issuing continually fresh editions of his book, with
expansions and later thoughts, until it got to be a
sort of philosophical library in itself. He appeared
in society in order to give his admirers opportunity
to offer up their grateful homage, and to settle for
them all questions relative to the meaning of man
and of religion. No misgivings troubled him; his
smile was as an unintermittent summer noonday.
He was accompanied by his wife, with whom he
seemed to be, as Tennyson says, "twinned, like
horse's ear and eye." She relieved him from the
embarrassing necessity of saying illuminative and
eulogistic things about himself and his great work.
The book, upon its first publication, was really read
by appreciable numbers of persons; later, I think,
"Festus Bailey" came to be, to the general mind,
an amusing kind of appanage of his own work,
which was now taken as read, but ceased to have
readers. How happy a little imperviousness may
make a good man!

Tom Taylor, the dramatist, *Punch* contributor,
and society wit, I remember only as a pale face and
a black beard. His wit had something of a professional tang. There are many like him in club-land
and hanging about the stage; they catch up and remember all the satirical sayings, the comicalities,
and quips that they hear, and they maintain a sort
of factory for the production of puns. Their repar-
tee explodes like an American boy's string of toy

crackers, and involves, to set it going, no greater intellectual effort. They are not, in their first state, less intelligent than the common run of men— rather the contrary; but as soon as they have gone so far as to acquire a reputation for wit, their output begins to betray that sad, perfunctory quality which we find in wound-up music-boxes, and that mechanical rattle makes us forget that they ever had brains. However, Tom Taylor, with his century of plays and adaptations—among them "Our American Cousin," which the genius of an actor, if not its own merit, made memorable—should not be deemed unworthy of the reputation which, in his time and place, he won. He was at his best when, stimulated by applause and a good dinner, he portrayed persons and things with a kind of laughable extravagance, in the mode introduced by Dickens. Men of his ilk grow more easily in our soil than in the English, and are much less regarded.

Henry Stevens—"the man of libraries," as my father calls him—was a New - Englander, born in Vermont; he took betimes to books, came abroad, and was employed by the British Museum in getting together *Americana*, and by various collectors as an agent to procure books, and in these innocent pursuits his amiable life was passed. He had a pleasing gift of drollery, which made his companionship acceptable at stag-parties and in the smoking-room of the clubs, and he had also a fund of special information on literary subjects which was often of value. I met him in after-life—twenty-five years after—and age had not altered him, though, perhaps, custom had somewhat staled his variety. He was of medium stature, dark haired and bearded. With him was often seen the egregious Mr. Pecksniff (as Samuel Carter Hall was commonly known to his acquaintances since the publication of *Martin Chuzzlewit* ten years before). Hall was a genuine comedy figure. Such oily and voluble sanctimoniousness needed no modification to be fitted to appear before the footlights in satirical drama. He might be called an ingenuous hypocrite, an artless humbug, a veracious liar, so obviously were the traits indicated innate and organic in him rather than acquired. Dickens, after all, missed some of the finer shades of the character; there can be little doubt that Hall was in his own private contemplation as shining an object of moral perfection as he portrayed himself before others. His perversity was of the spirit, not of the letter, and thus escaped his own recognition. His indecency and falsehood were in his soul, but not in his consciousness; so that he paraded them at the very moment that he was claiming for himself all that was their opposite. No one who knew him took him seriously, but admired the ability of his performance, and so well was he understood that he did little or no harm beyond the venting of a spite here and there and the boring of his auditors after the absurdity of him became tedious. Self-worshippers of the *os-rotundus* sort are seldom otherwise mischievous. He may be sufficiently illustrated by two anecdotes.

They both occurred at a dinner where I was a guest, and Bennoch sat at the head of the table. Hall sat at Bennoch's left hand, and my place was next to Hall's. The old gentleman—he was at this period panoplied in the dignity of a full suit of snow-white hair, and that unctuous solemnity and simpering self-complacency of visage and demeanor which were inflamed rather than abated by years—began the evening by telling in sesquipedalian language a long tale of an alleged adventure of his with my father, which, inasmuch as there was no point to it, need not be rehearsed here; but I noticed that Bennoch was for some reason hugely diverted by it, and found difficulty in keeping his hilarity within due bounds of decorum, Hall's tone being all the while of the most earnest gravity. Later I took occasion to ask Bennoch the secret of his mirth; was the tale a fiction? "Not a bit of it," Bennoch replied; "it's every word of it true; but what tickled me was that it was myself and not Hall who was in the adventure with your father; but Hall has been telling it this way for twenty years past, and has long since come to believe that his lie is the truth." So ended the first lesson.

The second was administered shortly before the company dispersed. Mr. Hall again got the floor to deliver one of his more formal moral homilies. "And, my dear friends—my very dear friends," he went on, resting his finger-ends upon the table, and inclining his body affectionately towards his auditors, "may I, as an old man—I think the oldest of

any of you here present—conclude by asking your
indulgence for an illustration from the personal experience and custom of one who may, I think—
who at least has ever striven to be, a humble Christian gentleman—may I, my dear friends, cite this
simple example of what I have been attempting to
inculcate from my own personal practice, and that
of my very dear and valued wife, Mrs. Hall? It
has for very many years been our constant habit,
before seeking rest at night, to kneel down together
at our bedside, and to implore, together, the Divine
blessing upon the efforts and labors of the foregoing day. And before offering up that petition to
the Throne of Grace, my friends"—here the orator's
voice vibrated a little with emotion—"we have
ever been sedulous to ask each other, and to question our own hearts, as to whether, during that day,
some human fellow-creature had been made better,
or happier, because we had lived. And very seldom has it happened—very seldom, indeed, my
dear friends, has it happened—that we were unable
to say to ourselves, and to each other, that, during
that day, some fellow-creature, if not more than
one, had had cause for thankfulness because we
had lived. And now I will beg of you, my dear
friends," added Mr. Hall, producing his large, white
pocket-handkerchief and patting his eyes with it,
"to pardon a personal allusion, made in fulness of
heart and brotherly feeling, and if there be found in
it anything calculated to assist any of you towards
a right comprehension of our Christian responsibil-

ities towards our fellow-man, I entreat that you take it into your hearts and bosoms, and may it be sanctified unto you. I have done."

This report may be relied upon as substantially accurate, for the reporter made a note of the apologue and exhortation soon afterwards. Mrs. Hall, like her husband, was of Irish birth, and an agreeable and clever woman. They were both born in 1800, and died, she in her eighty-second, he in his ninetieth year. He remained the same Hall to the very end of his long chapter, and really, if no one was the better because he had lived, I don't know that any one was the worse, in the long run, either; and there have been Pecksniffs of whom as much could hardly be affirmed. There is, however, an anecdote of Hall which my father tells, and seems to have credited; if it be true, it would appear that once at least in his life he could hardly have implored the Throne of Grace for a blessing on the deeds of the day. "He told me," writes my father, "(laughing at the folly of the affair, but, nevertheless, fully appreciating his own chivalry) how he and Charles Lever, about ten years since, had been on the point of fighting a duel. The quarrel was made up, however, and they parted good friends, Lever returning to Ireland, whence Mr. Hall's challenge had summoned him." I suspect good Mr. Hall must have once more appropriated somebody else's adventure; it was not in the heat of youth that the bloody-minded and unchristian episode is supposed to have occurred, but when Mr. Hall was in his forty - seventh year.

Durham, the sculptor, was a lifelong friend of Bennoch's, and was often in my father's company, and he manifested a friendly feeling towards my father's son long afterwards. He was a man of medium height, compactly built, with slightly curling hair, and a sympathetic, abstracted expression of countenance. He was at this time making a bust of Queen Victoria, and he told us that it was contrary to court etiquette for her Majesty, during these sittings, to address herself directly to him, or, of course, for him directly to address her; they must communicate through the medium of the lady-in-waiting. The Queen, however, said Durham, sometimes broke through this rule, and so did the sculptor, the democracy of art, it would seem, enabling them to surmount the obligation to filter through the mind of a third person all such remarks as they might wish to make to each other. Durham also said that when the bust was nearly finished the Queen proposed that a considerable thickness of the clay should be removed from the model, which was done. The bust, as an ideal work, was thereby much improved, but the likeness to her Majesty was correspondingly diminished. Years afterwards I was talking with W. G. Wills, the painter and dramatist, a delightful Irishman of the most incorrigibly republican and bohemian type. He had, a little while before, been giving lessons in painting to the Princess Louise, who married the Marquis of

Lorne, and who was, herself, exceptionally emancipated for a royal personage. One day, said Wills (telling the story quite innocently), the Princess was prevented from coming as usual to his studio, and he received a message from Windsor Castle, where the Princess and the Queen were staying, from the Queen's secretary, commanding his presence there to give the Princess her lesson, and to spend the night. This would be regarded by the ordinary British subject not only as an order to be instantly and unhesitatingly obeyed, but as a high honor and distinction. "But the fact is," said Wills, with his easy smile, "I'd promised to be at my friend Corkran's reception that evening, and, of course, I couldn't think of disappointing him; there was no time to write, so I just sent a telegram to the castle saying I was engaged." Probably English society history does not contain a parallel to this piece of audacity, and one would have liked to see the face of the private secretary of her Majesty when he opened the telegram. But Wills could not be made to recognize anything singular in the affair.

Commenting in one of his private note-books, at this time, upon the subject of modern sculpture in general, my father utters one of his unregenerate opinions. "It seems to me," he says, "time to leave off sculpturing men and women naked; such statues mean nothing, and might as well bear one name as another; they belong to the same category as the ideal portraits in books of beauty or in the

windows of print-shops. The art does not naturally belong to this age, and the exercise of it, I
think, had better be confined to manufacture of
marble fireplaces." As we shall see, he modified
this radical view before he left Italy; but there is
some ground of truth in it, nevertheless.

Here is another bit of art criticism. He has been
giving a detailed description of the sitting-room in
one of our lodgings, and of the objects contained in
it, evidently as a part of his general practice to record the minor facts of English life, to serve as a
background for the English romance he hoped to
write afterwards. "On the mantle-piece," he
writes, "are two little glass vases, and over it a
looking-glass (not flattering to the beholder), and
above hangs a colored view of some lake or sea-
shore, and on each side a cheap colored print of
Prince Albert and one of Queen Victoria. And,
really, I have seen no picture, bust, or statue of her
Majesty which I feel to be so good a likeness as this
cheap print. You see the whole line of Guelphs in
it—fair, blue-eyed, shallow-brained, commonplace,
yet with a simple kind of heartiness and truth that
make one somewhat good-natured towards them."

"I must see Dickens before I leave England," he
wrote, commenting upon the various tales he heard
of him from henchmen and critics; but he never
did see him, nor Thackeray either, whom he perhaps wished still more to meet. Thackeray visited
America while we were abroad; and when Dickens
came to Boston to read, my father was dead. Nor

did he see Bulwer, an apostrophe by whom he quotes: "Oh, that somebody would invent a new sin, that I might go in for it!" Tennyson he saw, but did not speak with him. He sat at table, on one occasion, with Macaulay, and remarked upon the superiority over his portraits of his actual appearance. He made the acquaintance, which ripened into friendship, in Italy, of Robert Browning and his wife, and of Coventry Patmore, the author of "The Angel in the House," a poem which he greatly liked. But, upon the whole, he came in contact with the higher class of literary men in England less than with others, whom he was less likely to find sympathetic.

One afternoon, when I had accompanied him to the consulate, there entered a tall, active man, very well dressed, with black, thick-curling hair and keen, blue eyes. He seemed under thirty years of age, but had the self-confident manner of a man of the world, and a great briskness of demeanor and speech. He sat down and began to tell of his experiences; he had been all over the world, and knew everything about the world's affairs, even the secrets of courts and the coming movements of international politics. He was a striking, handsome, indomitable figure, and aggressively American. When he went away, he left with my father a book which he had written, with an engraved portrait of the author for frontispiece. This volume, faded and shelf-worn, but apparently unread, bound in the execrable taste of a generation and a half ago, I recently found among my father's volumes. It bore on the title-page the dashing signature of George Francis Train. Train saw things in the large—in their cosmic relations; from us he was going forth to make a fortune compared with which that of Monte Cristo would be a trifle. He did make fortunes, I believe; but there seems to have been in his blood a little too much of the elixir of life—more than he could thoroughly digest. His development was arrested, or was continued on lines which carried him away from practical contact with that world which he believed he held in the hollow of his hand. My father suspected his soundness; but in 1856 there seemed to be no height to which he might not rise. The spiritual steam-engine in him, however, somehow got uncoupled from the mass of the machinery of human affairs, and has been plying *in vacuo*, so to say, ever since.

On the 9th of June came a telegram from Southampton; my mother and sisters had arrived from Madeira. My father and I left Liverpool the next day, feeling that our troubles were over. In the afternoon we alighted at the little seaport and took a cab to the Castle Hotel, close to the water. My father, with a face full of light, sprang up-stairs to the room in which my mother awaited him; I found myself with my sisters and Fannie Wrigley, the faithful nurse and companion who had accompanied them on their travels. How tall and mature Una was! What a big girl baby Rose had become! There was a little strangeness between us, but great good-will; we felt that there were a great many explanations to be made. In a few minutes I was called up-stairs to my mother. At the first glance she seemed smaller than formerly; her face appeared a little different from my memory of it; I was overcome by an odd shyness. She smiled and held out her arms; then I saw my beloved mother, and a great passion of affection poured through me and swept me to her. I was whole again, and indescribably happy.

There was never such another heavenly room as that parlor in the Castle Hotel; never another hotel so delightful, or another town to be compared with Southampton. I was united to all I loved there, and in my thoughts sunshine will always rest on it.

XII

Talked familiarly with kings and queens—Half-witted
girl who giggled all the time—It gnawed me terribly—
A Scotch terrier named Towsey—A sentiment of diplomatic etiquette—London as a physical entity—Ladies
in low-necked dresses—An elderly man like a garden-
spider—Into the bowels of the earth—The inner luminousness of genius—Isolated and tragic situation—"Ate
ever man such a morsel before!"—The great, wild, mysterious Borrow—Her skeleton, huddled, dry, and awful
—"Ma'am, you expose yourself!"—Plane, spokeshave,
gouge, and chisel—"I — passed — the — *Lightning!*"—
Parallel-O-grams—A graduate of Antioch—"Continual
cursing" — A catastrophe — "Troubles are a sociable
sisterhood"—"In truth I was very sorry"—He had
dreamed wide-awake of these things—A friend of Emerson and Henry James—Embarked at Folkestone for
France.

WE spent our first reunited week at the Castle Hotel, which was founded on an ancient castle wall, or
part of it; traces of it were shown to guests. The
harbor lapped the sea-wall in front; the Isle of
Wight, white-ramparted, gleamed through the haze
in the offing. I suppose, during that week, we were
enough employed in telling one another our histories during our separation; and naturally that of
my mother and sisters filled the larger space. They

had brought home words and phrases in a foreign tongue, which made me feel very ignorant; they had talked familiarly with kings and queens; they had had exciting experiences in Madeira; they brought with them photographs and colored prints of people and places, unlike anything that I had seen. My mother, who was an unsurpassed narrator of events, gave us wonderful and vivid accounts of all they had seen and done, which I so completely assimilated that to this day I could repeat a great deal of them; my father listened with eyes like stars (as my mother would have said), and with a smile in the corners of his mouth. It was glorious weather all the time, or so it seems to have been to me. My sisters and I renewed our acquaintance, and found one another none the worse. Nobody called on us except a Mrs. Hume, with whom a stay of a fortnight was projected; she kept a girls' school, and, this being vacation, she would take us as boarders. We were starved there, as only a pinching, English, thin - bread - and - butter housekeeper can starve people; and my sisters and I had for our playmate a half-witted girl who was staying over the vacation, and who giggled all the time. Mrs. Hume had aroused my enthusiasm by telling me that there were endless sea-anemones along the coast; but Providence seemed hostile to my sea-anemone proclivities; for it turned out that what Mrs. Hume understood by sea-anemones was a small, white-flowering weed that grew on the low bluff beside the water. I never told her my disappointment, imagining that it would distress her; but it gnawed me terribly, and she did not merit such forbearance.

We would much better have stayed at the hotel, only that they charged us fourteen dollars a day, which was considered exorbitant in those days. There were seven of us, including Fanny, the nurse. What an age, when two dollars a head was exorbitant! What Mrs. Hume charged us I know not, but it is only just to admit that it must have been a good deal less than one hundred dollars a week; though, again, it must not be forgotten that translucent bread-and-butter is not expensive. We were sent there, I suppose, in order to remind us that this was still the world that we were living in, after all, and not yet Paradise. We came out from her sobered and chastened, but cheerful still; and meanwhile we visited Stonehenge and other local things of beauty or interest. Then Mr. Bennoch (who, to tell the truth, had introduced Mrs. Hume to us) invited us to spend a month at his house in Blackheath, while he and his wife were making a little tour in Germany, and we arrived at this agreeable refuge during the first half of July. My father records that he was as happy there as he had ever been since leaving his native land. It was a pleasant little house, in a semi-countrified spot, and it contained, besides the usual furniture proper to an English gentleman and his wife of moderate fortune, a little Scotch terrier named Towsey, who commanded much of the attention of us children, and one day inadvertently bit my thumb; and I carry the scar, for remembrance, to this day.

Many well-known persons passed across our stage here; and London, with all its wonders, was at our doors, the wide expanse of its smoke-piercing towers visible in our distance. All the while my father kept the official part of himself at Liverpool, where his consular duties still claimed his attention; he went and came between Mrs. Blodgett's and Blackheath. The popularity of the incomparable boarding-house in Duke Street had continued to increase, and he was obliged to bestow himself in a small room at the back of the building, which was reputed to be haunted by the spirit of one of his predecessors in office, who had not only died in it, but had often experienced there the terrors of delirium tremens; but the ghost, perhaps from a sentiment of diplomatic etiquette, never showed itself to my father. Or it may have been that the real self of him being in Blackheath, what remained was not sufficient to be conscious of a spiritual presence. He came and went, like sunlight on a partly cloudy day. I recollect taking a walk over the Heath at evening with him and the doctor who was attending my mother; Mr. Bennoch was with us; it must have been just before he and his wife went to the Continent. After walking some distance (the gentlemen chatting together, and I gambolling on ahead) we came to the summit of a low rise, from which we beheld London, flung out, all its gloomy length, before us; and in all my thoughts of London as a physical entity the impression then received of it returns to me. It lay vast, low, and obscure in front of the dull red of the sunset, with dim lights twinkling dispersedly throughout it, and the dome of St. Paul's doubtfully defining itself above the level. There is no other general view of London to be compared with this, seen under those conditions. Soon after, we came to some ridges and mounds, which, said Bennoch, marked the place where were buried the heaps of the slain of some great prehistoric battle—one, at least, which must have taken place while the Romans yet ruled Britain. It was a noble scene for such an antique conflict, when man met man, foot to foot and hand to hand, with sword and spear. My mind was full of King Arthur and his Round-Table knights of the Pendragonship, and I doubted not that their mightiest fight had been fought here.

There were many walks in London itself. One day, going west along the Strand, we found ourselves drawn into the midst of a vast crowd near Charing Cross; some royal function was in progress. Threading our way slowly through the press, we saw a troop of horsemen in steel breastplates, with nodding plumes on their helmets, and drawn swords carried upright on their thighs—the famous Horse Guards; and farther on we began to see carriages with highly ornamental coachmen and footmen passing in dilatory procession; within them were glimpses of ladies in low-necked dresses, feathers in their hair, and their necks sparkling with jewels.

At length we turned off towards the north, and by-and-by were entering a huge building of gray stone, with tall pillars in front of it, which my father told me was the British Museum. What a place for a boy! Endless halls of statues; enormous saloons filled with glass-cases of shells; cases of innumerable birds; acres of butterflies and other insects; strange objects which I did not understand—magic globes of shining crystal, enormous masses of iron which were said to have fallen from the sky; vases and jewels; and finally, at the farther end of a corridor, a small door, softly opening, disclosed a circular room of stupendous proportions, domed above, the curving walls filled with myriads of books. In the centre was a circular arrangement of desks, and in the midst of these an elderly man, like a garden-spider in his web; but it was his duty to feed, not devour, the human flies who sat or walked to and fro with literary meat gathered from all over the world. It was my first vision of a great library.

Another time we went—all of us, I think—to the Tower of London. I vibrated with joy at the spectacle of the array of figures in armor, and picked out, a score of times, the suit I would most gladly choose to put on. Here were St. George, King Arthur, Sir Scudamour, Sir Lancelot—all but their living faces and their knightly deeds! Then I found myself immured in dungeons with walls twenty feet thick, darksome and low - browed, with tiny windows, and some of them bearing on their stones strange inscriptions, cut there by captives who were nevermore to issue thence, save to the block. Here the great Raleigh had been confined; here, the lovable, rash-tempered Essex; here, the noble Sir Henry Vane, who had once trod the rocky coast of my own New England. Everywhere stood on the watch or paced about the Beef-eaters in their brilliant fifteenth-century motley. I have never since then passed the portals of the Tower, nor seen again the incomparable gleam of the Koh-i-noor—if it were, indeed, the Koh-i-noor that I saw, and not a glass model foisted on my innocence.

Again, I followed my father down many flights of steps, into the bowels of the earth; but there were lights there, and presently we passed through a sort of turnstile, and saw lengthening out before us two endless open tubes, of diameter twice or thrice the height of a man, with people walking in them, and disappearing in their interminable perspective. We, too, entered and began to traverse them, and after we had proceeded about half-way my father told me that the river Thames was flowing over our heads, with its ships on its surface, and its fishes, and its bottom of mud and gravel—under all these this illuminated corridor, with ourselves breathing and seeing and walking therein. Would we ever again behold the upper world and the sky? The atmosphere was not pleasant, and I was glad to find myself climbing up another flight of stairs and emerging on the other side of the river, which we had crossed on foot, dry-shod.

Of the famous personages of this epoch I did not

see much; only I remember that a woman who seemed taller than common, dressed in a dark silk gown, and moving with a certain air of composure, as if she knew she was right, and yet meant to be considerate of others; whose features were plain, and whose voice had a resonance and modulation unlike other voices, was spoken of in my hearing as bearing a name which I had heard often, and which had a glamour for my boyish imagination—Jenny Lind. There also rises before me the dark, courteous visage and urbane figure of Monckton Milnes; but there was something more and better than mere courtesy and urbanity about him; the inner luminousness, I suppose, of what was nearly genius, and would have been altogether that but for the swaddling-clothes of rank and society which hampered it. My father thought him like Longfellow; but there was an English materialism about Milnes from which the American poet was free. Henry James told me long afterwards a comical tale of how, being left to browse in Milnes's library one afternoon, he strayed into an alcove of pretty and inviting volumes, in sweet bindings, mellowed by age, and was presently terrified by the discovery that he was enmeshed in the toils of what bibliophiles term, I think, "Facetiæ"—of which Milnes had a collection unmatched among private book-owners. Milnes's social method was The Breakfast, which he employed constantly, and nothing could be more agreeable—in England; we cannot acclimate it here, because we work in the afternoon. Of Miss Bacon, of the Bacon-

wrote - Shakespeare theory, I saw nothing, but
heard much, for a time, in our family circle; my
father seemed to have little doubt of her insanity,
and absolute certainty of the despotic attitude she
adopted towards her supporters, which was far
more intolerable than the rancor which she visited
on those who disregarded her monomaniacal convictions. My mother, out of pure compassion, I
believe, for the isolated and tragic situation in
which the poor woman had placed herself, tried
with all her might to read the book and believe the
theory; she would take up the mass of manuscript
night after night, and wade through it with that
truly saintlike self-abnegation which characterized
her, occasionally, too, reading out a passage which
struck her. The result was that she could not
bring herself to disbelieve in Shakespeare, but she
conceived a higher admiration than ever of Bacon;
and that, too, was characteristic of her.

We made several incursions into the surrounding
country. One was to Newstead, where, from the
talkative landlady of the hotel, we heard endless
stories about Byron and his wife; this was before
Mrs. Harriet Beecher Stowe published her well-in-
tended but preposterous volume about the poet.
Then we visited Oxford, and were shown about by
the mayor of the town, and by Mr. S. C. Hall, and
were at one moment bathed in the light emanating
from Lady Waldegrave, of which interview my
father, in his private note-book, speaks thus: " Lady
Waldegrave appeared; whereupon Mr. Speirs (the

mayor) instantly was transfigured and transformed —like the English snob he is, worthy man—and looked humbler than he does in the presence of his Maker, and so respectful and so blest that it was pleasant to behold him. Nevertheless, she is but a brummagem kind of countess, after all, being the daughter of Braham, the famous singer, and married first to an illegitimate son of an Earl Waldegrave—not to the legitimate son and possessor of the title (who was her first love)—and after the death of these two to the present old Mr. Harcourt. She is still in her summer, even if it be waning, a lady of fresh complexion and light hair, a Jewish nose (to which her descent entitles her), a kind and generous expression of face, but an officer-like figure and bearing. There seems to be a peculiarity of manner, a lack of simplicity, a self-consciousness, which I suspect would not have been seen in a lady born to the rank which she has attained. But, anyhow, she was kind to all of us, and complimentary to me, and she showed us some curious things which had formerly made part of Horace Walpole's collection at Twickenham — a missal, for instance, splendidly bound and beset with jewels, but of such value as no setting could increase, for it was exquisitely illuminated by the own hand of Raphael himself! I held the precious volume in my grasp, though I fancy (and so does my wife) that the countess scarcely thought it safe out of her own hands. In truth, I suppose any virtuoso would steal it if he could; and Lady Waldegrave has reason to

look to the safe-keeping of her treasures, as she ex-
emplified by telling us a story while exhibiting a
little silver case. This once contained a portion of
the heart of Louis XII. (how the devil it was got
I know not), and she was showing it one day to
Strickland, Dean of Westminster, when, to her horror and astonishment, she saw him open the case
and swallow the royal heart! Ate ever man such
a morsel before! It was a symptom of insanity in
the dean, and I believe he is since dead, insane."
It was after this interview with the countess that
we visited Old Boston, and when my parents told
old Mr. Porter about the missal his jolly eyes took
on a far-away expression, as if he saw himself in
the delightful act of purloining it, "in obedience
to a higher law than that which he broke."

The man who, of all writing men, was nearest to
my heart in those years, and long after, was George
Borrow, whose book, *Lavengro*, I had already begun to read. The publication of this work had
made him famous, though he had written two or
three volumes before that, and was at this very
time bringing out its sequel, *Romany Rye*. But
Borrow was never a hanger-on of British society,
and we never saw him. One day, however, Mr.
Martineau turned up, and, the conversation chanc-
ing to turn on Borrow, he said that he and George
had been school-mates, and that the latter's gypsy
proclivities had given him a singular influence over
other boys. Finally, he had persuaded half a dozen
of them to run away from the school and lead a life

of freedom and adventure on the roads and lanes of
England. To this part of Mr. Martineau's tale I
lent an eager and sympathetic ear; but the narrator
was lowered in my estimation by the confession
that he himself had not been a member of Borrow's
party. He went on to say that the fugitives had
been pursued and captured and brought back to
bondage; and upon Borrow's admitting that he had
been the instigator of the adventure, he was sen-
tenced to be flogged, and that it was on the back of
this very Martineau that he had been "horsed" to
undergo the punishment! Imagine the great, wild,
mysterious Borrow mounted upon the ascetic and
precise cleric that was to be, and the pedagogue
laying on! My father asked concerning the accuracy of some of Borrow's statements in his books,
to which Martineau replied that he could not be
entirely depended on; not that he meant to mis-
lead or misrepresent, but his imagination, or some
eccentricity in his mental equipment, caused him
occasionally to depart from literal fact. Very possibly; but Borrow's imagination brought him much
nearer to essential truth than adherence to what
they supposed to be literal facts could bring most
men.

One of the most interesting expeditions of this
epoch—though I cannot fix the exact date—was to
an old English country-seat, built in the time of
Henry VIII., or earlier, and added to from age to
age since then, until now it presented an irregularity
and incongruousness of plan which rendered it an

interminable maze of delight to us children wandering through it. We were taken in charge by the children of the family, of whom there were no fewer than fourteen, all boys, with only twelve years between the eldest and the youngest (some of them being twins). Hide-and-seek at once suggested itself as the proper game for the circumstances, but no set game was needed; the house itself was Hide-and-seek House; you could not go twenty feet without getting lost, and the walls of many of the rooms had sliding panels, and passages through the thickness of them, and even staircases, so that when one of us went into a room there was no predicting where he would come out. Finally they brought us to a black, oaken door with a great, black lock on it, and bolts at the top and bottom; it was near the end of a corridor, in the oldest wing of the building. The door, in addition to its native massiveness, was studded with great nails, and there were bands of iron or steel crossing it horizontally. When we proposed to enter, our friends informed us that this door had been closed one hundred and eighty years before and had never been opened since then, and that it had shut in a young woman who, for some reason, had become very objectionable or dangerous to other persons concerned. The windows of the room, they added, had been walled up at the same time; so there this unhappy creature slowly starved to death in pitch darkness. There, doubtless, within a few feet of where we stood, lay her skeleton, huddled, dry, and awful in the garments she wore in life. Sometimes, too, by listening long at the key-hole, you could hear a faint sound, like a human groan; but it was probably merely the sigh of the draught through the aperture. This story so horrified me and froze my young blood that the fancies of Mrs. Radcliffe and Edgar Allan Poe seemed like frivolous chatter beside it.

About the middle of September the Bennochs returned from the Continent, and we made ready to transfer ourselves to the lodgings in Southport which had been prepared for us. Bennoch, who was soon to meet with the crucial calamity of his career, was in abounding spirits, and he told my father an anecdote of our friend Grace Greenwood, which is recorded in one of the private note-books. "Grace, Bennoch says," he writes, "was invited to a private reading of Shakespeare by Charles Kemble, and she thought it behooved her to manifest her good taste and depth of feeling by going into hysterics and finally fainting away upon the floor. Hereupon Charles Kemble looked up from his book and addressed himself to her sternly and severely. 'Ma'am,' said he, 'this won't do! Ma'am, you disturb the company! Ma'am, you expose yourself!' This last hit had the desired effect, for poor Grace probably thought that her drapery had not adjusted itself as it ought, and that perhaps she was really exposing more of her charms than were good to be imparted to a mixed company. So she came to herself in a hurry, and, after a few flutterings, subsided into a decorous listener. Bennoch says he had this story from an eye-witness, and that he fully believes it; and I think it not impossible that, betwixt downright humbug and a morbid exaggeration of her own emotions, Grace may have been betrayed into this awful fix. I wonder how she survived it!''

At Southport we remained from the middle of September to the following July, 1857. In addition to my aquarium, I was deeply involved in the ship-building industry, and, the more efficiently to carry out my designs, was apprenticed to a carpenter, an elderly, shirt-sleeved, gray-bearded man, who under a stern aspect concealed a warm and companionable heart. There were boys at the beach who had little models of cutters and yachts, and I conceived the project of making a sail-boat for myself. My father seems to have thought that some practical acquaintance with the use of carpenter's tools would do me no harm—by adding a knowledge of a handicraft to my other culture—so he arranged with Mr. Chubbuck that I should attend his work-shop for instruction. Mr. Chubbuck, accordingly, gave me thorough lessons in the mysteries of the plane, the spokeshave, the gouge, and the chisel, and finally presented me with a block of white pine eighteen inches long and nine wide, and I set to work on my sloop. He oversaw my labors, but conscientiously abstained from taking a hand in them himself; the model gradually took shape, and there began to appear a bluff-bowed, broad-beamed craft, a good deal resembling the French fishing-boats which I afterwards saw off the harbors of Calais and Havre. The outside form being done, I entered upon the delightful and exciting work of hollowing it out with the gouge, narrowly avoiding, more than once, piercing through from the hold into the outer world. But the little ship became more buoyant every day, and finally stood ready for her deck. This I prepared by planing down a bit of plank to the proper thickness—or thinness—and carefully fitted it into its place, with companionways fore and aft, covered with hatches made to slide in grooves. Next, with chisel, spokeshave, and sand-paper, I prepared the mast and fitted a top-mast to it, and secured it in its place with shrouds and stays of fine, waxed fishing-line. The boom and gaff were then put in place, and Fanny Wrigley (who had aforetime made my pasteboard armor and helmet) now made me a main-sail, top-sail, and jib out of the most delicate linen, beautifully hemmed, and a tiny American flag to hoist to the peak. It only remained to paint her; I was provided with three delectable cans of oil-paint, and I gave her a bright-green under-body, a black upper-body, and white portholes with a narrow red line running underneath them. Thus decorated, and with her sails set, she was a splendid object, and the boys with bought models were depressed with envy, especially when I called their attention to the stars and stripes. This boat-building mania of mine had originated while we were at Mrs. Blodgett's, where the captain of one of the clippers gave me a beautiful model of his own ship, fully rigged, and perfect in every detail; only it would not sail, being solid. Concerning his clipper, by-the-way, I once overheard a bit of dialogue in Mrs. Blodgett's smoking-room between my captain and another. "Do you mean to say," demanded the latter, "that you passed the *Lightning?*" To which my captain replied, in measured and impressive tones, "I—passed—the —*Lightning!*" The *Lightning*, it may be remarked, was at that time considered the queen of the Atlantic passage; she had made the trip between Boston and Liverpool in ten days. But my captain had once shown her his heels, nevertheless. I wanted to christen my sloop *The Sea Eagle*, but my father laughed so much at this name that I gave it up; he suggested *The Chub*, *The Mud-Pout*, and other ignoble titles, which I indignantly rejected, and what her name finally was I have forgotten. She afforded me immense happiness.

At Southport we had a queer little governess, Miss Brown, who came to us highly recommended both as to her personal character and for ability to instruct us in arithmetic and geometry, geography, English composition, and the rudiments of French. She was barely five feet in height, and as thin and dry as an insect; and although her personal character came up to any eulogium that could be pronounced upon it, her ignorance of the "branches" specified was, if possible, greater than our own. She was particularly perplexed by geometry; she

aroused our hilarity by always calling a parallelo-
gram a parallel-O-gram, with a strong emphasis on
the penultimate syllable; and she spent several
days repeating over to herself, with a mystified
countenance, the famous words, "The square of the
hypothenuse is equal to the sum of the squares of
the two legs." What were legs of a triangle, and
how, if there were any, could they be square? She
never solved this enigma; and although we liked
little Miss Brown very much, she speedily lost all
shadow of control over us; we treated her as a
sort of inferior sister, and would never be serious.
"English governess" became for us a synonym for
an amiable little nonentity who knew nothing; and
I was surprised to learn, later, from the early works
of Miss Rhoda Broughton, that they could be beautiful and intelligent. Miss Brown did not outlast
our residence in Southport.

From Southport we removed to Manchester, and
thence, after exhausting the exposition, to Leamington, where we spent September and October of
1857. We expected to proceed direct from Leamington to France and Italy, but we were destined to
be delayed in London till January of 1858.

It was in Leamington that we were joined by
Ada Shepard. She was a graduate of Antioch, a
men-and-women's college in Ohio, renowned in its
day, when all manner of improvements in the human race were anticipated from educating the sexes
together. Miss Shepard had got a very thorough
education there, so that she knew as much as a

professor, including — what would be of especial service to us—a knowledge of most of the modern European languages. What seemed, no doubt, of even more importance to her was her betrothal to her classmate, Henry Clay Badger; they were to be married on her return to America. Meanwhile, as a matter of mutual convenience (which rapidly became mutual pleasure), she was to act as governess of us children and accompany our travels. Ada (as my father and mother presently called her) was then about twenty-two years old; she had injured her constitution — never robust — by addiction to learning, and had incidentally imbibed from the atmosphere of Antioch all the women's-rights fads and other advanced opinions of the day. These, however, affected mainly the region of her intellect; in her nature she was a simple, affectionate, straightforward American maiden, with the little weaknesses and foibles appertaining to that estate; and it was curious to observe the frequent conflicts between these spontaneous characteristics and her determination to live up to her acquired views. But she was fresh-hearted and happy then, full of interest in the wonders and beauties of the Old World; she wrote, weekly, long, criss-crossed letters, in a running hand, home to "Clay," the king of men; and periodically received, with an illuminated countenance, thick letters with an American foreign postage-stamp on them, which she would shut herself into her chamber to devour in secret. She was a little over the medium height, with a blue-eyed face, not beautiful, but gentle and expressive, and wearing her flaxen hair in long curls on each side of her pale cheeks. She entered upon her duties as governess with energy and good-will, and we soon found that an American governess was a very different thing from an English one (barring the Rhoda Broughton sort). Her special aim at present was to bring us forward in the French and Italian languages. We had already, in Manchester, made some acquaintance with the books of the celebrated Ollendorff; and my father, who knew Latin well, had taught me something of Latin grammar, which aided me in my Italian studies. I liked Latin, particularly as he taught it to me, and it probably amused him, though it must also often have tried his patience to teach me. I had a certain aptitude for the spirit of the language, but was much too prone to leap at conclusions in my translations. I did not like to look out words in the lexicon, and the result was sometimes queer. Thus, there was a sentence in some Latin author describing the manner in which the Scythians were wont to perform their journeys; relays of fresh horses would be provided at fixed intervals, and thus they were enabled to traverse immense distances at full speed. The words used were, I think, as follows: "*Itaque conficiunt iter continuo cursu.*" When I translated these, "So they came to the end of their journey with continual cursing," I was astonished to see my father burst into inextinguishable laughter, falling back in his chair and throwing up his feet in the ebullience of his mirth. I heard a good deal of that "continual cursing" for some years after, and I believe the incident prompted me to pay stricter attention to the dictionary than I might otherwise have done.

However, what with Ollendorff and Miss Shepard, we regarded ourselves, by the time we were ready to set out for the Continent, as being in fair condition to ask about trains and to order dinner. My mother, indeed, had from her youth spoken French and Spanish fluently, but not Italian; my father, though he read these languages easily enough, never attained any proficiency in talking them. After he had wound up his consular affairs, about the first week in October, we left Leamington and took the train for a few days in London, stopping at lodgings in Great Russell Street, close to the British Museum.

We were first delayed by friendly concern for the catastrophe which at this moment befell Mr. Bennoch. He was a wholesale silk merchant, but his literary and social tendencies had probably led him to trust too much to the judgment and ability of his partners; at all events, on his return from Germany he had found the affairs of his establishment much involved, and he was now gazetted a bankrupt. In the England of those days bankruptcy was no joke, still less the avenue to fortune which it is sometimes thought to be in other countries; and a man who had built up his business during twenty years by conscientious and honorable work, and who was sensitively proud of his commercial honor, was for a time almost overwhelmed by the disaster. My father felt the most tender sympathy and grief for him, and we were additionally depressed by a report, circumstantially detailed (but which proved to be unfounded), that Mrs. Bennoch had died in childbirth—they had never had children. "Troubles," commented my father "(as I myself have experienced, and many others before me), are a sociable sisterhood; they love to come hand-in-hand, or sometimes, even, to come side by side, with long-looked-for and hoped-for good-fortune." He was doubtless thinking of that dark and bright period when his mother lay dying in his house in Salem and *The Scarlet Letter* was waiting to be born.

A few days later he went by appointment to Bennoch's office in Wood Street, Cheapside, and I will quote the account of that interview for the light it casts on the characters of the two friends:

"When I inquired for Bennoch, in the warehouse where two or three clerks seemed to be taking account of stock, a boy asked me to write my name on a slip of paper, and took it into his peculiar office. Then appeared Mr. Riggs, the junior partner, looking haggard and anxious, poor man. He is somewhat low of stature, and slightly deformed, and I fancied that he felt the disgrace and trouble more on that account. But he greeted me in a friendly way, though rather awkwardly, and asked me to sit down a little while in his own apartment, where he left me. I sat a good while, reading an old number of *Blackwood's Magazine*, a pile of which I found on the desk, together with some well-worn ledgers and papers, that looked as if they had been pulled out of drawers and pigeon-holes and dusty corners, and were not there in the regular course of business. By-and-by Mr. Riggs reappeared, and, telling me that I must lunch with them, conducted me up-stairs, and through entries and passages where I had been more than once before, but could not have found my way again through those extensive premises; and everywhere the packages of silk were piled up and ranged on shelves, in paper boxes, and otherwise—a rich stock, but which had brought ruin with it. At last we came to that pleasant drawing-room, hung with a picture or two, where I remember enjoying the hospitality of the firm, with their clerks all at the table, and thinking that this was a genuine scene of the old life of London City, when the master used to feed his 'prentices at a patriarchal board. After all, the room still looked cheerful enough; and there was a good fire, and the table was laid for four. In two or three minutes Bennoch came in—not with that broad, warm, lustrous presence that used to gladden me in our past encounters—not with all that presence, at least—though still he was not less than a very genial man, partially bedimmed. He looked paler, it seemed to me, thinner, and rather smaller, but nevertheless he smiled at greeting me, more brightly, I suspect, than I smiled back at him, for in truth I was very sorry. Mr. Twentyman, the middle partner, now came in, and appeared as much or more depressed than his fellows in misfortune, and to bear it with a greater degree of English incommunicativeness and reserve. But he, too, met me hospitably, and I and these three poor ruined men sat down to dinner—a good dinner enough, by-the-bye, and such as ruined men need not be ashamed to eat, since they must needs eat something. It was roast beef, and a boiled apple-pudding, and —which I was glad to see, my heart being heavy—a decanter of sherry and another of port, remnants of a stock which, I suppose, will not be replenished. They ate pretty fairly, but scarcely like Englishmen, and drank a reasonable quantity, but not as if their hearts were in it, or as if the liquor went to their hearts and gladdened them. I gathered from them a strong idea of what commercial failure means to English merchants—utter ruin, present and prospective, and obliterating all the successful past; how little chance they have of ever getting up again; how they feel that they must plod heavily onward under a burden of disgrace—poor men and hopeless men and men forever ashamed. I doubt whether any future prosperity (which is unlikely enough to come to them) could ever compensate them for this misfortune, or make them, to their own consciousness, the men they were. They will be like a woman who has once lost her chastity: no after-life of virtue will take out the stain. It is not so in America, nor ought it to be so here; but they said themselves they would never again have put unreserved confidence in a man who had been bankrupt, and they could not but apply the same severe rule to their own case. I was touched by nothing more than by their sorrowful patience, without any fierceness against Providence or against mankind, or disposition to find fault with anything but their own imprudence; and there was a simple dignity, too, in their not assuming the aspect of stoicism. I could really have shed tears for them, to see how like men and Christians they let the tears come to their own eyes. This is the true way to do; a man ought not to be too proud to let his eyes be moistened in the presence of God and of a friend. They talked of some little annoyances, half laughingly. Bennoch has been dunned for his gas-bill at Blackheath (only a pound or two) and has paid it. Mr. Twentyman seems to have received an insulting message from some creditor. Mr. Riggs spoke of wanting a little money to pay for some boots. It was very sad, indeed, to see these men of uncommon energy and ability, all now so helpless, and, from managing great enterprises, involving vast expenditures, reduced almost to reckon the silver in their pockets.

TO BEGIN LIFE OVER AGAIN

"Bennoch and I sat by the fireside a little while after his partners had left the room, and then he told me that he blamed himself, as holding the principal position in the firm, for not having exercised a stronger controlling influence over their operations. The two other men had recently gone into speculations, of the extent of which he had not been fully aware, and he found the liabilities of the firm very much greater than he had expected. He said this without bitterness, and said it not to the world, but only to a friend. I am exceedingly sorry for him; it is such a changed life that he must lead hereafter, and with none of the objects before him which he might heretofore have hoped to grasp. No doubt he was ambitious of civic, and even of broader public distinction; and not unreasonably so, having the gift of ready and impressive speech, and a behavior among men that wins them, and a tact in the management of affairs, and many - sided and never-tiring activity. To be a member of Parliament—to be lord mayor—whatever an eminent merchant of the world's metropolis may be—beyond question he had dreamed wide-awake of these things. And now fate itself could hardly accomplish them, if ever so favorably inclined. He has to begin life over again, as he began it twenty-five years ago, only under infinite disadvantages, and with so much of his working-day gone forever.

"At parting, I spoke of his going to America; but he appeared to think that there would be little hope for him there. Indeed, I should be loath to see him transplanted thither myself, away from the warm, cheerful, juicy English life into our drier and less genial sphere; he is a good guest among us, but might not do well to live with us."

Bennoch was never lord mayor or member of Parliament; I do not know that he cared to be either; but he lived to repay all his creditors with interest, and to become once more a man in easy circumstances, honored and trusted as well as loved by all who knew him, and active and happy in all good works to the end of his days. There could be no keeping down such a man, even in England; and when I knew him, in after years, he was the Bennoch of yore, grown mellow and wise.

We were now ready for the Continent, when symptoms of some malady began to manifest themselves among the younger persons of the family, which presently culminated in an attack of the measles. It was six weeks before we were in condition to take the road again. Meanwhile we were professionally attended by Dr. J. J. Garth Wilkinson, a homœopathist, a friend of Emerson and of Henry James the elder, a student of Swedenborg, and, at this particular juncture, interested in spiritualism. In a biography of my father and mother, which I published in 1884, I alluded to this latter circumstance, and some time afterwards I received from his wife a letter which I take this opportunity to print:

"4 FINCHLEY ROAD, N. W., *June* 19, 1885.

"DEAR SIR,—May I beg of you in any future edition of the Life of your father to leave out your passage upon my husband and spiritualism? He is utterly opposed to it now. On Mr. Home's first appearance in England very remarkable things did occur; but from the first I was a most decided opponent, and by my firmness I have kept all I know and love from having anything to do with it for at least thirty-five years. You may imagine, therefore, I feel hurt at seeing so spiritually minded a man as my husband really is to be mixed up with so evil a thing as spiritism. You will pardon a faithful wife her just appreciation of his character. One other author took the liberty of using his name in a similar way, and I wrote to him also. Believe me,

"Yours faithfully,

"E. A. WILKINSON."

The good doctor and his wife are now, I believe, both of them in the world where good spirits go, and no doubt they have long ere this found out all about the rights and wrongs of spiritism and other matters, but there is no doubt that at the time of my father's acquaintance with him the doctor was a very earnest supporter of the cult. He was a man of mark and of brains and of most lovable personal quality; he wrote books well worth deep study; Emerson speaks of "the long Atlantic roll" of their style. Henry James named his third son after him—the gentle and brave "Wilkie" James, who was my school-mate at San- born's school in Concord after our return to Amer- ica, and who was wounded in the fight at Fort Fisher while leading his negro soldiers to the assault. But for the present, Dr. Wilkinson, so far as we children knew him, was a delightful and impressive physician, who helped us through our measles in masterly style, under all the disadvantages of a foggy London winter.

On the 5th of January, 1858—we were ready to start the next day — Bennoch came to take tea with us and bid us farewell. " He keeps up a manly front," writes my father, "and an aspect of cheerfulness, though it is easy to see that he is a very different man from the joyous one whom I knew a few months since; and whatever may be his future fortune, he will never get all the sunshine back again. There is a more determinate shadow on him now, I think, than immediately after his misfortunes; the old, equable truth weighs down upon him, and makes him sensible that the good days of his life have probably all been enjoyed, and that the rest is likely to be endurance, not enjoyment. His temper is still sweet and warm, yet, I half fancy, not wholly unacidulated by his troubles—but now I have written it, I decide that it is not so, and blame myself for surmising it. But it seems most unnatural that so buoyant and expansive a character should have fallen into the helplessness of commercial misfortune; it is most grievous to hear his manly and cheerful allusions to it, and even his jokes upon it; as, for example, when we suggested how pleasant it would be to have him accompany us to Paris, and he jestingly spoke of the personal restraint under which he now lived. On his departure, Julian and I walked a good way down Oxford Street and Holborn with him, and I took leave of him with the truest wishes for his welfare."

The next day we embarked at Folkestone for France, and our new life began.

XIII

No doubt my father had grown fond of England during his four years' residence there. Except for its profits he had not, indeed, liked the consular work; but even that had given zest to his several excursions from it, which were in themselves edifying and enjoyable. The glamour of tradition, too, had wrought upon him, and he had made friends and formed associations. Such influences, outwardly gentle and unexacting, take deeper hold of the soul than we are at the time aware. They show their strength only when we test them by removing ourselves from their physical sphere.

Accordingly, though he looked forward with

239

pleasure to leaving England for the Continent, he was no sooner on the farther side of the narrow seas than he began to be conscious of discomfort, which was only partly bodily or sensible. An unacknowledged homesickness afflicted him—an Old-Home-sickness, rather than a yearning for America. He may have imagined that it was America that he wanted, but, when at last we returned there, he still looked back towards England. As an ideal, America was still, and always, foremost in his heart; and his death was hastened partly by his misgiving, caused by the civil war, lest her best days were past. But something there was in England that touched a deep, kindred chord in him which responded to nothing else. America might be his ideal home, but his real home was England, and thus he found himself, in the end, with no home at all outside of the boundaries of his domestic circle. A subconscious perception of this predicament, combined with his gradually failing health, led him to say, in a moment of frank self-communion, "Since this earthly life is to come to an end, I do not try to be contented, but weary of it while it lasts."

It is true that Rome, vehemently as at first he rebelled against it, came at last to hold a power over him. Rome, if you give it opportunity, subtly fastens its grasp upon both brain and heart, and claims sympathies which are as undeniable as our human nature itself. Yet there is something morbid in our love for the mystic city, like a passion for

some beautiful but perilous woman with a past—
such as Miriam in *The Marble Faun*, for example.
Only an exceptionally vigorous and healthy constitution can risk it without danger. Had my father visited Rome in his young manhood, he might
have both cared for it less and in a sense have
enjoyed it more than he did during these latter
years of his life.

But from the time we left London, and, indeed,
a little before that, he was never quite himself physically. Our departure was made at the most inclement moment of a winter season of unusual in-
clemency; they said (as *they* always do) that no
weather to be compared with it had been known
for twenty years. We got up before dawn in London, and after a dismal ride in the train to Folkestone, where the bitter waves of the English Channel left edgings of ice on the shingle beach where I
went to pick up shells, we were frost-bitten all our
two-hours passage across to Boulogne, where it
became cold in dead earnest, and so continued all
through Paris, Lyons, and Marseilles, and down the
Mediterranean to Genoa and Civita Vecchia, and
thence up the long, lonely, bandit-haunted road to
Rome, and in Rome, with exasperating aggrava-
tions, right up to April, or later. My own first recollection of St. Peter's is that I slid on the ice near
one of the fountains in the piazza of that famous
edifice; and my father did the same, with a savage
satisfaction, no doubt, at thus proving that everything was what it ought not to be. Either in Lon-

don, or at some intermediate point between that and Paris, he caught one of the heaviest colds that ever he had; and its feverish and debilitating effects were still perceptible in May. "And this is sunny Italy—and this is genial Rome!" he wrathfully exclaims. It was like looking forward to the Garden of Eden all one's life, and going to vast trouble and expense to get there, and, on arriving, finding the renowned spot to be a sort of Montreal ice-palace. The palaces of Rome are not naturally fitted to be ice-palaces, and the cold feels all the colder in them by consequence.

But I am going too fast. The first thing my father did, after getting on board the little Channel steamer, was to go down in the cabin and drink a glass of brandy-and-water, hot, with sugar; and he afterwards remarked that "this sea-passage was the only enjoyable part of the day." But the wind cut like a scimitar, and he came on deck occasionally only—as when I came plunging down the companion-way to tell him, with the pride of a discoverer, that France was broad in sight, and the sun was shining on it. "Oh!" exclaimed my mother, looking up from her pale discomfortableness on a sofa, with that radiant smile of hers, and addressing poor Miss Shepard, who was still further under the sinister influence of those historic alpine fluctuations which have upset so many. "Oh, Ada, Julian says the sun is shining on France!" Ada never stirred. She was the most amiable and philosophic of young ladies; but if thought could visit her reeling brain at that moment, she probably wondered why Providence had been so inconsiderate as to sever Britain from its Gallic base in those old geologic periods before man was yet born to sea-sickness.

Sunshine on the pale, smooth acclivities of France, and half a dozen bluff-bowed fishing-boats, pitching to the swell, were all that was notable on our trip across; and of Boulogne I remember nothing, except the confused mountain of the family luggage on the pier, and afterwards of its being fed into the baggage-car of the train. Ollendorff abandoned me thus early in my travels; nor was my father much better off. But Miss Shepard, now restored to life, made amends for her late incompetence by discoursing with excited French officials with what seemed to me preternatural intelligence; indeed, I half doubted whether there were not some conspiracy to deceive in that torrent of outlandish sounds which she and they were so rapidly pouring forth to one another. However, all turned out well, and there we were, in a compartment of a French railway-train, smelling of stale tobacco, with ineffective zinc foot-warmers, and an increasing veil of white frost on the window-panes, which my sisters and myself spent our time in trying to rub off that France might become visible. But the white web was spun again as fast as we dissipated it, and nothing was to be seen, at all events, but long processions of poplars, which interested me only because I imagined myself using them as lances in some romantic Spenserian adventure of knight - errantry — for the spell of that chivalric dream still hung about me. So we came to Amiens, a pallid, clean, chilly town, with high-shouldered houses and a tall cathedral, and thence went on to Paris at five o'clock. It was already dusk, and our transit to the Hôtel de Louvre in crowded cabs, through streets much unlike London, is the sum of my first impressions of the wonderful city.

Then, marshalled by princely yet deferential personages in rich costumes, we proceeded up staircases and along gilded corridors to a suite of sumptuous apartments, with many wax candles in candelabra, which were immediately lighted by an attendant, and their lustre was reflected from tall mirrors which panelled the rooms. The furniture thus revealed was costly and elegant, but hardly comfortable to an English-bred sense; the ceilings were painted, the floor rich with glowing carpets. But the glow of color was not answered by a glow of any other sort; a deadly chill pervaded this palatial place, which fires, as big as one's fist, kindled in fireplaces as large as hall bedrooms, did nothing to dissipate. Hereupon our elders had compassion on us, and, taking from the tall, awful bedsteads certain crimson comforters, they placed each of us in an easy-chair and tucked the comforters in over us. These comforters, covered with crimson silk, were of great thickness, but also of extraordinary lightness, and for a few minutes we had no confidence in their power to thaw us. But they were filled with swan's-down; and presently a novel and delightful sensation — that of warmth — began to steal upon us. It steadily increased, until in quarter of an hour there might be seen upon our foreheads and noses, which were the only parts of us open to view, the beads of perspiration. It was a marvellous experience. The memory of the crimson comforters has remained with me through life; light as sunset clouds, they accomplished the miracle of importing tropic warmth into the circle of the frozen arctic. I think we must have been undressed and night-gowned before this treatment; at any rate, I have forgotten how we got to bed, but to bed we somehow got, and slept the blessed sleep of childhood.

The next morning my father, apparently as an accompaniment of his cold, was visited by a severe nosebleed; no importance was attached to it, beyond its preventing him from going forth to superintend the examination of our luggage at the custom-house—the mountain having been registered through from London. This duty was, therefore, done by Miss Shepard and my mother. The next day, at dinner, the nosebleeding began again. "And thus," observed my father, "my blood must be reckoned among the rivers of human gore which have been shed in Paris, and especially in the Place de la Concorde, where the guillotines used to stand" —and where our restaurant was. But these bleedings, which came upon him at several junctures during his lifetime, and were uniformly severe and

prolonged, probably had a significance more serious
than was supposed. The last one occurred not
many weeks before his death, and it lasted twenty-
four hours; he was never the same afterwards. He
joked about it then, as now, but there was the fore-
warning of death in it.

But that day lies still unsuspected in the future,
six years away. For the present, we were in splendid Paris, with Napoleon III. in the Tuileries, and
Baron Haussmann regnant in the stately streets.
For a week we went to and fro, admiring and—
despite the cold, the occasional icy rains, and once
even a dark fog—delighted. In spirit and in substance, nothing could be more different from London. For my part, I enjoyed it without reser-
vation; the cold, which depressed my sick father,
exhilarated me. For Notre Dame, the Tuileries, the
Louvre, the Madeleine, the pictures, and the statues,
I cared little or nothing; I hardly even heeded the
column of the Place Vendôme or the mighty mass
of the Arc de Triomphe. But the Frenchiness of it
all captivated me. The throngs in the streets were
kaleidoscopic in costume and character: priests, soldiers, gendarmes, strange figures with turbans and
other Oriental accoutrements; women gayly dressed
and wearing their dresses with an air; men with curling mustachios, and with nothing to do, apparently,
but amuse themselves; romantic artists with soft
felt hats and eccentric beards; grotesque figures of
poverty in rags and with ominous visages, such as
are never seen in London; martial music, marching

regiments, with gorgeous generals on horseback, with shining swords; church processions; wedding pageants crowding in and out of superb churches; newspapers, shop-signs, and chatter, all in French, even down to the babble of the small children. And the background of this parade was always the pleasant, light-hued buildings, the majority of them large and of a certain uniformity of aspect, as if they had been made in co-operation, and to look pretty, instead of independently and incongruously, as in England. These people seemed to be all playing and prattling; nobody worked; even the shop-keepers held holiday in their shops. Such was my boyish idea of Paris. Napoleon had been emperor only five or six years; he had been married to Eugénie only four or five; and, so far as one could judge who knew nothing of political *coups d'état* and crimes, he was the right man in the right place. Moreover, the French bread was a revelation; it tasted better than cake, and was made in loaves six feet long; and the gingerbread, for sale on innumerable out-door stalls, was better yet, with quite a new flavor. I ate it as I walked about with my father. He once took a piece himself, and, said he, "I desired never to taste any more." How odd is, sometimes, the behavior of grown-up people!

But even my father enjoyed the French cookery, though he was in some doubt whether it were not a snare of the evil one to lure men to indulgence. We dined in the banquet-hall of our hotel once or twice only; in general we went to neighboring restaurants, where the food was just as good, but cost less. I was always hungry, but hungrier than ever in Paris. "I really think," wrote my father, "that Julian would eat a whole sheep." In his debilitated state he had little appetite either for dinners or for works of art; he looked even upon the Venus of Milo with coldness. "It seemed," wrote he, speaking of the weather one morning, "as if a cold, bitter, sullen agony were interposed between each separate atom of our bodies. In all my experience of bad atmospheres, methinks I never knew anything so atrocious as this. England has nothing to compare with it." The "grip" was a disease unnamed at that epoch, but I should suppose that it was very vividly described in the above sentence. He had the grip, and for nearly six months he saw everything through its medium.

Besides the Venus and the populace, we saw various particular persons. I went with my father to the bank, and saw a clerk give him a long roll of bright gold coins, done up in blue paper; and we visited, or were visited by, a Miss MacDaniel and her mother, two Salem women, "of plain, New England manners and appearance," wrote my father, "and they have been living here for nearly two years. The daughter was formerly at Brook Farm. The mother suffered so much from seasickness on the passage that she is afraid to return to America, and so the daughter is kept here against her will, and without enjoyment, and, as I judge, in narrow circumstances. It is a singular misfortune. She told me that she had been to the Louvre but twice since her arrival, and did not know Paris at all." This looks like a good theme for Mr. Henry James.

We called on the American minister to Paris, Judge John Young Mason, a simple and amiable personage. He was rubicund and stolid, and talked like a man with a grievance; but, as my father afterwards remarked, it was really Uncle Sam who was the aggrieved party, in being mulcted of seventeen thousand dollars a year in order that the good old judge should sleep after dinner in a French arm-chair. The judge was anticipating being superseded in his post, but, as it turned out, was not driven to seek second-rate employment to support himself in his old age; he had the happiness to die in Paris the very next year.

But the most agreeable of our meetings was with Miss Maria Mitchell, the astronomer, who, like ourselves, was stopping a few days in Paris on her way to Rome. She desired the protection of our company on the journey, though, as my father remarked, she looked well able to take care of herself. She was at this time about forty years old; born in Nantucket; the plainest, simplest, heartiest of women, with a face browned by the sun, of which she evidently was accustomed to see as much as of the other stars in the heavens. Her mouth was resolute and full of expression; but her remarkable feature was her eyes, which were dark and powerful, and had the kindest and most magnetic look of comradeship in them. Her dark hair was a little grizzled. She was dressed in plain gray, and was active and energetic in her movements. She was, as the world knows, a woman of unusual intellect and character; but she had lived alone with her constellations, having little contact with the world or practical knowledge of it, so that in many respects she was still as much a child as I was, and I immediately knew her for my friend and playmate and loved her with all my heart. There was a charming quaintness and innocence about her, and an immense, healthy curiosity about this new old world and its contents. She had a great flow of native, spontaneous humor, and could say nothing that was not juicy and poignant. She was old-fashioned, yet full of modern impulses and tendencies; warm-hearted and impulsive, but rich in homely common-sense. Though bold as a lion, she was, nevertheless, beset with the funniest feminine timidities and misgivings, due mainly, I suppose, to her unfamiliarity with the ways of the world. There was already a friendship of long standing between her and Miss Shepard, and they did much of their sight-seeing during the coming year together, and debated between themselves over the statues and pictures. Her talk with us children was of the fine, countrified, racy quality which we could not resist; and in the evenings, as we journeyed along, she told us tales of the stars and gave us their names. On the steamer going to Genoa, one night, she pointed out to me the constellation Orion, then riding high

MARIA MITCHELL

aloft in glittering beauty, and I kindly communicated to my parents the information that the three mighty stars were known to men as O'Brien's Belt. This was added to the ball of jolly as a household word.

Miss Mitchell's trunk was contributed to our mountain, when we set out anew on our pilgrimage, with a result at first deplorable, for the number of our own pieces of luggage being known and registered in the official documents, it turned out, at our first stopping-place, that the trunk of our new companion had been substituted for one of our own, which, of course, was left behind. It was ultimately recovered, I believe, but it seemed as if the entire world of French officialdom had to be upheaved from its foundations in order to accomplish it.

Our route lay through Lyons to Marseilles. At Lyons I remember only the enormous hotel where we slept the first night, with corridors wandering like interminable streets, up-stairs and down, turning corners, extending into vistas, clean-swept, echoing, obscure, lit only by the glimmering candle borne by our guide. We seemed to be hours on our journey through these labyrinths; and when at last we reached our rooms, they were so cold and so unwarmable that we were fain to journey back again, up and down, along and athwart, marching and countermarching past regiments of closed doors, until at length we attained the region of the hotel dining-saloon, where it was at least two or three degrees less cold than elsewhere. After dinner we had to undertake a third peregrination to bed, and a fourth the next morning to get our train. The rooms of the hotel were on a scale suited to the length of the connecting thoroughfares, and the hotel itself stood hard by a great, empty square with a statue in the middle of it. But the meals were not of a corresponding amplitude. And I think it was at the railway station of this town that the loss of the trunk was discovered.

The region from Lyons to Marseilles, along the valley of the Rhône, with the lower ranges of the Alps on our left hand, was much more picturesque than anything France had shown us hitherto. Ancient castles crowned many of the lower acclivities; there were villages in the vales, and presently vineyards and olive groves. The Rhône, blue and swift as its traditions demanded, kept us close company much of the way; the whole range of country was made for summer, and the wintry conditions under which we saw it seemed all the more improper. It must have been near midnight when our train rolled into the station at Marseilles, and my pleasure in "sitting up late" had long become stale.

The sun shone the next morning, and, being now in the latitude of Florence and such places, it could not help being hot, though the shaded sides of the streets were still icy cold; and most of the streets were so narrow that there was a great deal of shade. The whole population seemed to be out-of-doors and collecting in the sun, like flies, a very animated and voluble population and of a democratic complexion; the proportion of poor folks was noticeable, and the number of women, who seemed to camp out in the squares and market-places, and there gossip and do their knitting, as other women might at their firesides; but here the sun is the only fire. But a good deal of the bustle this morning was occasioned by the news from Paris that an attempt to assassinate Napoleon III. had been made the day before; had we remained one day longer in Paris we might have assisted at the spectacle. The Marseilles people seemed to take it comfortably; nobody was very sorry that the attempt had been made, nor very glad that it had not succeeded. It was something to talk about. It was ten years more before the French got thoroughly used to the nephew of his uncle and decided that he was, upon the whole, a good thing; and soon after they lost him. And for a decade after Sedan, chatting with the boulevardiers in Paris, they would commonly tell me that they wished they had the empire back again. Perhaps they will have it, some day.

There was a great deal of filth in Marseilles streets and along her wharves and in the corners of her many public squares; and even our hotel, the "Angleterre," was anything but clean; it was a tall, old rookery, from the windows of our rooms in which I looked down into an open space between the strange, old buildings, and saw a juggler do his marvels on a bit of carpet spread on the pavement, while a woman handed him the implements of magic out of a very much travelled and soiled deal-box. Later in the day, when the place was deserted, I heedlessly flung out of the window the contents of a glass of water, and, looking after it in its long descent, I was horrified to see approaching a man of very savage and piratical aspect, with a terrible black beard and a slouch hat. As luck would have it, the water struck him full on the side of the face, probably the first time in many a year that he had felt the impact of the liquid there. I withdrew my head from the window in alarm, mingled with the natural joy that a boy cannot help feeling at such a catastrophe; and by-and-by, when I felt certain that he must have passed on, I peeped out again, but what were my emotions at beholding him planted terribly right under the window where he had been baptized, and staring upward with a blood-thirsty expression. I immediately drew back again, but too late—our eyes had met, and he had made a threatening gesture at me. I now felt that a very serious thing had happened, and that if I ventured out upon the streets again I should assuredly be assassinated; that it would be no mere attempt, as in the case of the Emperor, but a pronounced success. I did not tell my fears to any of my family—I had not, to say the truth, informed any of them of the incident which had imperilled my life, but I no longer felt any curiosity to see more of Marseilles, and was sincerely thankful when I found myself, betimes next morning, on board the *Calabrese*, bound for Genoa. I never saw my murderer again, but I could make a fair likeness of him, I believe, to-day.

The trip to Genoa, and onward to Civita Vecchia, lasted two or three days, the steamer generally pursuing her course by night and laying up by day. The first morning, soon after sunrise, found us approaching the bay of Genoa, with the sun rising over the Mediterranean on our right and throwing its light upon the curving acclivity on which the city stands. The water had a beautiful blue-green color and was wonderfully clear, so that, looking down through it over the ship's side, as we glided slowly to our moorings, I saw sea-weeds and blocks of marble and other marine curiosities which reawakened my old passion for aquariums. Indeed, to be candid with the reader—as is my study throughout this narrative—nothing in Genoa the Superb itself has, I find, remained with me so distinctly as that glimpse of the floor of the bay through the clear sea-water. I did not care to go up into the town and see the palaces and churches; I wanted to stay on the beach and hunt for shells— Italian shells—and classical or mediæval sea-anemones. Of course, I had to go up into the town; and I saw, no doubt, the churches and the palaces, with their rooms radiant with the mellow brilliance of precious marbles and painted ceilings, and statues and pictures, under the personal conduct of no less an individual than Salvator Rosa himself—for that was the name of our guide—and for years afterwards I never doubted that he was the creator of the paintings which, in Rome and elsewhere, bore his signature. I say I must have seen these things, but in memory I cannot disentangle them from the innumerable similar objects which I beheld, later, in other Italian cities; their soft splendor and beautiful art could not hold their own for me beside that cool translucence of the Mediterranean inlet, with its natural marvels dimly descried as I bent over the boat's side. It was for that, and not for the other, that my heart yearned, and that became a part of me, all the more, no doubt, that it was denied me. Our aim in the world is beauty and happiness; but we are late in learning that they exist in the will and imagination, and not in this or that accredited and venerable thing or circumstance that is mechanically obtruded on our unready attention. If you were put down in the Garden of Eden, and told that you might stay there an hour and no more, what would you do? How would you "improve" your time? Would you run to and fro, and visit the spot where Adam first stood erect, and the place where he sat when he named the animals, and the thymey bank on which he slept while Eve was taking form from his rib, and the tree on which grew the fruit of the knowledge of good and evil, and the precise scene of the temptation and the fall, and the spot on which stood the altars on which Cain and Abel offered their sacrifices, and where, presently, wrathful Cain rose up against his brother and slew him? Would you make sure of all these set sights in order that you might reply satisfactorily to the cloud of interviewers awaiting you outside the Garden? Or would you simply throw yourself down on the grass wherever the angel happened to leave you, and try to see or to realize or to recall nothing, but passively permit your soul to feel and experience and grow what way it would, prompted by the inner voice and guided by the inner light, heedless of what the interviewers were expecting and of what duty and obligation and the unique opportunity demanded? It is worth thinking about. It may be conceded that there is some risk to run.

I next find myself in a coach, with four horses harnessed to it, trundling along the road from Civita Vecchia to Rome; for of Monaco I recall nothing, nor of Leghorn; and though we passed within sight of Elba, I saw only a lonely island on our starboard beam. As for the coach, it was a necessity, if we would continue our journey, for the railroad was still in the future in 1858. The coach-road was not only as rugged and uneasy as it had been any time during the past three hundred years, but it was outrageously infested by banditti; and, indeed, a robbery had taken place on it only a week or two before. For miles and miles on end it was totally destitute of dwellings, and those that we saw might well have been the harboring-places of iniquity. Moreover, we were so long delayed in making our start that it was already afternoon before we were under way, and finally one of our horses gave out ere we were many miles advanced, compelling us to hobble along for the remainder of the trip at reduced speed. As the shades of evening began to fall, we saw at intervals sundry persons lurking along the roadway, clad in long cloaks and conical hats, with the suggestion of the barrel of a musket about them, and it is probable that we were preserved from a tragic fate only by the fortunate accident that we were just behind the mail-coach and might theoretically have hailed it for help had we been attacked. Meanwhile, my father, with ostensible pleasantry, suggested that we should hide our gold coin (of which we carried a considerable store) in various queer, out-of-the-way receptacles. I remember that an umbrella was filled with a handful or two of the shining pieces, and stuck with studied carelessness through the straps in the roof of the vehicle. This was regarded by us children as excellent sport, though I think there was a lingering feeling of apprehension in the bottom of my soul. My father kept a moderate sum in napoleons in his pockets, so that, should the worst happen, the bandits might fancy it was our all. But then there was our mountain of luggage, incredibly strapped on the top of the conveyance, and behind it, and no reasonable bandits, one would suppose, could have failed to be satiated with that. However, it was written that we were to reach Rome unscathed, albeit long after dark, and though we did not get past the Porta del Popolo without suffering legalized robbery on the part of the custom-house officials. But by that time we were so weary, downcast, and chilled that depredation and outrage could not rouse or kindle us.

"OH, BYRON!"

We ended, at last, in one of those refrigerator hotels to which our travels had made us accustomed, in one of the hollow, dull, untoward caverns of which I was presently put to bed and to sleep. "Oh, Rome, my country, City of the Soul!" Oh, Byron, were you an Esquimau?

XIV

Our unpalatial palace—"Cephas Giovanni"—She and
George Combe turned out to be right—A rousing temper—Bright Titian hair—"All that's left of him"—The
pyramidal man of destiny—The thoughts of a boy are
long, long thoughts—Clausilia Bubigunia—Jabez Hogg
and the microscope—A stupendous surprise—A lifetime in fourteen months — My father's jeremiades—
"Thank Heaven, there is such a thing as whitewash!"
—"Terrible lack of variety in the old masters"—"The
brazen trollop that she is!"—Several distinct phases of
feeling—Springs of creative imagination roused—The
Roman fever—A sad book—Effects of the death-blow—
The rest is silence.

WE arrived in Rome on the 17th of January,
1858, at eleven o'clock at night. After a day or
two at Spillman's Hotel, we moved into lodgings
in the Via Porta Pinciana, the Palazzo Larazani.
The street extended just below the ridge of the
Pincian Hill, and was not far from the broad flight
of steps mounting upward from the Piazza d' Espagna, on the left as you go up. In spite of its resounding name, our new dwelling had not a palatial
aspect. It was of no commanding height or architectural pretensions; a stuccoed edifice, attached
on both sides to other edifices. The street, like
other Roman streets, was narrow; it was dirty like

them, and, like them, was paved with cobble-stones. The place had been secured for us by (I think) our friends the Thompsons; Mr. Thompson—the same man who had painted my father's portrait in 1853— had a studio hard by. The Thompsons had been living in Rome for five years or more, and knew the Roman ropes. They were very comfortable people to know; indeed, Rome to me would have been a very different and less delightful place without them, as will hereafter appear. The family consisted of Cephas Giovanni Thompson, the father and artist; his wife and his two sons and one daughter. "Cephas Giovanni," being interpreted, means plain Peter John; and it was said (though, I believe, unjustifiably) that Peter John had been the names originally given to Thompson by his parents at the baptismal-font, but that his wife, who was a notable little woman, a sister of Anna Cora Mowatt, the actress, well known in America and England seventy years ago, had persuaded him to translate them into Greek and Italian, as more suitable to the romantic career of an artist of the beautiful. I fancy the story arose from the fact that Mrs. Thompson was a woman who, it was felt, might imaginably conceive so ambitious a project. She was small, active, entertaining, clever, and "spunky," as the New-Englanders would have said; indeed, she had a rousing temper, on occasion. Her husband, on the other hand, had the mildest, wisely smiling, philosophic air, with a low, slow voice, and a beard of patriarchal fashion and size, though as yet it was a rich brown, with scarcely a thread of silver in it. Brown and abundant, also, was his hair; he had steady, bright, brown eyes, and was rather under the average height of Anglo-Saxon man. But for all this mild-shining aspect of his, his dark eyebrows were sharply arched, or gabled rather; and my mother, who had absorbed from her former friend, George Combe, a faith in the betrayals of phrenology, expressed her private persuasion that good Mr. Thompson had a temper, too. She and George Combe turned out to be right in this instance, though I am not going to tell the tale of how we happened to be made acquainted with the fact. Little thunder-storms once in a while occur in human skies as well as in the meteorological ones; and the atmosphere is afterwards all the sweeter and softer. No people could be more good, honest, and kind than the Thompsons.

There was no other artist in Rome who could paint as well as Mr. Thompson. That portrait of my father, to which reference has been made, which now hangs in my house, looks even better, as a painting, to-day than it did when it was fresh from his easel. Rubens could not have laid on the colors with more solidity and with truer feeling for the hues of life. But the trouble with Thompson was that he had never learned how to draw correctly; and this defect appeared to some extent in his portraits as well as in his figures. The latter were graceful, significant, full of feeling and character; but they betrayed a weakness of anatomical knowledge and of perspective. They had not the conventional incorrectness of the old masters preceding Raphael, but an incorrectness belonging personally to Thompson; it was not excessive or conspicuous to any one, and certainly not to Thompson himself. But his color redeemed all and made his pictures permanently valuable. He was at this time painting a picture of Saint Peter being visited by an angel, which was rich and beautiful; and he had some sketches of a series based on Shakespeare's *Tempest;* and standing on one side in the studio was a glowing figure of a woman in Oriental costume, an odalisque, or some such matter, which showed that his sympathy with life was not a restricted one. Later in our acquaintance he fell in love with the bright Titian hair of my sister Rose, and made a little portrait of her, which was one of his best likenesses, apart from its admirable color; it even showed the tears in the child's eyes, gathering there by reason of her antipathy to posing.

Cora Thompson, the daughter, was the most good-natured and sunny-tempered of girls; she may have been fifteen at this time; she inherited neither the handsomeness of her father nor the sharp-edged cleverness of her mother; but she was lovable. Of the two boys, the younger was named Hubert; he was about ten years old, small of his age, and not robust in make or constitution. He was, however, a smart, rather witty youth, a little precocious, perhaps, and able to take care of himself. Some five and twenty years after the date of which I am now writing I was at a large political dinner in New York and was there introduced to a Mr. Thompson, who was the commissioner of public works, and a party boss of no small caliber and power. He was an immense personage, physically likewise, weighing fully three hundred pounds, and, though not apparently advanced in years, a thorough man of the world and of municipal politics. After we had conversed for a few minutes, I was struck by a certain expression about my interlocutor's eyebrows that recalled long-forgotten days and things. I remembered that his name was Thompson, and had an impression that his initials were H. O. "Are you little Hubert Thompson?" I suddenly demanded. "Why, of course I am—all that's left of him!" he replied, with a laugh. So this was the boy whom, a quarter of a century before, I could have held out at arm's-length. We talked over the old days when we played together about the Roman streets and ruins. Nothing more reveals the essential strangeness of human life than this meeting after many years with persons we have formerly known intimately, who are now so much changed in outward guise. We feel the changes to be unreal, and yet, there they are! Grover Cleveland was being groomed for his first Presidential term then; Hubert was one of his supporters in New York, and he presented me to the pyramidal man of destiny. Poor Hubert died, lamentably, not long after. He was a good and affectionate son. He was perhaps too kind - hearted and loyal for the political rôle which he enacted.

The elder Thompson boy was called Edmund, or, in my vernacular, Eddy. There were in his nature a gravity, depth, and sweetness which won my heart and respect, and we became friends in that intimate and complete way that seems possible only to boys in their early teens. For that matter, neither of us was yet over twelve; I think Eddy was part of a year my junior. But you must search the annals of antiquity to find anything so solid and unalterable as was our friendship. He was the most absolutely good boy I ever knew, but by no means goody-goody; he had high principles, noble ambitions, strong affections, the sweetest of tempers; his seriousness formed a healthy foil to my own more impetuous and hazardous character. "The thoughts of a boy are long, long thoughts"; and not in many long lifetimes could a tithe of the splendid projects we resolved upon have been carried out. We were together from morning till night, month after month; we walked interminably about Rome and frequented its ruins, and wandered far out over the Campagna and along the shores of famous Tiber. We picked up precious antique marbles, coins, and ancient curiosities of all sorts; we hunted for shells and butterflies and lizards; our hearts were uplifted by the martial music of the French army bands, which were continually resounding throughout Rome; and we admired the gleaming swords of the officers and the sharp, punctual drill and marching of the red-legged rank and file. We haunted the lovely Villa Borghese, the Pincian Hill, the Villa Pamphili Doria; we knew every nook and cranny of the Palace of the Cæsars, the Baths of Caracalla, the Roman Forum, the Coliseum, the Egerian Grove; we were familiar with every gate that entered Rome; we drank at every fountain; we lingered through the galleries of the Vatican and of the Capitol; we made St. Peter's Church our refuge in inclement weather; we threaded every street and by-way of the city; we were on friendly and confidential terms with the *custode* of every treasure. And all the time we talked about what we thought, what we felt, what we would do; there is no looking backward in boys' confidences; they live in the instant present and in the infinite future. Eddy and I arranged to spend one lifetime in Central Africa, in emulation of the exploits of David Livingstone; there, freed from all civilized burdens, we would live, and we would run, catch the wild goat by the hair, and hurl our lances in the sun. At another epoch of our endless lives we would enter the army and distinguish ourselves in heroic war; we would have swords like sunbeams and ride steeds like Bucephalus. Then, and interleaved with all this, as it were, there was an immense life of natural history; we would have a private museum to rival the famous ones of nations. Eddy was especially drawn towards insects, while my own predilection was still for conchology; and both of us spent hours every week in classifying and arranging our respective collections, not to speak of the time we devoted to hunting for specimens. Eddy had a green net at the end of a stick, and became very skilful in making his captures; and how we triumphed over a "swallow-tail," so difficult to catch, or an unfamiliar species! Eddy had his pins and his strips of cork, and paper boxes; and his collections certainly were fairer to look upon, to the ordinary view, than mine; moreover, his was the more scientific mind and the nicer sense of order. For the display of my snail-shells I used bits of card-board and plenty of gum-arabic; and I was affluent in "duplicates," my plan being to get a large card and then cover it with specimens of the shell, in serried ranks. I also called literature to my aid, and produced several little books containing labored descriptions of my collection, couched, so far as possible, in the stilted and formal phraseology of the conchological works to which I had access, but with occasional outbursts after a style of my own. Here is a chapter from one of them; a pen-and-ink portrait of the shell is prefixed to the original essay:

"CLAUSILIA BUBIGUNIA

"This handsome and elegant little shell is found in mossy places, or in old ruins, such as the Coliseum—where it is found in immense numbers—or the Palace of the Cæsars. But in Italy it is common in any mossy ruin, in the small, moss-covered holes, where it is seen at the farthest extremity. After a rain they always crawl out of their places of concealment in such numbers that one would think it had been raining clausilias. The shell, in large and fine specimens, is five-eighths of an inch in length. The young are very small and look like the top part of the spire of the adults. This shell is also largest in the middle, shaped something like a grain of wheat. It has nine whorls, marked by small white lines, which look like fine white threads of sewing-cotton; and just below them are marks which look like very fine and very small stitches of white cotton. The color of the shell, down to next to the last whorl, is a brown color, but the very last whorl is a little lighter. The shell is covered all over with fine lines, but they need to be looked at through a magnifying-glass, they are so fine. The lip is turning out, and very thin; inside there are three ridges, two on the top part of the mouth, and the other, which is very small, is below. The shell, when the animal is out of it, is semi-transparent, and the little colomella, or pillar, can be indistinctly seen through."

There follows a detailed and loving description of the animal inhabiting the shell, which I must reserve for a future edition. Of another species of snail, *Helix strigata*, our learned author observes that "This shell is, when dead, one of those which is found on the banks of the Tiber. It is a strange circumstance that, although it is a land shell, it should be found more on the banks of a river than anywhere else, and also *only* on the banks of the Tiber, for it is not found on the banks of any other river. Any one would think that dead shells were gifted with the power of walking about, for certainly it is an inexplicable wonder how they got there." Of *Helix muralis* we are informed that "The Romans eat these snails, not the whole of them, but only their feet. In ancient times the most wealthy people used to eat snails, and perhaps they ate the very ones which the poorest people eat nowadays. It is most probable, for there are a great many different kinds of snails round Rome, and the Romans would probably select the best." I may perhaps be permitted to remark that the correct orthography of this writer fills me with astonishment, inasmuch as in later life I have reason to know that he often went astray in this respect. Of the uniform maturity of the literary style, I have no need to speak.

Eddy's father was in the habit of giving him an income of two or three pauls a week, dependent on his good behavior and punctual preparation of his lessons; and since Eddy was always well behaved and faithful in his studies, the income came in pretty regularly. Eddy saved up this revenue with a view to buying himself a microscope, for the better prosecution of his zoological labors; being, also, stimulated thereto by the fact that I already possessed one of these instruments, given me by my father a year or two before. Mine cost ten shillings, but Eddy meant to get one even more expensive. I had, too, a large volume of six hundred pages on *The Microscope, Its History, Construction, and Uses*, by Jabez Hogg, the contents of which I had long since learned by heart, and which I gladly communicated to my friend. At length Eddy's economies had proceeded so far that he was able to calculate that on his twelfth birthday he would possess a fortune of five scudi, and he decided that he would buy a microscope at that figure; it is needless to add that the microscope had long since been selected in the shop, and was decidedly superior to mine. We could hardly contain our impatience to enter upon the marvellous world whereof this instrument was the key; that twelfth birthday seemed long in coming, but at last it came.

I was to go with my friend to the shop to see him make the purchase; and I was at his house betimes in the morning. But what a stupendous surprise awaited me! Eddy was too much excited to say anything; with a face beaming with emotion, he led me into the sitting-room, and there, upon the table, was a microscope. But such a microscope! It was of such unheard-of magnificence and elaborateness that it took my breath away, and we both stood gazing at it in voiceless rapture. It was tall and elegant, shining with its polished brass and mirrors, and its magnifying powers were such as to disclose to us the very heart of nature's mystery. It was quiet Mr. Thompson's birthday present to his son. That gentleman sat smiling in his arm-chair by the window, and presently he said, with a delightful archness, "Well, Eddy, I suppose you are ready to give me back all that money you've been collecting?" Eddy grinned radiantly. He spent his savings for microscope-slides and other appurtenances, and for weeks thereafter he could hardly take his eye away from the object-lens. He was luminous with happiness, and I reflected his splendor from my sympathetic heart. Dear old Eddy! In after years he entered West Point and became a soldier, and he died early; I never saw him after parting from him in Italy in 1859. But he is still my first friend, and there has been no other more dear.

I am not aware that Rome has ever been described from the point of view of a twelve-year-old boy, and it might be worth doing; but I have delayed attempting it somewhat too long; the moving pictures in my mind have become too faded and confused. And yet I am surprised at the minuteness of some of my recollections; they have, no doubt, been kept alive by the numerous photographs of Rome which one carries about, and also by the occasional perusal of *The Marble Faun* and other Roman literature. But much is also due to the wonderful separateness which Rome retains in the mind. It is like nothing else, and the spirit of it is immortal. It seems as if I must have lived a lifetime there; and yet I cannot make out that our total residence in the city extended over fourteen months. Certainly no other passage of my boyhood time looms so large or is rooted so deep.

But the passion for Rome (unless one be a Byron) is not a plant of sudden growth, and I dare say that, during those first frigid weeks, I may have shared my father's whimsical aversion to the city. He has described, in his journals, how all things seemed to be what they should not; and he was terribly disgusted with the filth that defiled the ruins and the street corners. He was impressed by the ruins, but deplored their nakedness. "The marble of them grows black or brown, it is true," says he, "and shows its age in that way; but it remains hard and sharp, and does not become again a part of nature, as stone walls do in England; some dry and dusty grass sprouts along the ledges of a ruin, as in the Coliseum; but there is no green mantle of ivy spreading itself over the gray dilapidation." We stumbled upon the Fountain of Trevi in one of our early rambles, not knowing what it was. "One of these fountains," writes my father, referring to it, "occupies the whole side of a great edifice, and represents Neptune and his steeds, who seem to be sliding down with a cataract that tumbles over a ledge of rocks into a marble-bordered lake, the whole—except the fall of water itself—making up an exceedingly cumbrous and ridiculous affair." He goes to St. Peter's, and "it disappointed me terribly by its want of effect, and the little justice it does to its real magnitude externally; as to the interior, I am not sure that it would not be even more grand and majestic if it were less magnificent, though I should be sorry to see the experiment tried. I had expected something dim and vast, like the great English cathedrals, only more vast and dim and gray; but there is as much difference as between noonday and twilight." The pictures, too, were apt in these first days to go against the grain with him. Contemplating a fresco representing scenes in purgatory, he broke forth: "I cannot speak as to the truth of the representation, but, at all events, it was purgatory to look at this poor, faded rubbish. Thank Heaven, there is such a thing as whitewash; and I shall always be glad to hear of its application to old frescoes, even at the sacrifice of remnants of real excellence!" Such growlings torture the soul of the connoisseur; but the unregenerate man, hearing them, leaps up and shouts for joy. He found the old masters, in their sacred subjects, lacking in originality and initiative; and when they would represent mythology, they engendered an apotheosis of nakedness. His conclusion was that "there is something forced, if not feigned, in our taste for pictures of the old Italian school." Of the profane subjects, he instances the Fornarina, "with a deep bright glow on her face, naked below the waist, and well pleased to be so, for the sake of your admiration—ready for any extent of nudity, for love or money—the brazen trollop that she is! Raphael must have been capable of great sensuality to have painted this picture of his own accord, and lovingly." These are the iconoclasms of the Goth and Vandal at their first advent to Rome. They remained to alter their mood, and extol what they had before assaulted; and so did my father, as we shall see presently. But at first he was sick and cold and uncomfortable; and he consoled himself by hitting out at everything, in the secret privacy of his diary, since opened to the world. With warmer weather came equanimity and kinder judgments; but there is a refreshing touch of truth and justice even in these mutterings of exasperation.

It was not so much, I suppose, that Rome was cold as that my father had expected it to be otherwise. When one is in a place where tradition and association invite the soul forth to be warmed and soothed and rejoiced, and the body, venturing out, finds nothing but chill winds and frigid temperature and discomfort, the shock is much greater and more disagreeable than if one had been in some northern Canada or Spitzbergen, where such conditions are normal. Ice in the arctic circle is all right and exhilarating, but in the Piazza of St. Peter's it is an outrage, and affects the mind and heart even more than the flesh.

Circumstances caused my father to pass through several distinct phases of feeling while he was in Rome. First, his own indisposition and the inclement weather depressed and exasperated him. Time, in due course, brought relief in these respects, and he began to enjoy himself and his surroundings. Anon, the springs of creative imagination, long dormant in him, were roused to activity by thoughts connected with the Faun of Praxiteles in the Capitol. He now became happy in the way of his genius and immediately took a new interest in all things, looking at them from the point of view of possible backgrounds or incidents for the romance which had begun to take form in his mind. He describes what he saw *con amore*, and all manner of harmonious ideas bloom through his thoughts, like anemones and other flowers in the Villa Pamphili and the Borghese. This desirable mood continued until, after our return to Rome from the Florentine visit, my sister caught the Roman fever. She lay for weeks in danger of death; and her father's anxiety about her not only destroyed in him all thoughts of literary production and care for it, but made even keeping his journal no longer possible for him. That strain, so long continued, broke him down, and he never recovered from it so as to be what he had been before. Nevertheless, when she became convalescent, the reaction from his dark misgivings made him, for a time, as light-hearted as a boy; and, the carnival happening to be coincident with her recovery, he entered into the fun of it with a zest and enjoyment that surprised himself. But, again, it presently became evident that her recovery was not complete, and probably never would be so; the injury to her health was permanent, and she was liable to recurrences of disease. His spirits sank again, not so low as before, but, on the other hand, they never again rose to their normal level. It was in this saddened mood that he once more took up the Roman romance and finished it; it is a sad book, and when there is a ray of sunshine across the page, it has a melancholy gleam. After we returned to Concord, his apprehensions concerning Una's unsound condition were confirmed; and, in addition, the bitter cleavage between North and South inspired in him the gloomiest forebodings. A wasting away of his whole physical substance ensued; and he died, almost suddenly, while in years he might be considered hardly past the prime of his life. A sensitive eye can trace the effects of the death-blow all through *The Marble Faun*, and still more in *Septimius* and *Grimshawe*, published after his death. In *The Dolliver Romance* fragment, which was the last thing he wrote, there is visible once more some reminiscence of the old sunshine of humor that was so often apparent in his time of youth and vigor; but it, too, has a sad touch in it, such as belongs to the last rays of the star of day before it sinks below the horizon forever. Night follows, and the rest is silence.

XV

The Roman carnival in three moods—Apples of Sodom—
Poor, battered, wilted, stained hearts—A living protest
and scourge—*Dulce est desipere in loco*—A rollicking
world of happy fools—Endless sunshine of some sort—
Greenwich Fair was worth a hundred of it—They thundered past, never drawing rein—"*Senza moccolo!*"—
Nothing more charming and strange could be imagined
—Girls surprised in the midst of dressing themselves—
A Unitarian clergyman with his fat wife—Apparent
license under courteous restraint—He laughed and pelted and was pelted—William Story, as vivid as when I
saw him last—A too facile power—A deadly shadow
gliding close behind—Set afire by his own sallies—"Thy
face is like thy mother's, my fair child!"—Cleopatra in
the clay—"*Wer nie sein Brod mit thränen ass.*"

THE Roman carnival opened about a month after
our arrival in Rome.   The weather was bad nearly all the time, and my father's point of view was
correspondingly unsympathetic.   The contrast between his mood now and a year later, when he was
not only stimulated by his daughter's recovery from
illness, but, also, was looking at everything rather
as the romancer than as the man, is worth bringing
out.   My father likewise describes the carnival in
the romance; there we see it in a third phase—as
art.   But the passages in the note-books are written

from the realistic stand-point. In her transcriptions of the journals for the press my mother was always careful to omit from the former everything that had been "used" in the book; the principle, no doubt, was sound, but it might be edifying for once, in a way, to do just the opposite, in order to mark, if we choose to take the trouble, what kind of changes or modifications Hawthorne the romancer would make in the work of my father the observer of nature. Take your *Marble Faun* and turn to two of the latter chapters and compare them with the corresponding pages in my excerpts from the journals in the *Biography*. In the latter you will find him always in a critical and carping humor; seeing everything with abundant keenness, but recognizing nothing worth while in it. The bouquets, he noticed, for example, were often picked up out of the street and used again and again; "and," he adds, "I suppose they aptly enough symbolized the poor, battered, wilted, stained hearts that had flown from one hand to another along the muddy pathway of life, instead of being treasured up in one faithful bosom. Really, it was great nonsense."

It is true—such uncongenial interpretation—if you feel that way about it. And I remember, in my rambles along the famous thoroughfare, seeing a saturnine old fellow in a dingy black coat and slouch hat, with a sour snarl on his unprepossessing features, who made it his business, all day, to cuff and kick the little boys whom he caught throwing confetti, or picking up the fallen bouquets, and to shove the latter down into the sewer which ran beneath the street, through the apertures opening underneath the curb. He seemed to have stationed himself there as a living protest and scourge against and of the whole spirit of the carnival; to hate it just because the rest of the world enjoyed it, and to wish that he might make everybody else as miserable and uncharitable as he was. He was like a wicked and ugly Mrs. Partington, trying to sweep back the Atlantic of holiday merriment with his dirty mop. But this crabbed humor of his, while it made him conspicuous against the broad background of gayety, of course had no effect on the gayety itself. The flood of laughter, jocundity, and semi-boisterous frolic continued to roll up and down the Corso all day long, never attempting to be anything but pure nonsense, indeed, but achieving, nevertheless, the wise end of nonsense in the right time and place—that of refreshing and lightening the mind and heart. *Dulce est desipere in loco*—that old saw might have been made precisely to serve as the motto of the Roman carnival; and very likely it was actually suggested to its renowned author by some similar sport belonging to the old Roman days, before Christianity was thought of. The young fellows—English, American, or of whatever other nationality—would stride up and down the overflowing street hour after hour, clad in linen dust-coats down to their heels, with a bag of confetti slung on one side and another full of bouquets on the other;

and they would plunge a warlike hand into the
former and hurl ammunition at their rivals; or they
would pick out a bunch of flowers from the latter
for a pretty girl—not that the flowers were worth
anything intrinsically, nor was that their fault—
but just to show the fitting sentiment. There was
only one rule, the unwritten one that everybody
was to take everything that came with a smile or
a laugh, and never get angry at anything; and this
universal good-humor lifted the whole affair into a
wholesome and profitable sphere. Then there was
the double row of carriages forever moving in opposite directions, and passing within easy arm's-
reach of each other; and the jolly battle was waged
between their occupants, with side conflicts with
the foot-farers at the same time. And as the same
carriages would repass one another every forty minutes or so, the persons in them would soon get to
recognize one another; and, if they were of the
sterner sex, they would be prepared to renew desperate battle; or if there was a pretty girl or two in
one of them, she would be the recipient of a deluge
of flowers or of really pretty bonbons. It was all
play, all laughter, all a new, rollicking world of happy fools, of comic chivalry, of humorous gallantry.
For my part, I thought it was the world which I
had been born to live in; and I was too happy in it
to imagine even that anybody could be less happy
than I was. My sole grief was when my supply of
confetti had given out, and I had no money to buy
more. I used to look at those great baskets at the

street-corners, filled with the white agglomeration, with longing eyes, and wish I had it all in my pockets. I picked up the fallen bouquets, muddy or not, with no misgiving, and flung them at the girls with the unquestioning faith of boyhood. I looked up at the people in the windows and on the draped balconies with romantic emotions, and exchanged smiles and beckonings with them. The February days were never long enough for me; I only wished that the whole year was made up of those days; if it rained, or was cold, I never knew it. There was an endless sunshine of some sort which sufficed for me. But my father, at this epoch, could catch not a glimpse of it. " I never in my life knew a shallower joke than the carnival at Rome; such a rainy and muddy day, too; Greenwich Fair (at the very last of which I assisted) was worth a hundred of it."

The masking day, and the ensuing night of the *moccolo*, were the culminating features of the carnival; and it was on the afternoon of this day, I think, that the horse-race, with bare-backed horses, took place. The backs of these horses, though bare of riders, had attached to them by strings little balls with sharp points in them, which, as the horses ran, bobbed up and down, and did the office of spurs. The race was preceded by a thundering gallop of cavalry down the whole length of the Corso (the street having been cleared of carriages beforehand), ostensibly to prevent anybody from being run over by the race-horses; but, as a matter of fact, if any one were killed, it was much more likely to be by the ruthless riding of these helmeted dragoons than by the riderless steeds. They thundered past, never drawing rein, no matter what stood or ran in their way; and then, after an interval, during which the long crowds, packed back on the opposite sidewalks, craned forward as far as they dared to see them, came the eight or ten racers at a furious pace. They were come and gone in a breath; and finally, after the body of them were passed, came a laggard, who had been left at the post, and was trying to make up for lost time. I believe it was this horse who actually killed somebody on the course. The race over, back into the street thronged the crowd, filling it from wall to wall; then there was a gradual thinning away, as the people went home for supper; and finally came the night and the *moccoli*, with the biggest crowd of all. I was there with my twist of *moccolo* and a box of matches; except the *moccoli*, there was no other illumination along the length of the Corso. But their soft lights were there by myriads, and made a lovely sight, to my eyes at least. "*Senza moccolo!*" was the universal cry; young knights-errant, singly or in groups, pressed their way up and down, shouting the battle-cry, and quenching all lights within reach, while striving to maintain the flame of their own; using now the whisk of a handkerchief, now a puff of breath, now the fillip of a finger; contriving to extinguish a fair lady's taper with the same effusion of vain words wherewith they told her of their passion. Most of the ladies thus assailed sat in the lower balconies, elevated only a foot or two above the level of the sidewalk; but those in the higher retreats made war upon one another, and upon their own cavaliers; none was immune from peril. The cry, uttered at once by such innumerable voices far and near, made a singular murmur up and down the Corso; and the soft twinkling of the lights, winking in and out as they were put out or relighted, gave a singular fire-fly effect to the whole illumination. It seemed to me then, and it still seems in the retrospect, that nothing more charming and strange could be imagined; and through it all was the constant blossoming of laughter, more inextinguishable than the *moccoletti* themselves. The colors of the tapestries and stuffs dependent from the windows and balconies glowed out in light, or were dimmed by shadow; and the faces of the thousandfold crowd of festival-makers glimmered forth and were lost again on the background of the night, like the features of spirits in the glimpses of a dream. How long it all lasted I know not; but it had its term, like other mortal things, even in this fairyland of carnival; and when the last light was out the carnival was no more, and Lent, unawares, had softly settled down upon us with the darkness.

But let us now listen to my father when, for the second time, he made proof of the carnival in the year following our return from Florence, and after Una had left her sick-room and could be at his side. "The weather has been splendid," he writes, "and the merriment far more free and riotous than as I remember it in the preceding year. Tokens of the festival were seen in flowers on street - stands, or borne aloft on people's heads, while bushels of confetti were displayed, looking like veritable sugarplums, so that a stranger might have thought that the whole commerce and business of stern old Rome lay in flowers and sweets. One wonders, however, that the scene should not be even more rich and various when there has been so long a time (the immemorial existence of the carnival) to prepare it, and adorn it with shapes of gayety and humor. There was an infinite number of clowns and particolored harlequins; a host of white dominoes; a multitude of masks, set in eternal grins, or with monstrous noses, or made in the guise of monkeys, bears, dogs, or whatever beast the wearer chooses to be akin to; a great many men in petticoats, and almost as many girls and women, no doubt, in breeches; figures, too, with huge, bulbous heads and all manner of such easy monstrosities and exaggerations. It is strange how the whole humor of the thing, and the separate humor of each individual character, vanishes the moment I try to grasp it and describe it; and yet there really was fun in the spectacle as it flitted by—for instance, in the long line of carriages a company of young men in flesh-colored tights and chemises, representing a party of girls surprised in the midst of dressing themselves, while an old nurse in the midst of them expressed ludicrous horror at their predicament. Then the embarrassment of gentlemen who, while quietly looking at the scene, are surrounded by groups of maskers, grimacing at them, squeaking in their ears, hugging them, dancing round them, till they snatch an opportunity to escape into some doorway; or when a poor man in a black coat and cylinder hat is whitened all over with a half-bushel of confetti and lime-dust; the mock sympathy with which his case is investigated by a company of maskers, who poke their stupid, pasteboard faces close to his, still with the unchangeable grin; or when a gigantic female figure singles out some shy, harmless personage, and makes appeals to his heart, avowing her passionate love in dumb show, and presenting him with her bouquet; and a hundred other nonsensicalities, among which the rudest and simplest are not the least effective. A resounding thump on the back with a harlequin's sword, or a rattling blow with a bladder half full of dried pease or corn, answers a very good purpose. There was a good deal of absurdity one day in a figure in a crinoline petticoat, riding on an ass and almost filling the Corso with the circumference of crinoline from side to side. Some figures are dressed in old-fashioned garbs, perhaps of the last century, or, even more ridiculous, of thirty years ago, or in the stately Elizabethan (as we should call them) trunk hose, tunics, and cloaks of three centuries since. I do not know anything that I have seen queerer than a Unitarian clergyman (Mr. Mountford), who drives through the Corso daily with his fat wife in a one-horse chaise, with a wreath of withered flowers and oak leaves round his hat, the rest of his dress remaining unchanged, except that it is well powdered with the dust of confetti. That withered wreath is the absurdest thing he could wear (though, perhaps, he may not mean it to be so), and so, of course, the best. I can think of no other masks just now, but will go this afternoon and try to catch some more." You see, he has that romance in view again. "Clowns, or zanies," he resumes, after fresh inspection, "appear in great troupes, dancing extravagantly and scampering wildly; everybody seems to do whatever folly comes into his head; and yet, if you consider the matter, you see that all this apparent license is kept under courteous restraint. There is no rudeness, except the authorized pelting with confetti or blows of harlequins' swords, which, moreover, are within a law of their own. But nobody takes rough hold of another, or meddles with his mask, or does him any unmannerly violence. At first sight you would think that the whole world had gone mad, but at the end you wonder how people can let loose all their mirthful propensities without unchaining the mischievous ones. It could not be so in America or in England; in either of those countries the whole street would go mad in earnest and come to blows and bloodshed were the populace to let themselves loose to the extent we see here. All this restraint is self - imposed and quite apart from the presence of the soldiery."

This mood, we see, is far more gentle and sympathetic than the former one; there is sunshine within as well as without; and, indeed, I remember with what glee my father took part in the frolic, as well as looked on at it; he laughed and pelted and was pelted; he walked down the Corso and back again; he drove to and fro in a carriage; he mounted to Mr. Motley's balcony and took long shots at the crowd below. The sombre spirit of criticism had ceased, for a time, to haunt him.

We went quite often to the studio of William Story, whom my father had slightly known in Salem before he became a voluntary exile from America. Mr. Story was at this time a small, wiry, nervous personage, smiling easily, but as much through nervousness as from any inner source or outward provocation of mirth, and as he smiled he would stroke his cheeks, which were covered with a short, brown beard, with the fingers and thumb of his right hand, while wrinkles would appear round his bright, brown eyes. "He looks thin and worn already," wrote my father; "a little bald and a very little gray, but as vivid as when I saw him last; he cannot, methinks, be over thirty-seven." He was thirty-nine in 1858. "The great difficulty with him, I think, is a too facile power," my father goes on; "he would do better things if it were more difficult for him to do merely good ones. Then, too, his sensibility is too quick; being easily touched by his own thoughts, he cannot estimate what is required to touch a colder and duller person, and so stops short of the adequate expression." He commented on the vein of melancholy beneath the sparkle of his surface, as if, in the midst of prosperity, he was conscious of a "deadly shadow gliding close behind." Boys of twelve are not troubled with insight, unless of that unconscious, intuitive kind that tells them that a person is likeable, or the reverse, no matter what the person may do or say. I liked Mr. Story, and thought him as light of spirit as he seemed; not that he was not often earnest enough in his talks with my father, to whom he was wont to apply himself with a sort of intensity, suggesting ideas, and watching, with his nervous smile, my father's reception of them; plunging into deep matters, beyond my comprehension, dwelling there a few minutes, and then emerging again with a sparkle of wit; he was certainly very witty, and the wit was native and original, not memorized. When he got into the current of drollery, he would, as it were, set himself afire by his own sallies, and soar to astonishing heights, which had an irresistible contagion for the hearers; and he would sometimes, sitting at a table with pen and paper at hand, illustrate his whimsicalities with lightning sketches of immense cleverness, considering their impromptu character. I have preserved a sheet of letter-paper covered with such drawings. The conversation had got upon Byron, whom Mr. Story chose to ridicule; as he talked, he drew a head of "Byron as he thought he was," followed by one of "Byron as he was," and by another of "Byron as he might have been," showing a very pronounced negro type. Then he made a portrait of "Ada, sole daughter of

WILLIAM WETMORE STORY

my house and heart," and wrote under it, "Thy face was like thy mother's, my fair child!" a hideous, simpering miss, with a snub nose and a wooden mouth—"A poet's dream!" He also showed the appearance of the Falls of Terni, "as described by Byron," and added studies of infant phenomena, mother's darlings, a Presidential candidate, and other absurdities, accompanying it all with a running comment and imaginative improvisations which had the charm of genius in them, and made us ache with laughter, young and old alike. Such a man, nervous, high-strung, of fine perceptions and sensibilities, must inevitably pass through rapid and extreme alternations of feeling; and, no doubt, an hour after that laughing seance of ours, Mr. Story was plunged deep in melancholy. Yet surely his premonitions of evil were unfulfilled; Story lived long and was never other than fortunate. Perhaps he was unable to produce works commensurate with his conceptions; but unhappiness from such a cause is of a noble sort, and better than most ordinary felicities.

I remember very well the statue of Cleopatra while yet in the clay. There she sat in the centre of the large, empty studio, pondering on Augustus and on the asp. The hue of the clay added a charm to the figure which even the pure marble has not quite maintained. Story said that he never was present while the cast of one of his statues was being made; he could not endure the sight of the workmen throwing the handfuls of plaster at the delicate clay. Cleopatra was substantially finished, but Story was unwilling to let her go, and had no end of doubts as to the handling of minor details. The hand that rests on her knee—should the forefinger and thumb meet or be separated? If they were separated, it meant the relaxation of despair; if they met, she was still meditating defiance or revenge. After canvassing the question at great length with my father, he decided that they should meet; but when I saw the marble statue in the Metropolitan Museum the other day I noticed that they were separated. In the end the artist had preferred despair. Such things indicate the man's character, and, perhaps, explain his failure to reach the great heights of art. He could not trust a great idea to manage itself, but sought subtler expression through small touches, and thus, finally, lost the feeling of the larger inspiration. A little more of the calm, Greek spirit would have done him good.

He had many projects for other statues, which he would build up in fancy before my father and discuss with him. His words and gestures made the ideas he described seem actual and present, but he seldom got them into marble; he probably found, upon trial, that they did not belong to sculpture. He had the ambition to make marble speak not its own language merely, but those of painting and of poetry likewise; and when this proved impossible he was unhappy and out of conceit with himself. On the other hand, he did good work in poetry and in prose; but neither did these content him. After all, my father's observation hit the mark; things came too easy to him. Goethe speaks the word for him:

> " *Wer nie sein Brod mit thränen ass,*
> *Er kennt euch nicht. ihr ewige Mächte!*"

XVI

Drilled in Roman history—Lovely figures made of light and morning—What superb figures!—The breath and strength of immeasurable antiquity—Treasures coming direct from dead hands into mine—A pleasant sound of coolness and refreshment — Receptacles of death now dedicated to life—The Borghese is a forest of Ardennes —Profound and important communings—A smiling deceiver—Of an early-rising habit—Hauling in on my slack—A miniature cabinet magically made Titanic—"If I had a murder on my conscience"—None can tell the secret origin of his thoughts—A singularly beautiful young woman—She actually ripped the man open—No leagues of chivalry needed in Rome—A resident army—Five foot six—Corsets and padding—She was wounded in the house of her friends.

WE children had been drilled in Roman history, from Romulus to Cæsar, and we could, and frequently did, repeat by heart the *Lays of Ancient Rome* by Macaulay, which were at that period better known, perhaps, than they are now. Consequently, everything in Rome had a certain degree of meaning for us, and gave us a pleasure in addition to the intrinsic beauty or charm that belonged thereto. Our imagination thronged the Capitol with senators; saw in the Roman Forum the contentions of the tribunes and the patricians; heard

the populus Romanus roar in the Coliseum; beheld
the splendid processions of victory wind cityward
through the Arch of Titus; saw Cæsar lie bleeding
at the base of Pompey's statue; pondered over the
fatal precipice of the Tarpeian Rock; luxuriated
in the hollow spaces of the Baths of Caracalla; lost
ourselves in gorgeous reveries in the palace of the
Cæsars, and haunted the yellow stream of Tiber, beneath which lay hidden precious treasures and forgotten secrets.   And we were no less captivated by
the galleries and churches, which contained the preserved relics of the great old times, and were in
themselves so beautiful.   My taste for blackened
old pictures and faded frescoes was, indeed, even
more undeveloped than my father's; but I liked
the brilliant reproductions in mosaic at St. Peter's
and certain individual works in various places.   I
formed a romantic attachment for the alleged Bea-
trice Cenci of Guido, or of some other artist, and
was very sorry that she should be so unhappy,
though, of course, I was ignorant of the occasion of
her low spirits.   But I liked much better Guido's
large design of Aurora, partly because I had long
been familiar with it on the head - board of my
mother's bedstead.   Before her marriage she had
bought a set of bedroom furniture, and had painted
it a dull gold color, and on this surface she had
drawn in fine black lines the outlines of several
classical subjects, most of them from Flaxman; but
in the space mentioned she had executed an outline
of this glorious work of the Italian artist.   I knew

every line of the composition thoroughly; and, by-the-way, I doubt if a truer, more inspired copy of the picture was ever produced by anybody. But the color had to be supplied by the observer's imagination; now, for the first time, I saw the hues as laid on by the original painter. In spite of time, they were pure and exquisite beyond description; these lovely figures seemed made of light and morning. Another favorite picture of mine was the same artist's "Michael Overcoming the Evil One," and I even had the sense to like the painting better than the mosaic copy. Raphael's "Transfiguration" I also knew well from the old engraving of it that used to hang on our parlor wall from my earliest recollections; it still hangs yonder. But I never cared for this picture; it was too complicated and ingenious—it needed too much co-operation from the observer's mind. Besides, I had never seen a boy with anything approaching the muscular development of the epileptic youth in the centre. The thing in the picture that I most approved of was the end of the log in the little pool, in the foreground; it looked true to life.

But my delight in the statues was endless. It seems to me that I knew personally every statue and group in the Vatican and in the Capitol. Again and again, either with my parents, or with Eddy, or even alone, I would pass the warders at the doors and enter those interminable galleries, and look and look at those quiet, stained - marble effigies. My early studies of Flaxman had, in a measure, educated me towards appreciation of them. I never tired of them, as I did of the Cleopatras and the Greek Slaves. What superb figures! What power and grace and fleetness and athletic loins! The divine, severe Minerva, musing under the shadow of her awful helmet; the athlete with the strigil, resting so lightly on his tireless feet; the royal Apollo, disdaining his own victory; the Venus, half shrinking from the exquisiteness of her own beauty; the swaying poise of the Discobulus, caught forever as he drew his breath for the throw; the smooth-limbed, brooding Antinous; the terrible Laocoon, which fascinated me, though it always repelled me, too; the austere simplicity of the Dying Gladiator's stoop to death—the most human of all the great statues; the heads of heroic Miltiades, of Antony, of solitary Cæsar, of indifferent Augustus; the tranquil indolence of mighty Nile, clambered over by his many children—these, and a hundred others, spoke to me out of their immortal silence. I can conceive of no finer discipline for a boy; I emulated while I adored them. Power, repose, beauty, nobility, were in their message: "Do you, too, possess limbs and shoulders like ours!" they said to me; "such a bearing, such a spirit within!" I cannot overestimate even the physical good they did me; it was from them that I gained the inspiration for bodily development and for all athletic exercise which has, since then, helped me over many a rough passage in the path of life. But they also awoke higher ambitions and conferred finer benefits.

From these excursions into the ideal I would return to out-of-doors with another inexhaustible zest. That ardent, blue Roman sky and penetrating, soft sunshine filled me with life and joy. The breath and strength of immeasurable antiquity emanated from those massive ruins, which time could deface but never conquer. Emerald lizards basked on the hot walls; flowers grew in the old crevices; butterflies floated round them; they were haunted by spirits of heroes. There is nothing else to be compared with the private, intimate, human, yet sublimated affection which these antique monuments wrought in me. They were my mighty brothers, condescending to my boyish thoughts and fancies, smiling upon me, welcoming me, conscious of my love for them. Each ruin had its separate individuality for me, so that to-day I must play with the Coliseum, to-morrow with the Forum, or the far-ranging arches of the Aqueduct, or the Temple of Vesta. Always, too, my eyes were alert for treasures in the old Roman soil, coming, as it seemed, direct from the dead hands of the vanished people into mine. I valued the scraps that I picked up thus more than anything to be bought in shops or seen in museums. These bits of tinted marble had felt the touch of real Romans; their feet had trodden on them, on them their arms had rested, their hands had grasped them. Two thousand years had dulled the polish of their surfaces; I took them to the stone - workers, who made them glow and bloom again—yellow, red, black, green, white.

They were good-natured but careless men, those marble-polishers, and would sometimes lose my precious relics, and when I called for them would say, every day, "Domane — domane," or try to put me off with some substitute—as if a boy could be deceived in such a matter! I once found in the neighborhood of a recent excavation a semi-transparent tourmaline of a cool green hue when held to the light; it had once been set in the ring of some Roman beauty. It had, from long abiding in the earth, that wonderful iridescent surface which ancient glass acquires. Rose, my sister, picked up out of a rubbish heap a little bronze statuette, hardly three inches high, but, as experts said, of the best artistic period. Such things made our Roman history books seem like a tale of yesterday, or they transported us back across the centuries, so that we trod in the footsteps of those who had been but a moment before us.

In those warm days, after our walks and explorations, Eddy and I, and little Hubert, who sometimes was permitted to accompany us, though we deemed him hardly in our class, would greatly solace ourselves with the clear and gurgling fountains which everywhere in Rome flow forth into their marble and moss-grown basins with a pleasant sound of coolness and refreshment. Rome without her fountains would not be Rome; every memory of her includes them. In the streets, in the piazzas, in the wide pleasaunces and gardens, the fountains allure us onward, and comfort us for our weariness.

In the Piazza d' Espagna, at the foot of the famous steps, was that great, boat-shaped fountain whose affluent waters cool the air which broods over the wide, white stairway; and not far away is the mighty Trevi, with its turmoil of obstreperous figures swarming round bragging Neptune, and its cataract of innumerable rills welling forth and plunging downward by devious ways to meet at last in the great basin, forever agitated with baby waves lapping against the margins. These, and many similar elaborate structures, are for the delight of the eye; but there are scores of modest fountains, at the corners of the ways, in shady or in sunny places, formed of an ancient sarcophagus receiving the everlasting tribute of two open-mouthed lion-heads, or other devices, whose arching outgush splashes into the receptacle made to hold death, but now immortally dedicated to the refreshment of life. It was at these minor fountains that we quenched our boyish thirst, each drinking at the mouth of a spout; and when we discovered that by stopping up one spout with our thumb the other would discharge with double force, we played roguish tricks on each other, deluging each other at unawares with unmanageable gushes of water, till we were forced to declare a mutual truce of honor. But what delicious draughts did we suck in from those lion-mouths into our own; never elsewhere did water seem so sweet and revivifying. And then we would peer into the transparent depths of the old sarcophagus, with its fringes of green, silky moss waving slightly with the movement of the water, and fish out tiny-spired water-shells; or dip in them the bits of ancient marbles we had collected on our walk, to see the hues revive to their former splendor. Many-fountained Rome ought to be a cure for wine-bibbers; yet I never saw an Italian drink at these springs; they would rather quaff the thin red and white wines that are sold for a few *baiocchi* at the inns.

The Pincian Hill and the adjoining grounds of the Borghese Palace came at length to be our favorite haunts. The Borghese is a delectable spot, as my father remarks in one of those passages in his diary which was afterwards expanded into the art-picture of his romance. "Broad carriage-ways," he says, "and wood-paths wander beneath long vistas of sheltering boughs; there are ilex-trees, ancient and sombre, which, in the long peace of their lifetime, have assumed attitudes of indolent repose; and stone-pines that look like green islands in the air, so high above earth are they, and connected with it by such a slender length of stem; and cypresses, resembling dark flames of huge, funereal candles. These wooded lawns are more beautiful than English park scenery; all the more beautiful for the air of neglect about them, as if not much care of men were bestowed upon them, though enough to keep wildness from growing into deformity, and to make the whole scene like nature idealized—the woodland scenes the poet dreamed of—a forest of Ardennes, for instance. These lawns and gentle valleys are beautiful, moreover, with fountains flashing into marble basins, or gushing like natural cascades from rough rocks; with bits of architecture, as pillared porticos, arches, columns, of marble or granite, with a touch of artful ruin on them; and, indeed, the pillars and fragments seem to be remnants of antiquity, though put together anew, hundreds of years old, perhaps, even in their present form, for weeds and flowers grow out of the chinks and cluster on the tops of arches and porticos. There are altars, too, with old Roman inscriptions on them. Statues stand here and there among the trees, in solitude, or in a long range, lifted high on pedestals, moss-grown, some of them shattered, all grown gray with the corrosion of the atmosphere. In the midst of these sunny and shadowy tracts rises the stately front of the villa, adorned with statues in niches, with busts, and ornamented architecture blossoming in stone-work. Take away the malaria, and it might be a very happy place.''

Here was a playground for boys of imaginative but not too destructive proclivities, such as the world hardly furnishes elsewhere. But much of my enjoyment of it I ascribe to my friend Eddy. My conversation with no person since then has rivalled the profundity and importance of my communings with his sympathetic soul. We not only discussed our future destinies and philosophical convictions, but we located in these delicious retreats the various worlds which we purposed to ex-

PENCIL SKETCHES IN ITALY, BY MRS. NATHANIEL
HAWTHORNE

plore and inhabit during the next few hundred years. Here we passed through by anticipation all our future experiences. Sometimes we were accompanied by other boys; but then our visits lost their distinction; we merely had good times in the ordinary way of boys; we were robber barons, intrenched in our strongholds, and attacked by other robbers; or we ran races, or held other trials of strength and activity, or we set snares for the bright-colored fishes which lurked in some of the fountains. The grounds were occasionally invaded by gangs of Italian boys, between whom and ourselves existed an irreconcilable feud. We could easily thrash them in the Anglo-Saxon manner, with nature's weapons; but they would ambush us and assail us with stones; and once one of them struck at me with a knife, which was prevented from entering my side only by the stout leather belt which I chanced to wear. We denounced these assassins to the smiling *custode* of the grounds, and he promised, smilingly, to bar the entrance to them thenceforth; but he was a smiling deceiver; our enemies came just the same. After all, we would have regretted their absence; they added the touch of peril to our chronic romance which made it perfect. It is forty-four years since then. Are there any other Borghese Gardens to come for me in the future, I wonder?

There was a rough pathway along the banks of the Tiber, extending up the stream for two or three miles, as far as the Ponte Molle, where the cork-trees grew, and farther, for aught I know. This was a favorite walk of mine, because of the fragments of antique marbles to be found there, and also the shells which so mysteriously abounded along the margin, as shown by the learned conchological author hereinbefore cited. And, being of an early rising habit, it was my wont to get up long before breakfast and tramp up and down along the river for an hour or two, thinking, I suppose, as I gazed upon the turbulent flood, of brave Horatius disdainfully escaping from the serried hosts of Lars Porsena and false Sextus, or of Cæsar and Cassius buffeting the torrent on a "dare," and with lusty sinews flinging it aside. There were also lovely effects of dawn upon the dome of St. Peter's, and the redoubtable mass of St. Angelo, with its sword-sheathing angel. Moreover, sunrise, at twelve years of age, is an exhilarating and congenial phenomenon. And I painted my experiences in colors so attractive that our Ada Shepard was inflamed with the idea of accompanying me on my rambles. She was a child in heart, though so mature in intellect, and her spirit was valiant, though her flesh was comparatively infirm. It was my custom to set out about five o'clock in the morning, and Miss Shepard promised to be ready at that hour. But after keeping awake most of the night in order not to fail of the appointment, she fell asleep and dreamed only of getting up; and, after waiting for her for near an hour, I went without her. She was much mortified at her failure, and suggested a plan to insure her punctuality, in which I readily agreed to collaborate. When she went to bed she attached a piece of string to one of her toes, the other end of the filament being carried underneath doors and along passages to my own room. I was instructed to haul in on my slack at the proper hour; and this I accordingly did, with good-will, and was at once made conscious that I had caught something, not only by the resistance which my efforts encountered, but by the sound of cries of feminine distress and supplication, heard in the distance. However, my companion appeared in due season, and we took our walk, which, she declared, fulfilled all the anticipations which my reports had led her to form. Nevertheless, I cannot remember that we ever again made the expedition together; it is a mistake to try to repeat a perfect joy.

It seems to me that I must have been a pretty constant visitor at St. Peter's. The stiff, heavy, leathern curtain which protects the entrance having been strenuously pushed aside (always with remembrance of Corinne's impossible act of grace and courtesy in holding it aside with one hand for Lord Neville), the glorious interior expanded, mildly radiant, before me. As has been the case with so many other observers, the real magnitude of the spectacle did not at first affect me; the character of the decoration and detail prevented the impression of greatness; it was only after many times traversing that illimitable pavement, and after frequent comparisons with ordinary human measurements of the aerial heights of those arches and that dome, that

303

one comes to understand, by a sort of logical compulsion, how immense it all is. It is a miniature cabinet magically made titanic; but the magic which could transform inches into roods could not correspondingly enlarge the innate character of the ornament; so that, instead of making the miniature appear truly vast, it only makes us seem unnaturally small. Still, after all criticisms, St. Peter's remains one of the most delightful places in the world; its sweet sumptuousness and imperial harmonies seem somehow to enter into us and make us harmonious, rich, and sweet. The air that we inhale is just touched with the spirit of incense, and mellowed as with the still memories of the summers of five hundred years ago. The glistening surfaces of the colored marbles, dimmed with faint, fragrant mists, and glorified with long slants of brooding sunshine, soothe the eye like materialized music; and the soft twinkle of the candles on the altars, seen in daylight, has a jewel-like charm. As I look back upon it, however, and contrast it with the cathedrals of England, the total influence upon the mind of St. Peter's seems to me voluptuous rather than religious. It is a human palace of art more than a shrine of the Almighty. A prince might make love to a princess there without feeling guilty of profanation. St. Peter himself, sitting there in his chair, with his highly polished toe advanced, is a doll for us to play with. On one occasion I was in the church with my father, and the great nave was thronged with people and lined with soldiers, and down the midst went slowly a gorgeous procession, with Pope Pio Nono borne aloft, swayingly, the triple crown upon his head. He blessed the crowd, as he passed along, with outstretched hand. One can never forget such a spectacle; but I was not nearly so much impressed in a religious sense as when, forty years later, I stood in the portals of a Mohammedan mosque in Central India and saw a thousand turbaned Moslems prostrate themselves with their foreheads in the dust before a voice which proclaimed the presence of the awful, unseen God.

My father enjoyed the church more after each visit to it. But it was the confessionals and their significance that most interested him. "What an institution the confessional is! Man needs it so, that it seems as if God must have ordained it." And he dwells upon the idea with remarkable elaboration and persistence. Those who have followed the painful wanderings of heart-oppressed Hilda to the carven confessional in the great church, where she found peace, will recognize the amply unfolded flower of this seed. What I supposed to be my notion of St. Peter's looking like the enlargement of some liliputian edifice is also there, though I had forgotten it till I myself reread the pages. In this book of my memories, which is also the book of my forgettings, I must walk to and fro freely, if I am to walk at all. None can tell the secret origin of his thoughts.

Besides the monumental and artistic features of Rome, the human side of it appealed to me. There was something congenial in the Romans, and, indeed, in the Italians generally, so that I seemed to be renewing my acquaintance with people whom I had partly forgotten. I picked up the conversational language with unusual ease, perhaps owing to the drilling in Latin which my father had given me; and I liked the easy, objectless ways of the people, and the smiles which so readily took the place of the sallow gravity which their faces wore in repose. But it was the Transteverini women who chiefly attracted me; they wore an antique costume familiar enough in paintings, and they claimed to be descendants of the ancient race; they had the noble features and bearing which one would have looked for in such descendants, at all events. Looking in their dark, haughty eyes, one seemed to pass back through the terrible picturesqueness of mediæval Italy, with its Borgias and Bella Donnas, its Lorenzos and Fornarinas, to the Rome of Nero, Augustus, Scipio, and Tarquin. Eddy and I would sometimes make excursions across the river to Transtevere, and stroll up and down those narrow streets, imagining all manner of suitable adventures and histories for the inhabitants, stalking there in their black and scarlet and yellow habiliments, and glancing imperially from under the black brows of their dark countenances. One afternoon during the carnival I was in a dense crowd in the piazza towards the lower end of the Corso, and found myself pushed into the neighborhood of a singularly beautiful young woman of this class, dressed in the height of her fashion, who was slowly making her way in my direction through the press. All at once a man, smartly clad in the garb of recent civilization, stepped in front of her and said something to her; what it was I knew not. She drew herself back, as from something poisonous or revolting, and the expression of her face became terrible. At the same time her right hand went swiftly to the masses of her sable hair, and as swiftly back again, armed with the small, narrow dagger which these women wear by way of hair-pin. Before the unhappy creature who had accosted her knew what was happening, she thrust the dagger, with a powerful movement—while her white teeth showed, set edge to edge, through her drawn lips—deep into his body. · As he collapsed forward she drew the weapon upward, putting the whole strength of her body into the effort, and actually ripped the man open. Down he fell at her feet. There was a score or more of Roman citizens within arm's-reach of her at the moment; no one spoke, still less attempted to restrain her. On the contrary, as she turned they respectfully opened a way for her through the midst of them, and none made an offer to assist the dying wretch who lay writhing and faintly coughing on the cobble-stone pavement of the piazza. I was soon elbowed quietly away from the spot where he lay; I caught a glimpse of the crimson head-dress of his slayer passing away afar amid the crowd; presently the cocked hat of a gendarme appeared from another direction, advancing slowly against manifest obstructions; everybody seemed to get in his way, without appearing to intend it. Such was the attitude towards assassination of the Roman people in those days. I have often thought over the incident since then. Their sympathy is with private vengeance, never with ordained statute law. They love to use the poniard and to see it used, and will do their best to shield the users. Pity for the victim they have none; they assume that he has his deserts. For that matter, my own sympathies, filled though I was with horror at the spectacle of actual murder done before my eyes, were wholly with the savage beauty, and not with the fatuous creature who had probably insulted her. It is needless to say that the women of Transtevere were not so often called upon to resent insults as are the ladies of New York and other American cities. They did not wait for policemen or for "leagues of chivalry" to avenge them.

Towards the French soldiers I was cordially disposed. Their dark-blue tunics and baggy, red peg-tops were never out of sight, and though I had seen troops in England, and had once observed the march of a British regiment in Liverpool going to embark for the Crimea (whence, I believe, very few of this particular regiment returned), yet the conception of a resident army first came to me in Rome. About the French army of those days still hovered the lustre bestowed upon it by the deeds of the great Napoleon, which their recent exploits in the Crimea had not diminished. There were among

them regiments of fierce and romantic looking
zouaves, with Oriental complexions and semi-bar-
baric attire, marching with a long swing, and appearing savage and impetuous enough to annihilate
anything; and there was also a brigade, the special
designation of which I have forgotten, every man
of which was a trained athlete, and whose drill was
something marvellous to witness. But the average
French soldier was simply a first-class soldier, good-
natured, light-hearted, active, trim, and efficient;
in height averaging not more than five foot six;
carrying muskets which seemed out of proportion
large, though they handled them lightly enough,
and wearing at their sides a short sword, like the
sword of ancient Rome, which was also used as a
bayonet. There was always a drill or a march in
progress somewhere, and sentinels paced up and
down before the palaces. The officers were immensely impressive; the young ones had wasp
waists, surpassing those of the most remorseless
belles of fashion; and the old ones were, *en revanche*,
immensely stout in that region, as if outraged nature were resolved to assert herself at last. But,
young or old, their swords were sun-bright and
lovely to behold—I used to polish my own little
weapon in vain in the attempt to emulate them.
Hopelessly envious was I, too, of the heroic chests
of these warriors (not knowing them to be padded,
as the waists were corseted), and I would swell out
my own little pectoral region to its utmost extent
as I walked along the streets, thereby, though I

knew it not, greatly benefiting my physical organism. Of course I had no personal commerce with the officers, but the rank and file fraternized with me and my companions readily; there was always a number of them strolling about Rome and its environs on leave, in pairs or groups, and they were just as much boys as we were. They would let me heft their short, strong swords, and when they understood that I was gathering shells they would climb lightly about the ruins, and bring me specimens displayed in their broad, open palms. Our conversation was restricted to few words and many grunts and gestures, but we understood one another and were on terms of gay *camaraderie*. A dozen years afterwards, when there was war between France and Germany, my sympathies were ardently with the former, and great were my astonishment and regret at the issue of the conflict. Man for man, and rightly led and managed, I still believe that Gaul could wipe up the ground with the Teuton, without half trying. But there were other forces than those of Moltke and Bismarck fighting against poor France in that fatal campaign. She was wounded in the house of her friends.

XVII

WHILE my father was conscientiously making acquaintance with the achievements of old-time art,
modern artists were trying to practise their skill
on him; he had already sat to Cephas Giovanni
Thompson, and he was now asked to contribute his
head to the studio of a certain Miss Lander, late of
Salem, Massachusetts, now settled, as she intended,
permanently in Rome. "When I dream of home,"
she told him, "it is merely of paying a short visit
and coming back here before my trunk is unpack-
ed." Miss Lander was not a painter, but a sculptor, and, in spite of what my father had said against
the nude in sculpture, I think he liked clay and
marble as a vehicle of art better than paint and

canvas. At all events, he consented to give her sittings. He was interested in the independence of her mode of life, and they got on very comfortably together; the results of his observation of her appear in the references to Hilda's and Miriam's unhampered ways of life in *The Marble Faun*. She had, as I recall her, a narrow, sallow face, sharp eyes, and a long chin. She might have been thirty years old. Unlike Miss Harriet Hosmer, who lived not far away, Miss Lander had no attractiveness for us children. I have reason to think, too, that my father's final opinion of her was not so favorable as his first one. Except photographs, no really good likeness of my father was ever taken; the portrait painted in Washington, in 1862, by Leutze, was the least successful of them all. The best, in my opinion, was an exquisitely wrought miniature of him at the age of thirty, which I kept for a long time, till it was stolen by a friend in London in 1880.

Paul Akers, a Maine Yankee, with the twang of his native place still strong in him after ten years in Rome, was another sculptor of our acquaintance; he was very voluble, and escorted us about Rome, and entertained us at his own studio, where he was modelling his best group, "The Drowned Fisherboy," as he called it. The figure is supposed to be lying at the bottom of the sea, face upward, with a fragment of rock supporting on its sharp ridge the small of the back—a most painful and uncomfortable attitude, suggesting that even in death there could be no rest for the poor youth. Mr. Akers was rather sharply critical of his more famous brother-artists, such as Greenough and Gibson, and was accused by them, apparently not wholly without justification, of yielding too much to the influence of other geniuses in the designing of his groups. But he was a sensible and obliging little personage, and introduced us to the studios of several of his fellow-artists in Rome, some of which were more interesting than his own.

Bright little Miss Harriet Hosmer, with her hands in her jacket-pockets, and her short hair curling up round her velvet cap, struts cheerfully forth out of the obscurity of the past in my memory; her studio, I think, adjoined that of Gibson, of whom I remember nothing whatever. Her most notable production at that time was a Puck sitting on a toadstool, with a conical shell of the limpet species by way of a cap; he somehow resembled his animated and clever creator. Miss Hosmer's face, expressions, gestures, dress, and her manifestations in general were perfectly in keeping with one another; there never was a more succinct and distinct individuality; she was wholly unlike anybody else, without being in the least unnatural or affected. Her social manner was of a persistent jollity; but no doubt she had her grave moments or hours, a good and strong brain, and a susceptibility to tragic conceptions, as is shown by the noble figure of her Zenobia. This figure I saw in clay in her studio during our second season in Rome. Miss Hosmer's talk was quick, witty, and pointed; her big eyes redeemed her round, small-featured face from triviality; her warm heart glowed through all she said and did. Her studio was a contrast to the classicality of Gibson's, whose influence, though she had studied under him during her six years' residence in Rome, had affected her technique only, not her conceptions or aims in art. We all liked her much. She was made known to us, I believe, through the medium of grave, wise, humorous Sarah Clarke, the sister of the James Freeman Clarke who married my mother to my father, and who, twenty-two years later, read over my father the burial service. Sarah Clarke was often abroad; she was herself an admirable artist in water-color, and was always a dear friend of my mother's. After we had returned to Concord, in 1860, Miss Hosmer wrote to us, and one of her letters has been preserved; I quote it, because it is like her:

"MY DEAR MRS. HAWTHORNE,—It is not unlikely that you may be somewhat surprised to hear from me; but after you have received the four dozen letters which, sooner or later, I intend writing you, you will cease to be so. I begin at the present moment with the first of the forty-eight, partly for business and partly for pleasure. Reversing, then, the order of things which some unknown but well-regulated-minded individual considered to be correct, I will go in for pleasure first, under which head I seek information respecting the health and well-being of all members of your family. It seems cruel that you should go off to the glorious Republic when there are other places in Rome besides the Piazza Poli. Now that you are safely out of it, I must try to persuade you that it was the most unhealthy place in the whole city, not only because I really believe it to be so, but that malaria may not be mingled and cherished with *every* remembrance of this delicious, artistic, fleay, malarious paradise. But I suppose little short of a miracle would transport you here again, not only because Una is probably becoming the size of Daniel Lambert, in her native air, but because Julian is probably weaving a future President's chair out of the rattans he is getting at school. However that may be, the result is the same, I fear, as to your getting back to the Gods and the Fleas; and I must look forward to a meeting in America. Well, as that carries me over the ocean, in my mind's eye, Mrs. Hawthorne, the business clause of my epistle is suggested —and it is this: I have just had a letter from my best of friends, Mr. Crow, of St. Louis [she had studied anatomy in St. Louis before coming to Rome], who has been passing the summer in New York and Boston, and he writes: ' They are talking in Boston of a monument to the memory of Mr. Horace Mann, and I have said to one of the active men engaged in it that if you could have the commission I would subscribe handsomely towards it.' Now, it occurred to me that perhaps you or yours might have an opportunity of saying a good word for me, in which case I would have you know how pleased and grateful I should be. You may not have the occasion offered you, but if it chances, I commend myself to you *distintamente*, and trust to your good-nature not to consider me *pushing* for having suggested it. I send this through our well-beloved Sarah Clarke, and hope it will arrive before 1861. When you have nothing better to do, pray give me a line, always in care of Pakenham & Hooker. Good-bye, dear Mrs. Hawthorne — my best love to Mr. Hawthorne and the chicks—and the best wish I can make is that you are all as fat as yours always affectionately,

"HARRIET HOSMER."

All the influence which my father and mother possessed was given to Miss Hosmer's cause, but some other person got the commission. I remember, too, that my mother, at Mrs. Mann's request, was at great pains to make drawings for the face of the statue which now confronts from the slopes of Beacon Hill the culture and intelligence of Boston, which Horace Mann did so much to promote. But he was not a subject which accommodated itself readily to the requirements of plastic art. There is a glimpse of Miss Hosmer in one of my father's diaries, which I will reproduce, for the sake of indicating his amused and benevolent attitude towards her. "She had on," says he, "a neat little jacket, a man's shirt-bosom, and a cravat with a brooch in it; her hair is cut short, and curls jauntily round her bright and smart little physiognomy; and, sitting opposite me at table, I never should have imagined that she terminated in a petticoat any more than in a fish's tail. However, I do not mean to speak disrespectfully of Miss Hosmer, of whom I think very favorably; but, it seems to me, her reform of the female dress begins with its least objectionable part, and is no real improvement."

One evening we visited Miss Bremer, the novelist, of Sweden, who was then near the end of her foreign travels, which had begun with her visit to America in 1849. She had met my father in Lenox, and had written of him in the book of her travels. She was a small woman, with a big heart and broad mind, packed full of sense, sentiment, and philanthropy. She had an immense nose, designed, evidently, for some much larger person; her conversation in Eng-

lish, though probably correct, was so oddly accent-
ed that it was difficult to follow her. She was a
very lovable little creature, then nearing her six-
tieth year. Most of her voluminous literary work
was done. Her house in Rome was near the Capitol and the Tarpeian Rock; and after we had for-
gathered with her there for a while, she accompanied us forth—the moon being up—to see the
famous precipice. It was to this incident that we
owe the scene in *The Marble Faun*, the most visibly
tragic in my father's writings. "The court-yard,"
he writes in his notes, "is bordered by a parapet,
leaning over which we saw a sheer precipice of the
Tarpeian Rock, about the height of a four-story
house; not that the precipice was a bare face of
rock, but it appeared to be cased in some sort of
cement, or ancient stone-work, through which the
primeval rock, here and there, looked grimly and
doubtfully. Bright as the Roman moonlight was,
it would not show the front of the wall, or rock, so
well as I should have liked to see it, but left it pretty
much in the same degree of dubiety and half-
knowledge in which the antiquarians leave most of
the Roman ruins. Perhaps this precipice may have
been the Traitor's Leap; perhaps it was the one on
which Miss Bremer's garden verges; perhaps neither
of the two. At any rate, it was a good idea of the
stern old Romans to fling political criminals down
from the very height of the Capitoline Hill on which
stood the temples and public edifices, symbols of
the institutions which they sought to violate."

But there was no tragic suggestion in our little party, conducted about by the prattling, simple, affectionate little woman, so homely, tender, and charitable. "At parting," wrote my father, "she kissed my wife most affectionately on each cheek, 'because,' she said, 'you look so sweetly'; and then she turned towards myself. I was in a state of some little tremor, not knowing what might be about to befall me, but she merely pressed my hand, and we parted, probably never to meet again. God bless her good heart, and every inch of her little body, not forgetting her red nose, big as it is in proportion to the rest of her! She is a most amiable little woman, worthy to be the maiden aunt of the whole human race!"

Venerable Mrs. Jameson, author of a little library of writings on Italian art, was likewise of our company occasionally; and she evinced a marked liking for my father, which was remarkable, inasmuch as he was able to keep no sort of pace with her in her didactic homilies, which were delivered with a tranquil, *ex-cathedra* manner, befitting one who was *the* authority on her subject; one would no more have thought of questioning her verdicts than those of Ruskin; but I should have liked to see the latter and her together, with a difference between them. Her legs were less active than her mind, and most of our expeditions with her were made in carriages, from which she dispensed her wisdom placidly as we went along, laying the dust of our ignorance with the droppings of her erudition, like a watering-cart. However, she so far condescended from her altitudes as to speak very cordially of my father's books, for which he expressed proper acknowledgment; and she had a motherly way of holding his hand in hers when he took leave of her, and looking maternally in his face, which made him somewhat uneasy. "Were we to meet often," he remarked, "I should be a little afraid of her embracing me outright—a thing to be grateful for, but by no means to be glad of!" We drove one day to some excavations which had just been opened near the tomb of Cecilia Metella, outside the walls of Rome. Both Christian and Roman graves had been found, and they had been so recently discovered that, as my father observed, there could have been very little intervention of persons (though much of time) between the departure of the friends of the dead and our own visit. The large, excavated chambers were filled with sarcophagi, beautifully sculptured, and their walls were ornamented with free-hand decoration done in wet plaster, a marvellous testimony to the rapid skill of the artists. The sarcophagi were filled with the bones and the dust of the ancient people who had once, in the imperial prime of Rome, walked about her streets, prayed to her gods, and feasted at her banquets. My father remarked on the fact that many of the sarcophagi were sculptured with figures that seemed anything but mournful in their demeanor; but Mrs. Jameson said that there was almost always, in the subject chosen, some allusion to death, instancing the story of Meleager, an Argonaut, who, I think, slew the Calydonian boar, and afterwards his two uncles, who had tried to get the boar's hide away from Meleager's beloved Atalanta; whereupon the young hero was brought to death by his mother, who in turn killed herself. It is one of the most thorough-going of the classic tragedies, and was a favorite theme for the sculptors of sarcophagi. Certainly, in the sarcophagi of the Vatican the bas-reliefs are often scenes of battle, the rush of men and horses, and the ground strewn with dead; and in others, a dying person seems to be represented, with his friends weeping along the sides of the sarcophagus; but often, too, the allusion to death, if it exists at all, is very remote. The old Romans, like ourselves, had individual ways of regarding the great change; according to their mood and faith, they were hopeful or despairing. But death is death, think of it how we will.

I think it was on a previous occasion that I went with my father, afoot, along this same mighty Appian Way, beside which rise so many rounded structures, vast as fortresses, containing the remains of the dead of long ago, and culminating in the huge mass of the Cecilia Metella tomb, with the mediæval battlements on its summit. And it was on that walk that we met the calf of *The Marble Faun*: "A well-grown calf," my father says in his notes, "who seemed frolicsome, shy, and sociable all at the same time; for he capered and leaped to one side, and shook his head, as I passed him, but soon came galloping behind me, and again started aside when I looked round." How little I suspected then (or the bull-calf either, for that matter) that he was to frolic his way into literature, and go gambolling down the ages to distract the anxious soul of the lover of Hilda! Another walk of ours was to the huge, green mound of the Monte Testaccio; it was, at that period, pierced by numerous cavities, in the dark coolness of which stores of native wines were kept; and they were sold to customers at the rude wooden tables in front of the excavations, in flasks shaped like large drops of water, protected with plaited straw. When, nowadays, in New York or other cities here, I go to an Italian restaurant, I always call for one of these flasks, and think, as I drink its contents, of that afternoon with my father. It was the first time I had been permitted to taste a fermented liquor. I liked it very much, and got two glasses of it; and when we rose to depart I was greatly perplexed, and my father was vastly tickled, to discover a lack of coherence between my legs and my intentions. It speedily passed off, for the wines are of the lightest and airiest description; but when, a little later on in life, I came to read that Horatian verse describing how, turning from barbaric splendors such as the Persians affect, he binds his brows with simple myrtle, and sips, beneath the shadow of his garden bower, the pure vintage of the native grape, I better appreciated the poetry of the theme from having enjoyed that Testaccionesque experience.

It was in Rome, too, that I first came in contact with death. It aroused my liveliest curiosity, but, as I remember, no alarm; partly, I suspect, because I was unable to believe that there was anything real in the spectacle. The scene has been woven into the texture of the Italian romance; it is there described almost as it actually presented itself to the author's observation. A dead monk of the Capuchin order lay on a bier in the nave of their church, and while we looked at him a stream of blood flowed from his nostrils. We went down afterwards, I recollect, into the vaults, and saw the fine, Oriental loam in which the body was to lie; and it seems to me there were arches and other architectural features composed of skulls and bones of long-dead brothers of the order. He must have been a fantastic and saturnine genius who first suggested this idea.

Another subterranean expedition of ours was to the Catacombs, the midnight passages of which seemed to be made of bones, and niches containing the dust of unknown mortality, which were duskily revealed in the glimmer of our *moccoli* as we passed along in single file. Sometimes we came to chambers, one of which had in it a bier covered with glass, in which was a body which still preserved some semblance of the human form. There were occasional openings in the vaulted roof of the corridors, but for the most part the darkness was Egyptian, and for a few moments a thrill of anxiety was caused by the disappearance either of my sister Una or of Ada Shepard; I forget which. They were soon found, but the guide read us a homily upon the awful peril of lifelong entombment which encompassed us. But the air was dry and cool, and the whole adventure, from my point of view, enjoyable.

Again, we went down a long flight of steps somewhere near the Forum, till we reached a pitch-black place, where we waited till a guide came up from still lower depths, down into which we followed him — each with a *moccolo* — till we felt level earth or stone beneath our feet, and stood in what I suppose is as lightless a hole as can exist in nature. It was wet, too, and the smell of it was deadly and dismal. This, however, was the prison in which the old Romans used to confine important prisoners, such as Jugurtha and the Apostle Peter; and here they were strangled to death or left to starve. It was the Mamertine Prison. I did not like it. I also recall the opening of an oubliette in the castle of San Angelo, which affected me like a nightmare. Before leaving Concord, in 1853, I had once tumbled through a rotten board into a well, dug by the side of the road ages before, and had barely saved myself from dropping to the bottom, sixty feet below, by grabbing the weeds which grew on the margin of the hole. I was not much scared at the moment; but the next day, taking my father to the scene of the accident, he remarked that had I fallen in I never could have got out again; upon which I conceived a horror of the well which haunts me in my dreams even to this day. Only a tuft of grass between me and such a fate! I was, therefore, far from comfortable beside the oubliette, and was glad to emerge again into the Roman sunshine.

One night we climbed the Pincian Hill, and saw, far out across Rome, the outlines of St. Peter's dome in silver light. While we were thinking that nothing could be more beautiful, all of a sudden the delicate silver bloomed ðut into a golden glory, which made everybody say, "Oh!" Was it more beautiful or not? Theoretically, I prefer the silver illumination; but, as a matter of fact, I must confess that I liked the golden illumination better. We were told that the wonder was performed by convicts, who lay along the dome and applied their matches to the lamps at the word of command, and that, inasmuch as the service was apt to prove fatal to the operators, these convicts were allowed certain alleviations of their condition for doing it. I suppose it is done by electricity now, and the convicts neither are killed nor obtain any concessions. Such are the helps and hindrances of civilization!

Shortly after this, on a cool and cloudy night, I was down in the Piazza del Popolo and saw the fireworks, the only other pyrotechnic exhibition I had witnessed having been a private one in Rock Park, which, I think, I have described. This Roman one was very different, and I do not believe I have ever since seen another so fine. The whole front of the Pincian was covered with fiery designs, and in the air overhead wonderful fiery serpents and other de-

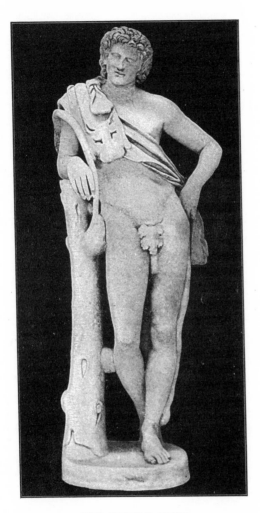

THE MARBLE FAUN

vices skimmed, arched, wriggled, shot aloft, and detonated. A boy accepts appearances as realities; and these fireworks doubtless enlarged my conceptions of the possibilities of nature, and substantiated the fables of the enchanters.

The Faun of Praxiteles, as the world knows, attracted my father, though he could not have visited it often; for both in his notes and in his romance he makes the same mistake as to the pose of the figure: "He has a pipe," he says in the former, "or some such instrument of music in the hand which rests upon the tree, and the other, I think, hangs carelessly by his side." Of course, the left arm, the one referred to, is held akimbo on his left hip. That my father's eyes were, however, already awake to the literary and moral possibilities of the Faun is shown by his further observations, which are much the same as those which appear in the book. "The whole person," he says, "conveys the idea of an amiable and sensual nature, easy, mirthful, apt for jollity, yet not incapable of being touched by pathos. The Faun has no principle, nor could comprehend it, yet is true and honest by virtue of his simplicity; very capable, too, of affection. He might be refined through his feelings, so that the coarser, animal part of his nature would be thrown into the background, though liable to assert itself at any time. Praxiteles has only expressed the animal part of the nature by one (or, rather, two) definite signs—the two ears, which go up in a little peak, not likely to be discovered on slight inspection, and, I suppose, they are covered with downy fur. A tail is probably hidden under the garment. Only a sculptor of the finest imagination, most delicate taste, and sweetest feeling would have dreamed of representing a faun under this guise; and, if you brood over it long enough, all the pleasantness of sylvan life, and all the genial and happy characteristics of the brute creation, seem to be mixed in him with humanity—trees, grass, flowers, cattle, deer, and unsophisticated man." This passage shows how much my father was wont to trust to first impressions, and even more on the moral than on the material side. He recognized a truth in the first touch—the first thought—which he was wary of meddling with afterwards, contenting himself with slightly developing it now and then, and smoothing a little the form and manner of its presentation. The finest art is nearest to the most veritable nature—to such as have the eye to see the latter aright.

Rome, like other ancient cities which have fallen from the positive activity of their original estate, has one great advantage over other places which one wishes to see (like London, for instance), that the whole business of whoever goes there, who has any business whatever, is to see it; and when the duty-sights have been duly done, the sight-seer then first begins to live his true life in independence and happiness, going where he lists, staying no longer than he pleases, and never knowing, when he sallies forth in the morning, what, or how many, or how few things he will have accomplished by nightfall.

THAT QUIET, OMNIVOROUS GLANCE

The duty to see is indeed the death of real vision;
the official cicerone leads you anywhere but to the
place or thing that you are in the mood to behold
or understand. But with his disappearance the
fun and the pageant begin; one's eyes are at last
opened, and beauty and significance flow in through
every pore of the senses. It is in this better phase
of his Roman sojourn that I picture my father; he
trudges tranquilly and happily to and fro, with no
programme and no obligations, absorbing all things
with that quiet, omnivorous glance of his; pausing
whenever he takes the fancy, and contemplating
for moments or minutes whatever strikes his fancy;
often turning aside from egregious spectacles and
giving his attention to apparent trifles, to the mere
passing show; pondering on the tuft of flowers in a
cranny of the Coliseum wall, on the azure silhouette
of the Alban Mountains, on the moss collected on
the pavement beneath the aperture in the roof of
the Pantheon, on the picturesque deformity of old,
begging Beppo on the steps of the Piazza d' Espagna. I am trudging joyously beside him, hanging
on to his left hand (the other being occupied with
his hook-headed cane), asking him innumerable
questions, to which he comfortably, or abstractedly,
or with humorous impatience, replies; or I run on
before him, or lag behind, busy with my endless occupation of picking up things to me curious and
valuable, and filling with them my much-enduring
pockets; in this way drinking in Rome in my own
way, also, and to my boyish advantage. He tells

me tales of old Rome, always apposite to the occasion; draws from me, sometimes, my private views as to persons, places, and scenes, and criticises those views in his own terse, arch, pregnant way, the force and pertinency whereof are revealed to me only in my later meditations upon them. It is only after one has begun to deal in this way with Rome that its magic and spell begin to work upon one; and they are never to be shaken off. Anxiety and pain may be mingled with them, as was the case with my father before we said our final farewell to the mighty city; but it is thereby only the more endeared to one. Rome is one of the few central facts of the world, because it is so much more than a fact. Byron is right—it is the city of the soul.

On one of the last evenings of our first season we went to the Thompsons', and were there shown, among other things, a portfolio of sketches. There is in *The Marble Faun* a chapter called "Miriam's Studio," in which occurs a reference to a portfolio of sketches by Miriam herself; the hint for it may have been taken from the portfolio of Mr. Thompson, though the sketches themselves were of a very different quality and character. The latter collection pleased me, because I was just beginning to fill an album of my own with such lopsided attempts to represent real objects, and yet more preposterous imaginative sallies as my age and nature suggested. My father was interested in them on account of the spiritual vigor which belongs to the artist's first vision of his subject. In their case, as well as in his own, he felt that it was impossible, as Browning put it, to "recapture that first, fine, careless rapture." But the man of letters has an advantage over the man of paint and canvas in the matter of being able to preserve the original spirit in the later, finished design.

Towards the close of this first season in Rome the Bryants came to town, and the old poet, old in aspect even then, called on us; but he was not a childly man, and we youngsters stood aloof and contemplated with awe his white, Merlin beard and tranquil but chilly eyes. Near the end of May William Story invited us to breakfast with him; the Bryants and Miss Hosmer and some English people were there; and I understood nothing of what passed except the breakfast, which was good, until, at the end of the session, my father and Story began to talk about the superstition as to Friday, and they agreed that, of course, it was nonsense, but that, nevertheless, it did have an influence on both of them. It probably has an influence on everybody who has ever heard of it. Many of us protest indignantly that we don't believe in it, but the protest itself implies something not unlike believing.

Finally, on the 24th of May, we left our Pincian palace, and got into and on the huge *vettura* which was to carry us to Florence, a week's journey. It was to be one of the most delightful and blessed of our foreign experiences; my father often said that he had enjoyed nothing else so much, the *vetturino* (who happened to be one of the honestest and sweetest-tempered old fellows in Italy) taking upon himself the entire management of everything, down to ordering the meals and paying the tolls, thus leaving us wholly unembarrassed and free from responsibility while traversing a route always historically and generally scenically charming. But we were destined, on the threshold of the adventure, to undergo one of those evil quarters of an hour which often usher in a period of special sunshine; for we were forced into a desperate conflict with our servant-girl, Lalla, and her mother over a question of wages. The girl had done chores for us during our residence at the Palazzo Larazani, and had seemed to be a very amiable little personage; she was small, slim, and smiling, and, though dirty and inefficient, was no worse, so far as we could discover, than any other Roman servant-girl. When we had fixed on the date of our departure, Lalla had been asked how much warning she wanted; she replied, a fortnight; which, accordingly, was given her, with a few days thrown in for good measure. But when the day arrived she claimed a week's more pay, and her old mother had a bill of her own for fetching water.

According to my observation, travelling Americans have little or no conscience; to avoid trouble they will submit to imposition, not to mention their habit of spoiling tradesmen, waiters, and other foreign attendants by excessive tips and payments. But my father and mother, though apt enough to make liberal bargains, were absolutely incorruptible and immovable when anything like barefaced robbery was attempted upon them; and they refused to present Lalla and her mother with a single *baioccho* more than was their due. Moreover, the *patrone*, or proprietor, of the Palazzo had mulcted them some six *scudi* for Lalla's profuse breakages of glass and crockery during our stay.

It was early morning when we set out, and only the faithful Thompsons were there to bid us farewell. Lalla and her tribe, however, were on hand, and violently demanded the satisfaction of their iniquitous claims. "No!" said my father, and "No!" said my mother, like the judges of the Medes and Persians. Thereupon the whole House of Lalla, but Lalla and her mother especially, gave us an example of what an Italian can do in the way of cursing an enemy. Ancient forms of malediction, which had been current in the days of the early Roman kings, were mingled with every damning invention that had been devised during the Middle Ages, and ever since then; and they were all hurled at us in shrill, screaming tones, accompanied by fell and ominous gestures and inarticulate yells of superheated frenzy. Nothing could surpass the volubility of this cursing, unless it were the animosity which prompted it; no crime that anybody, since Cain slew Abel, had or could have committed deserved a tenth part of the calamities and evil haps which this preposterous family called down upon our heads, who had committed no crime at all, but quite the contrary. When, in after-years, I heard Booth, as Richelieu, threaten "the curse of Rome" upon his opponents, I shuddered, wondering whether he had any notion what the threat meant. Through it all my mother's ordinarily lovely and peaceful countenance expressed a sad but unalterable determination; and my father kept smiling in a certain dangerous way that he sometimes had in moments of great peril or stress, but said nothing; while Mr. Thompson indignantly called upon the cursers to cease and to beware, and my dear friend Eddy looked distressed to the verge of tears. He squeezed my hand as I got into the *vettura*, and told me not to mind—the Lalla people were wicked, and their ill-wishes would return upon their own heads. A handful of ten-cent pieces, or their Roman equivalent, would have stopped the whole outcry and changed it into blessings; but I think my father would not have yielded had the salvation of Rome and of all Italy depended upon it. His eyes gleamed, as I have seen them do on one or two other occasions only, as we drove away, with the screams pursuing us, and that smile still hovered about his mouth. But we drove on; Gaetano cracked his long whip, our four steeds picked up their feet and rattled our vehicle over the Roman cobble-stones; we passed the Porta del Popolo, and were stretching along, under the summer sunshine, upon the white road that led to Florence. It was a divine morning; the turmoil and the strife were soon forgotten, and for a week thenceforward there was only unalloyed felicity before us. Poor, evil-invoking Lalla had passed forever out of our sphere.

XVIII

In Othello's predicament—Gaetano—Crystals and snail-shells—Broad, flagstone pavements—Fishing-rods and blow-pipes — Ghostly yarns — Conservative effects of genius—An ideal bust and a living one—The enigma of spiritualism — A difficult combination to overthrow — The dream-child and the Philistine—Dashing and plunging this way and that—Teresa screamed for mercy—Grapes and figs and ghostly voices—My father would have settled there—Kirkup the necromancer—A miraculous birth—A four-year-old medium—The mysterious touch—An indescribable horror—Not even a bone of her was left—Providence takes very long views.

THE railroad which now unites Rome with Florence defrauds travellers of some of the most agreeable scenery in Italy, and one of the most time-honored experiences; and as for the beggars who infested the route, they must long since have perished of inanition—not that they needed what travellers gave them in the way of alms, but that, like Othello, their occupation being gone, they must cease to exist. Never again could they look forward to pestering a tourist; never exhibit a withered arm or an artistic ulcer; never mutter anathemas against the obdurate, or call down blessings upon the profuse. What was left them in life? And what has become

of the wayside inns, and what of the *vetturinos?*   A
man like Gaetano, by himself, was enough to mod-
ify radically one's conception of the possibilities
of the Italian character.   In appearance he was a
strong-bodied Yankee farmer, with the sun-burned,
homely, kindly, shrewd visage, the blue jumper, the
slow, canny ways, the silent perception and enjoyment of humorous things, the infrequent but timely
speech.   It was astonishing to hear him speaking
Italian out of a mouth which seemed formed only
to emit a Down-East drawl and to chew tobacco.
In disposition and character this son of old Rome
was, so far as we, during our week of constant and
intimate association with him, could judge, absolutely without fault; he was mild, incorruptible, and
placid, as careful of us as a father of his children,
and he grew as fond of us as we were of him, so that
the final parting, after the journey was done, was
really a moving scene.   I have found the tribe of
cabbies, in all countries, to be, as a rule, somewhat
cantankerous and sinister; but Gaetano compen-
sated for all his horse-driving brethren.   To be sure,
vettura driving is not like cabbing, and Gaetano was
in the habit of getting out often and walking up the
hills, thus exercising his liver.   But he must have
been born with a strong predisposition to goodness,
which he never outgrew.

Save for a few showers, it was fine weather all the
way, and a good part of the way was covered on
foot by my father and me; for the hills were many,
and the winding ascents long, and we would alight

334

and leave the slow-moving vehicle, with its ponderous freight, behind us, to be overtaken perhaps an hour or two later on the levels or declivities. Gaetano was a consummate whip, and he carried his team down the descents and round the exciting turns at a thrilling pace, while the yards of whiplash cracked and detonated overhead like a liliputian thunder-storm. On the mountain-tops were romantic villages, surrounding rock - built castles which had been robber strongholds centuries before, and we traversed peaceful plains which had been the scenes of famous Roman battles, and whose brooks had run red with blood before England's history began. We paused a day in Perugia, and received the Bronze Pontiff's benediction; the silent voices of history were everywhere speaking to the spiritual ear. Meanwhile I regarded the trip as being, primarily, an opportunity to collect unusual snail-shells; and we passed through a region full of natural crystals, some of them of such size as to prompt my father to forbid their being added to our luggage. I could not understand his insensibility. Could I have had my way, I would have loaded a wain with them. I liked the villages and castles, too, and the good dinners at the inns, and the sound sleeps in mediæval beds at night; but the crystals and the snail-shells were the true aim and sustenance of my life. My mother and sister sketched continually, and Miss Shepard was always ready to tell us the story of the historical features which we encountered; it astounded me to note how much she knew about things which she had never before seen.

One afternoon we drove down from surrounding heights to Florence, which lay in a golden haze characteristic of Italian Junes in this latitude. Powers, the sculptor, had promised to engage lodgings for us, but he had not expected us so soon, and meanwhile we put up at a hotel near by, and walked out a little in the long evening, admiring the broad, flagstone pavements and all the minor features which made Florence so unlike Rome. The next day began our acquaintance with the Powers family, who, with the Brownings, constituted most of the social element of our sojourn.

Powers had an agreeable wife, two lovely daughters, and a tall son, a few years older than I, and a pleasant companion, though he could not take the place of Eddy Thompson in my heart. He was clever with his hands, and soon began to make fishing-rods for me, having learned of my predilection for the sport. There were no opportunities to fish in Florence; but the rods which Bob Powers produced were works of art, straight and tapering, and made in lengths, which fitted into one another—a refinement which was new to me, who had hitherto imagined nothing better than a bamboo pole. Bob finally confided to me that he straightened his rods by softening the wood in steam; but I found that they did not long retain their straightness; and, there being no use for them, except the delight of the eye, I presently lost interest in them. Then

Bob showed me how to make blow-pipes by pushing out the pith from the stems of some species of bushy shrub that grew outside the walls. He made pellets of clay from his father's studio; and I was deeply affected by the long range and accuracy of these weapons. We used to ensconce ourselves behind the blinds of the front windows of Powers's house, and practise through the slats at the passersby in the street. They would feel a smart hit and look here and there, indignant; but, after a while, seeing nothing but the innocent fronts of sleepy houses, would resume their way. Bob inherited his handiness from his father, who seemed a master of all crafts, a true Yankee genius. He might have made his fortune as an inventor had he not happened to turn the main stream of his energy in the direction of sculpture. I believe that the literary art was the only one in which he did not claim proficiency, and that was a pity, because Powers's autobiography would have been a book of books. He was a Swedenborgian by faith, but he also dabbled somewhat in spiritualism, which was having a vogue at that time, owing partly to the exploits of the American medium Home. Marvellous, indeed, were the ghostly yarns Powers used to spin, and they lost nothing by the physical appearance of the narrator, with his tall figure, square brow, great, black eyes, and impressive gestures; his voice, too, was deep and flexible, and could sink into the most blood-curdling tones. My recollection is that Powers was always clad in a long, linen pinafore, reaching from his chin to his feet, and daubed with clay, and on his head a cap made either of paper, like a baker's, or, for dress occasions, of black velvet. His homely ways and speech, which smacked of the Vermont farm as strongly as if he had just come thence, whereas in truth he had lived in Florence, at this time, about twenty years, and had won high fame as a sculptor, tempted one to suspect him of affectation—of a pose; and there is no doubt that Powers was aware of the contrast between his physical presentment and his artistic reputation, and felt a sort of dramatic pleasure in it. Nevertheless, it would be unjust to call him affected; he was a big man, in all senses of the term, and his instinct of independence led him to repudiate all external polish and ear-marks of social culture, and to say, as it were, "You see, a plain Vermont countryman can live half a lifetime in the centre of artificial refinement and rival by the works of his native genius the foremost living artists, and yet remain the same simple, honest old sixpence that he was at home!" It was certainly a more manly and wholesome attitude than that of the ordinary American foreign resident, who makes a point of forgetting his native ways and point of view, and aping the habits and traits of his alien associates. And, besides, Powers had such an immense temperament and individuality that very likely he could not have modified them successfully even had he been disposed to do so.

His daughters, as I have said, were lovely creat-

HIRAM POWERS

ures. Powers was at this time modelling an ideal bust of a woman, and one day I went into his studio expecting to find Bob there, but the studio was empty but for the bust, which I now had an opportunity to contemplate at my ease for the first time. I thought it very beautiful, and there was something about the face which reminded me of somebody, I could not decide who. Just then a portière in the doorway parted, and in came a living bust, a reality in warm flesh and blood, compared with which the ideal seemed second-rate. It belonged to one of Powers's daughters, who had come for a sitting; she was serving as her father's model. Upon seeing the unexpected boy, fixed there in speechless admiration, the young lady uttered a scream and vanished. I now knew whom the face of the clay effigy reminded me of, and afterwards when I saw beautiful statues I thought of her, and shook my head.

My father and Powers took a strong fancy to each other, and met and talked a great deal. As I just said now, spiritualism was a fad at that time, and Powers was pregnant with marvels which he had either seen or heard of, and which he was always ready to attempt to explain on philosophical grounds. My father would listen to it all, and both believe it and not believe it. He felt, I suppose, that Powers was telling the truth, but he was not persuaded that all the truth was in Powers's possession, or in any one else's. Powers also had a great deal to say concerning the exoteric and esoteric truths of sculpture; his racy individuality marked it all. He would not admit that there was any limit to what might be done with marble; and when my father asked him one day whether he could model a blush on a woman's cheek, he said, stoutly, that the thing was possible. My father, as his manner was with people, went with the sculptor as far as he chose to carry him, accepting all his opinions and judgments, and becoming Powers, so far as he might, for the time being, in order the better to get to the root of his position. And then, afterwards, he would return to his own self, and quietly examine Powers's assertions and theories in the dry light. My father was two men, one sympathetic and intuitional, the other critical and logical; together they formed a combination which could not be thrown off its feet.

We had already met the Brownings in London; but at this period they belonged in Italy more than anywhere else, and Florence formed the best setting for the authors both of *Aurora Leigh* and of *Sordello*. They lived in a villa called Casa Guidi, and with them was their son, a boy younger than myself, whom they called Pennini, though his real name was something much less fastidious. Penni, I believe, used to be an assistant of Raphael early in the sixteenth century, and Pennini may have been nicknamed after him. His mother, who was an extravagant woman on the emotional and spiritual plane, made the poor little boy wear his hair curled in long ringlets down his back, and clad him in a fancy costume of black velvet, with knickerbockers and black silk stockings; he was homely of face, and looked "soft," as normal boys would say. But his parents were determined to make an ideal dream-child of him, and, of course, he had to submit. I had the contempt for him which a philistine boy feels for a creature whom he knows he can lick with one hand tied behind his back, and I had nothing whatever to say to him. But Pennini was not such a mollycoddle and ass as he looked, and when he grew up he gave evidence enough of having a mind and a way of his own. My mother took him at his mother's valuation, and both she and my father have expressed admiration of the whole Browning tribe in their published journals. Mrs. Browning seemed to me a sort of miniature monstrosity; there was no body to her, only a mass of dark curls and queer, dark eyes, and an enormous mouth with thick lips; no portrait of her has dared to show the half of it. Her hand was like a bird's claw. Browning was a lusty, active, energetic person, dashing and plunging this way and that with wonderful impetus and suddenness; he was never still a moment, and he talked with extraordinary velocity and zeal. There was a mass of wild hair on his head, and he wore bushy whiskers. He appeared very different twenty years later, when I met him in London, after his wife's death; he was quiet and sedate, with close-cut silvery hair and pointed beard, and the rather stout, well-dressed figure of a British gentleman of the sober middle class. It is difficult to harmonize either of these outsides with the poet within—that remarkable imagination, intellect, and analytical faculty which have made him one of the men of the century. There was a genial charm in Browning, emphasized, in this earlier time, with a bewildering vivacity and an affluence of courtesy. In his mature phase he was still courteous and agreeable when he chose to be so, but was also occasionally supercilious and repellent, and assiduously cultivated smart society. I once asked him, in 1879, why he made his poetry so often obscure, and he replied, frankly, that he did so because he couldn't help it; the inability to put his thoughts in clear phrases had always been a grief to him. This statement was, to me, unexpected, and it has a certain importance.

After a few weeks in Casa Bella, opposite Powers's house, Florence grew so hot that we were glad of an opportunity to rent the Villa Montauto, up on the hill of Bellosguardo, less than a mile beyond the city gate. The villa, with two stories and an attic, must have been nearly two hundred feet long, and was two or three rooms deep; at the hither end rose a tower evidently much older than the house attached to it. Near the foot of the tower grew an ancient tree, on a projecting branch of which we soon had a swing suspended, and all of us children did some very tall swinging. There was a little girl of ten belonging to the estate, named Teresa, an amiable, brown-haired, homely little personage. We admitted her to our intimacy, and swung her in the swing till she screamed for mercy. The road from

Florence, after passing our big iron gate on the east, continued on westward, beneath the tower and the parapet of the grounds; beyond extended the wide valley of the Arno, with mountains hemming it in, and to the left of the mountains, every evening, Donati's comet shone, with a golden sweep of tail subtending twenty degrees along the horizon. The peasant folk regarded it with foreboding; and I remember seeing in the book shops of Rome, before we left, pamphlets in both Italian and English, with such titles as "Will the great comet, now rapidly approaching, strike the earth?" It did not strike the earth, but it afforded us a magnificent spectacle during our stay in Montauto, and the next year it was followed by war between Austria and France and the evacuation of Venice.

The elevation of Bellosguardo sloped from the villa north and east, and this declivity was occupied by a *podere* of some dozen acres, on which grew grape-vines, olive and fig trees. Every morning, about ten o'clock, the peasants on the estate would come in loaded with grapes, which they piled up on a large table in the reception-hall on the ground floor. We ate them by handfuls, but were never able to finish them. Between times we would go out among the fruit trees and devour fresh figs, luscious with purple pulp. I had three or four rooms to myself at the western extremity of the house; they were always cool on the hottest days. There I was wont to retire to pursue my literary labors; I was still writing works on conchology. My sister Una had rooms on the ground floor, adjoining the chapel. They were haunted by the ghost of a nun, and several times the candle which she took in there at night was moved by invisible hands from its place and set down elsewhere. Ghostly voices called to us, and various unaccountable noises were heard now and then, both within and without the house; but we children did not mind them, not having been bred in the fear of spirits. Indeed, at the instance of Mrs. Browning, who was often with us, we held spirit séances, Miss Shepard being the medium, though she mildly protested. Long communications were written down, but the sceptics were not converted, nor were the believers discouraged. " I discern in the alleged communications from my wife's mother," wrote my father, "much of her own beautiful fancy and many of her preconceived ideas, although thinner and weaker than at first hand. They are the echoes of her own voice, returning out of the lovely chambers of her heart, and mistaken by her for the tones of her mother."

Almost every day some of us made an incursion into Florence. The town itself seemed to me more agreeable than Rome; but the Boboli Gardens could not rival the Borghese, and the Pitti and Uffizi galleries were not so captivating as the Vatican and the Capitol. However, the Cascine and the Lung' Arno were delightful, and the Arno, shallow and placid, flowing through the midst of the city, was a fairer object than the muddy and turbulent Tiber. Men and boys bathed along the banks in the afternoons and evenings; and the Ponte Vecchio, crowded with grotesque little houses, was a favorite promenade of mine. There was also a large marketplace, where the peasant women sold the produce of their farms. My insatiable appetite for such things prompted me often to go thither and eat everything I had money to buy. One day I consumed so many fresh tomatoes that I had a giddiness in the back of my head, and ate no more tomatoes for some years. But the place I best liked was the great open square of the Palazzo Vecchio, with the statues of David and of Perseus under the Loggia dei Lanzi, a retreat from sun and rain; and the Duomo and Giotto's Campanile, hard by. The pavements of Florence, smooth as the surface of stone canals, were most soothing and comfortable after the relentless, sharp cobble-stones of Rome; the low houses that bordered them seemed to slumber in the hot, still sunshine. What a sunshine was that! Not fierce and feverish, as in the tropics, but soft and intense and white. Who would not live in Florence if he could? I think my father would have settled there but for his children, to whom he wished to give an American education. The thought was often in his mind; and he perhaps cherished some hope of returning thither later in life, and letting old age steal gently upon him and his wife in the delicious city. But the Celestial City was nearer to him than he suspected.

There was a magical old man in Florence named Kirkup, an Englishman, though he had dwelt

abroad so many years that he seemed more Florentine than the Florentines themselves. He had
known, in his youth, Byron, Shelley, Hunt, and
Edward Trelawney. After that famous group was
disparted, Kirkup, having an income sufficient for
his needs, came to Florence and settled there. He
took to antiquarianism, which is a sort of philtre,
driving its votaries mildly insane, and filling them
with emotions which, on the whole, are probably
more often happy than grievous. But Kirkup, in
the course of his researches into the past, came upon
the books of the necromancers, and bought and
studied them, and began to practise their spells and
conjurations; and by-and-by, being a great admirer
and student of Dante, that poet manifested himself to him in his lonely vigils and told him many
unknown facts about his career on earth, and incidentally revealed to him the whereabouts of the
now-familiar fresco of Dante on the wall of the
Bargello Chapel, where it had been hidden for ages
beneath a coat of whitewash. In these occult researches, Kirkup, of course, had need of a medium,
and he found among the Florentine peasants a
young girl, radiantly beautiful, who possessed an
extraordinary susceptibility to spiritual influences.
Through her means he conversed with the renowned
dead men of the past times. But one day Regina
(such was the girl's name), much to the old man's
surprise, gave birth to a child. She herself died, in
Kirkup's house, soon after, and on her death-bed
she swore a solemn oath on the crucifix that the

baby's father was none other than Kirkup himself.
The poor old gentleman had grown so accustomed
to believing in miracles that he made little ado
about accepting this one also; he received the child
as his daughter, and made provision for her in his
will.   No one had the heart or thought it worth
while to enlighten him as to certain facts which
might have altered his attitude; but it was well
known that Regina had a lover, a handsome young
Italian peasant, much more capable of begetting
children than of taking care of them afterwards.

These interesting circumstances I did not learn
until long after Florence had receded into the distance in my memory.   But one afternoon, with my
father and mother, I entered the door of a queer old
house close to the Ponte Vecchio; I was told that it
had formerly been a palace of the Knights Templars.
We ascended a very darksome flight of stairs, and a
door was opened by a strange little man. He may
have been, at that time, some seventy years my
senior, but he was little above my height; he had
long, soft, white hair and a flowing white beard;
his features bore a resemblance to those of Bulwer
Lytton, only Bulwer never lived to anything like
Mr. Kirkup's age. Old as he was, our host was
very brisk and polite, and did the honors of his
suite of large rooms with much grace and fantastic
hospitality.   Dancing about him, and making
friends freely with us all meanwhile, was the little
girl, Imogen by name, who was accredited as the
octogenarian's offspring. She was some four or five

years of age, but intellectually precocious, though
a complete child, too. Mr. Kirkup said that she,
like her beautiful mother, was a powerful medium,
and that he often used to communicate through her
with her mother, who would seem to have kept
her secret even after death. The house was stuffed
full of curiosities, but was very dirty and cobwebby;
the pictures and the books looked much in need of
a caretaker. The little child frolicked and flitted
about the dusky apartments, or seated herself like
a butterfly on the great tomes of magic that were
piled in corners. Nothing could be stronger or
stranger than the contrast between her and this
environment. My father wrote it all down in his
journal, and it evidently impressed his imagination;
and she and Kirkup himself—*mutatis mutandis*—
appear in *Dr. Grimshawe's Secret*, and again, in a
somewhat different form, in *The Dolliver Romance*.
There was even a Persian kitten, too, to bear little
Imogen company. But no fiction could surpass the
singularity of this withered old magician living
with the pale, tiny sprite of a child of mysterious
birth in the ghost-haunted rooms of the ancient
palace.

It seemed as if the world of the occult were making a determined attack upon us during this Florentine sojourn; whichever way we turned we came in
contact with something mysterious. In one of my
father's unpublished diaries he writes, in reference
to the stories with which he was being regaled by
Powers, the Brownings, and others, that he was

reminded " of an incident that took place at the old manse, in the first summer of our marriage. One night, about eleven o'clock, before either my wife or I had fallen asleep (we had been talking together just before), she suddenly asked me why I had touched her shoulder? The next instant she had a sense that the touch was not mine, but that of some third presence in the chamber. She clung to me in great affright, but I got out of bed and searched the chamber and adjacent entry, and, finding nothing, concluded that the touch was a fancied one. My wife, however, has never varied in her belief that the incident was supernatural and connected with the apparition of old Dr. Harris, who used to show himself to me daily in the reading-room of the Boston Athenæum. I am still incredulous both as to the doctor's identity and as to the reality of the mysterious touch. That same summer of our honeymoon, too, George Hillard and his wife were sitting with us in our parlor, when a rustling as of a silken robe passed from corner to corner of the room, right among my wife and the two guests, and was heard, I think, by all three. Mrs. Hillard, I remember, was greatly startled. As for myself, I was reclining on the sofa at a little distance, and neither heard the rustle nor believed it."

Nevertheless, such things affect one in a degree. Here is a straw to show which way the wind of doctrine was blowing with my father: We were in Siena immediately after the date of our Florentine residence, and he and I, leaving the rest of the family at our hotel, sallied forth in quest of adventures. "We went to the cathedral," he writes, "and while standing near the entrance, or about midway in the nave, we saw a female figure approaching through the dimness and distance, far away in the region of the high altar; as it drew nearer its air reminded me of Una, whom we had left at home. Finally, it came close to us, and proved to be Una herself; she had come, immediately after we left the hotel, with Miss Shepard, and was looking for objects to sketch. It is an empty thing to write down, but the surprise made the incident stand out very vividly." Una was to pass near the gates of the next world a little while later, and doubtless my father often during that dark period pictured her to himself as a spirit.

To make an end of this subject, I will quote here my father's account of a story told him by Mrs. Story when we were living in Rome for the second time. The incident of the woman's face at the carriage window reappears in *The Marble Faun*. "She told it," he says, "on the authority of Mrs. Gaskell, to whom the personages were known. A lady, recently married, was observed to be in a melancholy frame of mind, and fell into a bad state of health. She told her husband that she was haunted with the constant vision of a certain face, which affected her with an indescribable horror, and was the cause of her melancholy and illness. The physician prescribed travel, and they went first to Paris, where the lady's spirits grew somewhat better, and the vision haunted her less constantly. They purposed going to Italy, and before their departure from Paris a letter of introduction was given them by a friend, directed to a person in Rome. On their arrival in Rome the letter was delivered; the person called, and in his face the lady recognized the precise reality of her vision. By-the-bye, I think the lady saw this face in the streets of Rome before the introduction took place. The end of the story is that the husband was almost immediately recalled to England by an urgent summons; the wife disappeared that very night, and was recognized driving out of Rome, in a carriage, in tears, and accompanied by the visionary unknown. It is a very foolish story, but told as truth. Mrs. Story also said that in an Etruscan tomb, on the Barberini estate, the form and impression, in dust, of a female figure were discovered. Not even a bone of her was left; but where her neck had been there lay a magnificent necklace, all of gold and of the richest workmanship. The necklace, just as it was found (except, I suppose, for a little furbishing), is now worn by the Princess Barberini as her richest adornment. Mrs. Story herself had on a bracelet composed, I think, of seven ancient Etruscan *scarabei* in carnelian, every one of which has been taken from a separate tomb, and on one side of each was engraved the signet of the person to whom it had belonged and who had carried it to the grave with him. This bracelet would make a good connecting link for a series of Etruscan tales, the more fantastic the better!"

On the first day of October, 1859, we left Florence by railway for Siena on our way back to Rome. There had been no drawbacks to our enjoyment of the city and of our villa and of the people we had met. We departed with regret; had we stayed on there, instead, and not again attempted the fatal air of the Seven Hills, our after chronicles might have been very different. But we walk over precipices with our eyes open, or pass safely along their verge in the dark, and only the Power who made us knows why. Providence takes very long views.

Siena is distant from Florence, in a direct line, not
more than fifty miles, but the railway turns the
western flank of the mountains, and kept us full
three hours on the trip. I had long been familiar
with a paint in my color-box called Burnt Sienna,
and was now much interested to learn that it was
made of the yellow clay on which the city of Siena
stands; and when I discovered for myself that
this clay, having formed the bed of some antedilu-
vian ocean, was full of fossil shells, I thought that
Siena was a place where I would do well to spend
one of my lifetimes. The odd, parti-colored architecture of the town did not so much appeal to me,
and certainly the streets and squares were less attractive in themselves than either the Roman or
the Florentine ones. The shells were personally

ugly, but they were shells, and fossils into the bargain, and they sufficed for my happiness.

The Storys had a villa in Siena, and my father certainly had in the back part of his mind an idea of settling there, or elsewhere in Italy, now or later; but after ten days we were on our travels again. There were no ruins to be seen, that I remember, but many churches and frescoes and old oil-paintings, which I regarded with indifference. Mediæval remains did not attract me like classic ones. It was here that Story drew the caricatures which I have already spoken of, and from the windows of the room, as the twilight fell, we could see the great comet, then in its apogee of brilliance. Where will the world be when it comes again? We had rooms at the Aquila Nera, looking out on the venerable, gray Palazzo Tolomei. The narrow streets were full of people; the steepness and irregularity of the thoroughfares of the city produced a feeling of energy and activity in the midst of the ancient historic peace. Siena is, I believe, built about the crater of an extinct volcano. The old brick wall of the city was still extant, running up hill and down, and confining the rusty heaps of houses within its belt. There were projecting balconies, crumbling with age, and irregular arcades, resembling tunnels hewn out of the solid rock. From the windows of our sitting-room in the hotel we commanded the piazza in front of the Palazzo Tolomei, with a pillar in the midst of it, on which was a group of Romulus and Remus suckled by the wolf, the tradition of

the city being that it was founded during the epoch
of the Roman kings. My mother made a sketch of
this monument in her little sketch-book, and my
father, according to a common custom of his, sat for
an hour at the window one day and made a note of
every person who passed through the little square,
thus getting an idea of the character of the local
population not otherwise obtainable. I can imagine that, were one born in Siena, one might conceive
an ardent affection for it; but, in spite of its picturesqueness, it never touched my heart like Rome
or Florence, or even London or Paris. I left it
without regret, but with specimens of its fossils in
my pockets.

It often happens with miracles that they occur in
doubles or trebles, in order, I suppose, to suggest to
us that they may be simply instances of an undiscovered law. Gaetano was a miracle, and he was
followed by Constantino, who, though of an altogether different human type, was of no less sweet
and shining a nature than the other. He was a
grand, noble, gentle creature, and my mother soon
dubbed him "The Emperor," though it may be
doubted whether the original emperor of that name
was as good a man as ours; he was certainly not
nearly so good-looking. He was only the driver of
our *vettura* from Siena to Rome, but there was a
princely munificence in his treatment of us that
made us feel his debtors in an indefinitely greater
sum than that which technically discharged our obligations. He was massive, quiescent, oxlike, with

great, slow-moving, black eyes. He had the air of extending to us the hospitalities of Italy, and our journey assumed the character of a royal progress. He was especially devoted to my small sister Rose, and often, going up the hills, he would have her beside him on foot, one of his great hands clasping hers, while with the other he wielded the long whip that encouraged the horses. His garments were of the humblest fashion, but he so wore them as to make them seem imperial robes. My mother caught an excellent likeness of him as he sat before her on the driver's seat. The second trip was as enjoyable as the first, though it was two or three days shorter. The route was west of our former one, passing through Radicofani, incrusted round its hill-top; and Bolsena, climbing backward from the poisonous shore of its beautiful lake; and Viterbo, ugly and beggar-ridden, though famous forever on account of the war for Galiana waged between Viterbo and Rome. In the front of an old church in the town I saw the carved side of her sarcophagus, incorporate with the wall. She was the most beautiful woman in the world in her day, and in the fight for the possession of her her townsmen overcame the Romans, but the latter were permitted, as a salve for their defeat, to have one final glimpse of Galiana as they marched homeward without her. From a window in a tower of one of the gates of the city, therefore, her heavenly face looked forth and shed a farewell gleam over the dusty, defeated ranks of Rome as they filed past, up-looking. The

tale is as old as the incident itself, but I always love
to recall it; there is in it something that touches the
soul more inwardly than even the legend of Grecian
Helen.

By the middle of October we were back again in
Rome, and though we were now in new lodgings,
the feeling was that of getting home after travels.
The weather was fine, and we revisited the familiar
ruins and gardens, and renewed our acquaintance
with our favorite statues and pictures with fresh
enjoyment. Eddy Thompson and I found each other better friends than ever—we had written each
other laborious but sincerely affectionate letters
during our separation—and he and I, with one
or more favored companions sometimes, perambu-
lated Rome incessantly, and felt that the world had
begun again. But by the 1st of November there
came to pass an untoward change, and our rejoicing
was changed to lamentation. First, my father himself had a touch of malaria, which clouded his view
of all outward things; and then my sister Una,
disregarding the law which provides that all persons must be in-doors in Rome by six o'clock in the
evening, caught the veritable Roman fever, and
during four months thereafter a shadow brooded
over our snug little lodgings in the Piazza Poli. "It
is not a severe attack," my father wrote at the beginning, "yet it is attended by fits of exceeding
discomfort, occasional comatoseness, and even delirium to the extent of making the poor child talk
in rhythmic measure, like a tragic heroine—as if

357

the fever lifted her feet off the earth; the fever being seldom dangerous, but is liable to recur on slight occasion hereafter." But, as it turned out, Una's attack was of the worst kind, and she sank and sank, till it seemed at last as if she must vanish from us altogether. Eddy and I held melancholy consultations together, for Eddy, besides being my special crony and confidant, had allowed himself to conceive a heroic and transcendental passion for my sister—one of the antique, Spenserian sort—and his concern for her condition was only less than mine. So we went about with solemn faces, comforting each other as best we might. I remember, when the crisis of the fever was reached, taking him into a room and closing the door, and there imparting to him the news that Una might not recover. We stared drearily into each other's faces, and felt that the world would never again be bright for us. Boys are whole-souled creatures; they feel one thing at a time, and feel it with their might.

However, Una safely passed her crisis, thanks mainly to the wonderful nursing of her mother, and by carnival-time was able to be out again and to get her share of sugar-plums and flowers. But my mother was exhausted by her ceaseless vigils in the sick-room, and my father, as I have before intimated, never recovered from the long-drawn fear; it sapped his energies at the root, and the continued infirmity of Una's health prevented what chance there might have been of his recuperation. Yet for the moment he could find fun and pleasure in

the carnival, and he felt as never before the searching beauty of the Borghese, the Pincian, and the
galleries.   He was also comforted by the companionship of his friend Franklin Pierce, who, his Presidential term over, had come to Europe to get the
scent of Washington out of his garments.   There
was a winning, irresistible magnetism in the presence of this man.   Except my father, there was no
man in whose company I liked to be so much as in
his.   I had little to say to him, and demanded nothing more than a silent recognition from him; but
his voice, his look, his gestures, his gait, the spiritual
sphere of him, were delightful to me; and I suspect
that his rise to the highest office in our nation was
due quite as much to this power or quality in him
as to any intellectual or even executive ability that
he may have possessed.   He was a good, conscientious, patriotic, strong man, and gentle and tender
as a woman.   He had the old-fashioned ways, the
courtesy, and the personal dignity which are not
often seen nowadays.   His physical frame was immensely powerful and athletic; but life used him
hard, and he was far from considerate of himself,
and he died at sixty-five, when he might, under
more favorable conditions, have rounded out his
century.

My father had written nothing, not even his journal, during the period of Una's illness; but he began
to work again now, being moved thereto not only
as a man whose nature is spontaneously impelled
to express itself on the imaginative side, but also in

order to recoup himself for some part of the loss of the ten thousand dollars which he had loaned to John O'Sullivan, which, it was now evident, could never be repaid. His first conception of the story of *The Marble Faun* had been as a novelette; but he now decided to expand it so as to contain a large amount of descriptive matter; and although the strict rules of artistic construction may have been somewhat relaxed in order to admit these passages, there is no doubt that the book gained thereby in value as a permanent addition to literature, the plot, powerful though it is, being of importance secondary to the creation of an atmosphere which should soften the outlines and remove the whole theme into a suitable remoteness from the domain of matter-of-fact. The Eternal City is, after all, as vital a portion of the story as are the adventures of Miriam, Hilda, Kenyon, and Donatello. They could not have existed and played their parts in any other city of the world.

In selecting local habitations for the creatures of his imagination, he strolled into the Via Portoghese, and there found the "Virgin's Shrine," which, with minor modifications, was to become the home of Hilda. I quote from his journal the description of the actual place as he saw it. "The tower in the Via Portoghese," he says, "has battlements and machicolations, and the upper half of it is covered with gray, ancient-looking stucco. On the summit, at one corner, is the shrine of the Virgin, rising quite above the battlements, and with its lamp before it.

Beneath the machicolations is a window, probably belonging to the upper chamber; and there seems to be a level space on the top of the tower. Close at hand is the façade of a church, the highest pinnacle of which appears to be at about the same level as the battlements of the tower, and there are two or more stone figures (either angels or allegorical) ornamenting the top of the façade, and, I think, blowing trumpets. These personages are the nearest neighbors of any person inhabiting the upper story of the tower, and the sound of their angelic trumpets must needs be very loud in that close vicinity: The lower story of the palace extends out and round the lower part of the tower, and is surrounded by a stone balustrade. The entrance from the street is through a long, arched doorway and passage, giving admittance into a small, enclosed court; and deep within the passage there is a very broad staircase, which branches off, apparently, on one side, and leads to the height of the tower. At the base of the tower, and along the front of the palace, the street widens, so as to form something like a small piazza, in which there are two or three bakers' shops, one or two shoe-shops, a lottery-office, and, at one corner, the stand of a woman who sells, I think, vegetables; a little further, a stand of oranges. Not so many doors from the palace entrance there is a station of French soldiers and a sentinel on duty. The palace, judging from the broad staircase, the balustraded platform, the tower itself, and other tokens, may have been a grand one centuries ago;

but the locality is now a poor one, and the edifice itself seems to have fallen to unaristocratic occupants. A man was cleaning a carriage in the enclosed court-yard, but I rather conceive it was a cab for hire, and not the equipage of a dweller in the palace."

John Lothrop Motley, the historian of the Netherlands, had come to Rome this winter and brought his family with him. I believe my father had met Motley in America; at all events, we saw a good deal of him now. He was an exceedingly handsome man, not only on account of the beauty of physical features which marked him, but in the sensitiveness and vividness of expression which constantly illuminated them. He was at this time about five-and-forty years of age, and lacked a couple of inches of six feet in height. His hair, a dark, chestnut brown, had the hyacinthine wave through it, and was slightly streaked with gray; his beard, which was full and rather short, was likewise wavy; he was quietly and harmoniously dressed, but the artistic temperament declared itself in a touch of color in his cravat. His voice was melodious and finely modulated; his bearing gravely cheerful and very courteous. No type of man finer than Motley's has existed in modern times; all the elements of the best and purest society were illustrated in him. He had the depth of the scholar, the breadth and self-poise of the man of the world, the genial warmth of the human fellow-creature, and, over all, the harmonizing, individualizing charm of the artist. When

New England gathers her resources to make a man she achieves a result hardly to be surpassed.

The Storys were also in Rome during these last months of our stay, and Miss Mitchell, I think, still lingered in her little lodgings in the Via Bocca di Leone. Miss Cushman likewise reappeared for a time, with all her former greatness and fascination, and many other friends, new and old, made that spring season memorable. As the moment for our departure drew near, the magical allurement of Rome laid upon us a grasp more than ever potent; it was impossible to realize that we were leaving it forever. On the last evening we walked in the moonlight to the fountain of Trevi, near our lodgings, and drank of the water—a ceremony which, according to tradition, insures the return of the drinker. It was the 25th of May, forty-four years ago. None of us has gone back since then, and, of the five who drank, three have passed to the country whence no traveller returns. For my own part, as a patriotic American nearly thirteen years old, I had no wish ever again to see Rome, and declared myself glad to turn my back upon it, not that I had any fault to find with it—I had always had a good time there—but my imagination was full of my native land, with which nothing else could be comparable. I did not learn of the fabled spell of Trevi until afterwards; then I scoffed at and defied it, and possibly Rome may have decided that it could do without me.

The railway to Civita Vecchia had just been completed, and we passed swiftly over the route which had been so full of dangers and discomforts eighteen months before. Embarking on the steamer for Marseilles, we kept on thence to Avignon, where we spent about a week. This venerable town had few attractions for me; I did not much care for the fourteenth-century popes, nor for the eighteenth-century silks, nor even for Petrarch and Laura; and the architecture of the palace, after I had tried to sketch it, ceased to exhilarate me. My father was in no mood for sight-seeing, either, but he went through it all conscientiously. My mother, of course, enjoyed herself, but she met with an accident. While sketching some figures of saints and monsters that adorned the arch of the northern portal of the palace, she made an incautious movement and sprained her ankle. The pain was excessive for the moment, but it soon passed off, so as to enable her to limp back to our hotel. But the next day the pain was worse; my father had a headache, a rare affliction with him; I had caught a bad cold from swimming in the arrowy Rhône, and Una and Miss Shepard were both in a state of exhaustion from sight - seeing; and in this condition the journey to Geneva had to be made. We had intended to remain there but a day, but we stayed longer, breathing the pure air from the Alps, and feeling better as we breathed. I stood on a bridge and looked down at that wonderful azure water rushing into the lovely lake; I looked up and beheld those glorious mountains soaring into the sky, and

I forgot Rome and Florence, and almost America, in my joy.   Everything that life needs for life seemed present there.

We got into a little steamer and made the trip up the lake, the mountains all about us.   Up to this time I had imagined that the acclivities in the north of England and in Scotland were mountains.   We sat on deck, in the stern of the steamer, my father gazing out and up from beneath the rim of his soft felt hat, with his dark cloak over his shoulders.   He looked revived and vigorous again.   Shortly before we left Rome he had ceased to shave his upper lip, for what reason I know not; I think it was simply indisposition to take that trouble any longer.   My mother had at first gently protested; she did not want his upper lip and mouth to be hidden.   But as the brown mustache, thick and soldier-like, appeared, she became reconciled, and he wore it to the end of his life.   "Field-Marshal Hawthorne" James T. Fields used to call him after we got home. Owing to the preponderance of expression of the upper part of his head, the addition did not change his look as much as might have been expected; we soon got used to it, and, inasmuch as all his photographs were taken after the mustache was established, the world does not know him otherwise.

The view became more and more enchanting as we penetrated farther into the depths of the embrace of the mountains, and at last, at its most ravishing point, the lake ceased, and the lonely little pile of dingy white masonry, which is Chillon, appeared. Few works of man have a more romantic interest than this castle; but, seen from the lake, its environment was too much for it. Had it plunged downward into the smooth waters and vanished, its absence would not have been marked in that stupendous landscape. But it improved greatly upon closer acquaintance; and when we stood in its vaults, and saw the pillar to which the prisoner was chained, and the hole in the floor, with its three steps of stone, and the fourth of death, we felt that Chillon was not unequal to its reputation.

After leaving Chillon and Geneva our faces were turned homeward, and we hastened our steps. My father wrote to England to engage our passage for the first of August. We were now at midsummer. We returned to Paris, and after a few days there proceeded to Havre, in order to see Ada Shepard safe on board her steamer for home; her *Wanderjahre* was over, and she was now to be married to Henry Clay Badger. We were sorry to say good-bye to her; she had been a faithful and valuable element in our household, and she had become a dear friend and comrade. She stood waving her handkerchief to us as her steamer slipped away down the harbor. She, too, was sorry for the parting. She once had said to me: "I think your father is the wisest man I ever knew; he does not seem ever to say much, but what he does say is always the truest and best thing that could be said."

From Havre we crossed the Channel to Southampton, and were soon in London. Boston and

Concord were only six weeks distant. Such, at any rate, had been the original design. But after we reached London the subject of the English copyright of *The Marble Faun* came up for discussion. Henry Bright introduced Mr. Smith, of the firm of Smith, Elder & Company, who made such proposals for the English publication of the book as were not to be disregarded; but, in order to make them available, it was necessary that the manuscript should be completed in England. Nothing but the short sketch of it was as yet in existence; it could not be written in much less than a year; either the English offer must be rejected, or we must stay out that year in her Majesty's dominions. My father decided, not altogether unwillingly, perhaps, to stay. He had written in his journal a few weeks before: "Bennoch and Henry Bright are the only two men in England to whom I shall be much grieved to say farewell; but to the island itself I cannot bear to say that word as a finality. I shall dreamily hope to come back again at some indefinite time, rather foolishly, perhaps, for it will tend to take the substance out of my life in my own land. But this, I suspect, is apt to be the penalty of those who stay abroad and stay too long."

But my father could not write in London, and, casting about for a fitting spot, he finally fixed upon the remote hamlet of Redcar, far up on the bleak coast of Redcar, in Yorkshire. It was not far from Whitby, where we had been two or three years before. The gray German Ocean tumbled in there upon the desolate sands, and the contrast of the scene with those which we had been of late familiar with made the latter, no doubt, start forward intensely in the romancer's imagination. So there he wrote and wrote; and he walked far along the sands, with his boy dogging his steps and stopping for shells and crabs; and at a certain point of the beach, where the waves ran over a bar and formed a lake a few feet in depth, he would seat himself on a tussock of sand-grass, and I would undress and run into the cold water and continue my swimming-lessons, which had been begun in Stockbridge Bowl, continued in Lake Leman, and were now brought to a satisfactory conclusion. Both my feet were finally off the bottom, and I felt the wonderful sensation of the first cousin to flying. While I floundered there my father looked off towards the gray horizon, and saw the visions of Hilda, Miriam, Kenyon, and Donatello which the world of readers was presently to behold through his eyes. As we walked home in the twilight, the dull - red glow of the sunset would throw the outlines of the town into dark shadows, and shed a faint light on the surf roaming in from the east. I found, in my old album, the black silhouette of the scene which I made one day. The arms of an old mill are flung appealingly upward, the highest object of the landscape, above the irregular sky-line of the clustering houses. There is also, on the next page, a water-color drawing of a sailor in a blue jersey and a sou'wester, standing, with his hands in his pockets, on the beach beside one of the boats of the region—a slender, clipper-built craft, painted yellow below and black above, good for oars or sail. Her bow rests on a shaft connecting two wheels, for convenience of running her down into the water. There was a dozen or more of these boats always ready on the beach in front of our lodgings. These lodgings were just back of the esplanade, which, during our sojourn, was treated to a coat of tar from end to end—a delightful entertainment for us children— and I have loved the smell of tar ever since. There is little else that I remember about Redcar, ex- cept that, in the winter, there was skating on a part of the beach; but it was "salt ice," and not to be compared with the skating I was to enjoy a year or two later in Concord, which I shall describe if ever I come to that epoch in my nar- rative.

From Redcar, with the romance more than half done, we went south to our old Leamington, which seemed half like home; and there the loveliness of an English spring at its best came to greet us, and there the book was finished, and sent to the printer. We spent a month or two at Bath, and found it very pleasant; my father rested from his labors, ex- cept the proof-reading; and I was instructed in the use of the broadsword by an old Peninsular officer, Major Johnstone, who had fought at Waterloo, and had the bearing of such majors as Thackeray puts into *Vanity Fair*. I once asked him whether he had

ever killed a man; it was on the day when he first
allowed me to use a real broadsword in our lesson.
"Well," replied the major, hesitatingly, "I was riding in a charge, and there came a fellow at me, with
his sword up, and made a swing for my head. I
dodged, and his blade just grazed me; but I let him
have it, downright, at the same moment, and I
caught him where the neck joins the shoulder, and
he went down, and I went on, and what became of
him I don't know; I hope nothing serious!" The
major sighed and looked serious himself. "And
was this the sword?" I demanded, balancing the
heavy weapon in my hand. "No—no—it wasn't
that one," said the major, hastily. "I've never
used the other since! Now, then, sir, if you please,
on guard!"

We went to London, and there were our old
friends Bright and Bennoch, and the Motleys appeared from Italy, and a book called (by the publishers) *Transformation* came out in three volumes,
being the latest romance by the author of *The Scarlet Letter*. The title was not bestowed with my
father's consent. He had, at the publishers' request, sent them a list of several titles, beginning
with *The Marble Faun*, and among others on the list
was "The Faun's Transformation." The publishers took the "Transformation," and left out "The
Faun." My father laughed, but let it go. The
book was to come out under its proper title in
America, and he was indifferent as to what they
called it in England.

The end of our tarrying in the Old World was now at hand. Seven years had we lived there, and we were eager and yet loath to go. My father's friends gathered about him, men who had hardly so much as heard his name a little while ago, but who now loved him as a brother. For a few days Mrs. Blodgett's hospitable face glowed upon us once more, and pale Miss Williams, and trig little Miss Maria, and many of the old captains whom we had known. It was the middle of June, and the sun shone even in Liverpool. Our red-funnelled steamer lay at her moorings in the yellow Mersey, with her steam up. It was not *The Niagara*, but on her bridge stood our handsome little Captain Leitch, with his black whiskers, smiling at us in friendly greeting. How much had passed since we had seen him last! How much were we changed! What experiences lay behind us! What memories would abide with us always! My father leaned on the rail and looked across the river at the dingy, brick building, near the wharves, where he had spent four wearisome but pregnant years. The big, black steamer, with her little, puffing tug, slipped her moorings, and slid slowly down the stream. After a few miles the hue of the water became less turbid, the engines worked more rapidly and regularly. Liverpool was now a smoky mass off our starboard quarter. It sank and dwindled, till the smoke alone was left; the blue channel spread around us; we were at sea, and home lay yonder, across three thousand miles of tumbling waves. But my father still leaned on the rail, and looked backward towards the old home that he loved and would never see again. It was the hour for good-bye; there would come another hour for the other home and for welcome.

THE END